tempered but resolute defense of traditional values and institutions confronting
the rationalistic and materialistic excesses
of a faithless age. In the dark night of the
American soul, it flashes a warning to us
that the "bridge is out" and we had better
turn back or risk plunging into blackwater
chaos.

Bruce Frohnen, a speech writer for
United States Senator Spencer Abraham,
has served as Senior Research Fellow at
Liberty Fund and Bradley Resident
Scholar at the Heritage Foundation.
He has also taught at Reed College,
Oglethorpe University, and Emory
University.

The New Communitarians and the
Crisis of Modern Liberalism

The New Communitarians
and the Crisis of
Modern Liberalism

Bruce Frohnen

 University Press of Kansas

To Annette Kirk and Joseph Silverman
for coming to the rescue

Published by the University Press of Kansas (Lawrence, Kansas 66049), which was
organized by the Kansas Board of Regents and is operated and funded by Emporia State
University, Fort Hays State University, Kansas State University, Pittsburg State University,
the University of Kansas, and Wichita State University

Library of Congress Cataloging-in-Publication Data

Frohnen, Bruce.
    The new communitarians and the crisis of modern liberalism / Bruce
Frohnen.
        p.   cm.
Sequel to: Virtue and the promise of conservatism.
Includes bibliographical references and index.
ISBN 0-7006-0762-5 (alk. paper)
    1. Liberalism—United States.   2. Conservatism—United States.
3. Virtue.   4. Communitarianism—United States.   5. Civil religion—
United States.   I. Title.
JC574.2.U6F76   1996
320.5′1′0973—dc20   95-53769

British Library Cataloguing in Publication Data is available.

Printed in the United States of America

10 9 8 7 6 5 4 3 2 1

The paper used in this publication meets the minimum requirements of the American
National Standard for Permanence of Paper for Printed Library Materials Z39.48-1984.

Contents

Acknowledgments

This book is the product of several years of conversation and argument with friends and colleagues. George Carey first encouraged me to pursue my interest in the often blurred distinction between political and religious thought—a subject central to this current work. Professor Carey graciously read the manuscript for this book and provided comments based on his encyclopedic knowledge of American politics, and the Founding in particular.

I received early help and guidance from Robert Booth Fowler, James Stoner, and Stephen Macedo. I am indebted to all three men for their time, effort, and helpful comments. Guenter Lewy also was kind enough to read the manuscript and make a number of insightful comments that caused me to rethink several arguments. Joseph Fornieri provided helpful guidance through the works of Abraham Lincoln, whose thought is crucial to this work.

For their financial support, making possible a year spent doing research for this book, I would like to thank Antony Sullivan and the Earhart Foundation, Richard Larry of the Carthage Foundation, the Bradley Foundation, and another foundation whose generous donors and administrators prefer to remain anonymous. I also thank my parents for their support and generosity, which made possible the continuation of this project in spite of the uncertainties of life as an untenured academic.

I also must thank Rob Waters, who as always participated in many long telephone conversations, helping me develop my thoughts and hone my arguments. I am indebted as well to Bernadette Travers for her many helpful efforts.

Finally, I again must thank Mike Briggs, Susan Schott, and everyone at the University Press of Kansas for their consistent attention to quality and detail and for their civil and courteous attitude toward both author and work.

Introduction: The Rediscovery of Virtue

In November 1993, President Clinton went to Memphis, Tennessee, to ask a gathering of black ministers for their help in addressing "the great crisis of the spirit that is gripping America today." Speaking from the pulpit Martin Luther King used to deliver his final sermon, Clinton invoked the martyred civil rights leader's name in addressing the troubles of our age: "'I fought for freedom' [Reverend King] would say, 'but not for the freedom of people to kill each other with reckless abandonment, not for the freedom of children to have children and the fathers of the children to walk away from them and abandon them, as if they don't amount to anything.'"[1]

Clinton called on us as a nation to address our critical problems of violence and family breakdown. But, he continued, not even the national government can solve these problems for us. Ours is not a crisis of the state merely but also, and more fundamentally, a crisis of the spirit. And the state cannot provide all the answers in such a crisis. "Sometimes, all of the answers have to come from the values and the stirrings and the voices that speak to us from within."

In part Clinton echoed the worries of many Americans as they faced crime in the streets and the prospect of an entire generation of literally fatherless children entering adulthood. In part he echoed the first lady's sadness, expressed in a speech on "the politics of meaning," over the tragedy of our cities, "filled with hopeless girls with babies and angry boys with guns."[2]

Clearly Clinton's speech struck a responsive chord with many Americans. Liberal commentators including David Broder and E. J. Dionne of the Washington *Post* joined with more conservative observers in praising Clinton for seeking to inject moral concerns into public

1

debate. But Clinton was not just expressing his own concerns. He was joining a new consensus developing in response to the startling statistics on the country's social and cultural decline over the last several decades.

The statistics? Take for example former Reagan Education Secretary Bill Bennett's *Index of Leading Cultural Indicators*. Figures in that book show that while population increased only 41 percent between 1960 and 1990, the violent crime rate increased more than 500 percent. Also, since 1960 illegitimate births had increased more than 400 percent—in 1990 the illegitimacy rate among blacks actually exceeded 65 percent—the teen suicide rate had more than tripled, and the divorce rate had more than doubled.[3]

Observers on all sides now recognize that these "cultural" indicators show a nation in deep trouble. As Clinton argued in Memphis, we have weakened our communities, and this fact has made it more difficult to teach children how to act. "Where there are no families, where there is no order, where there is no hope . . . who will be there to give structure, discipline, and love to these children."

Years before the Republican congressional landslide of 1994 (which many claimed signaled a return to traditional values), Clinton and his political opponents joined in lamenting the loss of virtuous habits necessary for social stability and individual success. And the fingers of blame pointed largely to the Great Society programs begun in the 1960s by President Johnson. In a *Wall Street Journal* article published soon after Clinton's speech, social scientist Charles Murray singled out the welfare system as a primary source of social breakdown and a resulting underclass of whites as well as blacks in America. His analysis (which Clinton called "essentially right") showed that our welfare programs destroy the bonds of personal and family responsibility on which community and character formation rely. Confident that the state will take care of unwed mothers and their children, an increasing number of men feel free to abandon both.

A new consensus has emerged, according to which the war on poverty failed because it "freed" individuals from their communities. Few go as far as Murray in recommending a wholesale dismantling of our welfare system, but most now concede that the system was ill-designed. Our welfare system substituted impersonal bureaucratic rules and programs for neighborhood involvement, government checks for social interaction, and "entitlements" and the notion that we all should "do our own thing" for civic duty. The system made it seem unnecessary for individuals to learn the habits of honesty, decency, and hard work on which economies and societies rely.

Our predicament is in part the result of our desire to be "freed" from social constraints. Americans as a people are passionately fond of liberty in all its forms. They have attempted through most of their existence to free themselves from "oppressions," ranging from the British Parliament's taxation without representation to poverty (which lessens our freedom to choose where to live and so on) to the unwelcome restraints of rigid family ties.

The belief that marriages are confining and bad for everyone (including the children) if husband and wife do not both feel that they are getting the most they can out of life by staying together spawned calls for the institution of "no fault" divorce. The result was a revolution in American divorce law. Today either spouse may end a marriage for any or no reason in almost every state. In 40 percent of the states no other form of divorce is available. The result: divorces in the United States rose from 479,000 in 1965 to 1,215,000 in 1992. In 1985 alone more than a million children were involved in divorces. This rise in divorce rates directly coincided with the institutionalization of no fault divorce.[4]

Liberalized divorce was seen in part as a means to free wives from economic bondage to often domineering husbands. This view is subject to rethinking today because mothers and children are the primary victims of high divorce rates. In California, for example, when the average woman divorces she and her minor children suffer an almost 75 percent drop in their standard of living. Meanwhile, the average former husband actually improves his standard of living by over 40 percent. At least in part because divorce proceedings no longer consider who is to blame for the family's breakup, judges today require alimony less often and far less generously than in previous times.[5]

Liberalized divorce laws also have gone hand in hand with a marked diminution in the traditional prejudice against illegitimacy. In part because sexual mores have been significantly relaxed and because divorce now is so easy to obtain, the distinction between married and nonmarried couples has been blurred. Living together without benefit of marriage no longer is thought of by many Americans as living "in sin." Along with this change has come greater acceptance of the offspring of nonmarital unions. If marriage is generally more of a temporary arrangement, there is little reason to disapprove of people who have children out of wedlock. Thus children also have been "freed" from old prejudices.

But while few politicians or commentators are willing publicly to decry divorce, the consequences of illegitimacy and the effects of broken families on children have become topics of wide discussion. And there has been significant agreement, across the political spectrum, that children are harmed by the lack of two parents.

Barbara Whitehead of the *Atlantic Monthly* argued that former Vice President Dan Quayle "was right" when he criticized the popular television program *Murphy Brown*.[6] Accused of attacking the program's lead character for bearing a child out of wedlock, Quayle actually was criticizing the media for glorifying single motherhood. *Murphy Brown* made it look as if it were relatively easy and even glamorous for a woman to have and raise a child out of wedlock. But most single mothers are not well-off television broadcasters with large numbers of friends able and willing to lend support.

Having derided Quayle's stance during the 1992 presidential campaign, Clinton later joined in echoing it. He agreed substantially with Whitehead, who pointed out that children of single parents are six times as likely to be poor, and to be poor longer than other children. They are two to three times as likely to have emotional and behavioral problems and more likely to drop out of school, get pregnant as teenagers, abuse drugs, commit crimes, and even commit suicide. Without "family values"—that is, without a stable family life within which to learn how we should treat others—we will be more likely to fail economically, socially, and morally throughout our lives. We must learn habits like honesty, hard work, punctuality, and respect for superiors if we are to hold down jobs and develop good character.

Character can be defined as the collection of habits that makes up the bulk of our personality. In large measure we are a collection of character traits such as honesty (or dishonesty), hard work (or laziness), and lovingness (or hatefulness). Our character traits determine in large part how we treat others. And many people now recognize that the way we treat one another determines whether we will have a worthwhile life and live in a worthwhile society. If no one is willing to work and sacrifice for the good of others (most fundamentally his family) our neighborhoods and eventually our entire nation will become an armed camp in which none of us can trust the others; in which fear rules our lives.

Americans in their own eyes have become selfish, which has caused observers of all political stripes to worry that the fabric of our society soon may be irretrievably torn. The problem has spawned renewed interest in the sources of good and bad character; it has sparked new interest in a very old idea: virtue.

An Almost Forgotten Concept

Virtue is a fairly simple concept but one that has been out of fashion for many years. The old standards of virtue, which have been recognized if not always followed until recently, told us that we ought to do what is right even if that means giving up something we desire. In its simplest formulation, virtue means doing unto others as you would have them do unto you. It means being loyal to friends, family, and nation and trying to live up to their expectations of you.

Of course virtue rests on the notion that there are standards that tell us what is right. We cannot act as we ought if we do not know how we ought to act. And this is where virtue has run into trouble. It rests on a set of standards that are "imposed" on us by our past—by religion, tradition, and social and political institutions that existed before we were born. It may be a universal rule that we should do unto others as we would have them do unto us, but translating this rule into practice requires a certain knowledge of and adherence to tradition. To show respect is always good, but the manner of such displays varies widely between societies and even classes. Saluting one's superior officer is good, but saluting one's mother may be a sign of insolence because a mother expects (in America at least) more familiarity and affection than is indicated by a salute.

Virtue is "oppressive" because it imposes constraints on us to which we did not explicitly consent. But no one can be "against" virtue—against doing good—so, instead of attacking virtue, we let it languish until it shrank in the public mind from a vigorous concept of public service to a quaint notion of private chastity. In this way we came over time to think of virtue as unnecessary, as well as vaguely intrusive. We convinced ourselves that everyone would be happy if only we "tolerated"—in essence, ignored—those whose beliefs and practices were different from our own.

But the concept of virtue never completely disappeared; it is too integral a part of public discourse for that. The systematic study of public life began in ancient Greece with Plato's assertion that no one knowingly does evil and therefore that knowledge is the key to virtue. Plato's student Aristotle argued that we should call a man virtuous only if he has the proper character. For Aristotle only the moderate man, who seeks and as a rule finds the mean between excess and dearth (who avoids being, for example, either a spendthrift or a miser), is virtuous. It was the community's duty to use both political and social means to instill proper habits so that the citizens can lead good lives and join together to help the community survive.

Virtue has, however, been out of fashion among intellectuals for many years. Philosopher Alasdair MacIntyre wrote *After Virtue* in the early 1980s to decry the moral emptiness of public and intellectual discourse. *After Virtue* is a lament for premodern times, when our communities expected each of us to seek virtue and each of us sought the approval of our communities. In former times, MacIntyre argued, we included one another in the stories of our lives and sought to form a set of common characteristics rather than living only through our individual choices and whims.

Unfortunately, MacIntyre argues, we no longer converse with one another in any meaningful way. We have abandoned Aristotle's view that politics is the pursuit of a good life lived in common with our fellows. We have abandoned the moral standards that prescribe virtue, instead choosing the life of individual autonomy. We have "freed" ourselves from any shared conception of what it means to lead a moral life. In this way we have destroyed any basis on which to sustain common beliefs and practices, and thus any basis on which to come together to sustain and defend our society.

Lacking commonly accepted standards, we have come to question the very idea of moral authority. Thus, for MacIntyre, politics has become merely a contest between self-serving actors. Law and custom have lost their capacity to put us under the *moral* obligation to obey. Politics has become merely another means by which we pursue our own self-interest, and we have entered a dark age of selfish, materialistic battles over who shall gain power and use it to help friends and hurt enemies.

MacIntyre's criticism finally has hit home. The mass media has begun to address questions raised by the destruction of customary standards of conduct. Not only television violence but a whole array of moral and practical issues from crime to illegitimacy is coming to the fore as we debate how to defend and restore proper character to our children and our communities.

The Debate Continues

Almost everyone now recognizes our crisis of character, and the response often has been quite practical and nonideological. However, both the source of and the solution to our situation are matters of great controversy. Those who seek to resuscitate virtue may look to the standards of our traditional way of life, or they may seek to forge new standards of conduct. It is here that recent discussions of character tend to sort themselves out along partisan lines.

Most men of the right (usually called "conservatives") seek to preserve man's pre-existing character. They see mankind as largely and properly influenced by religious teaching and customary practice. Thus they see virtue, and the proper way to teach it, quite differently from men of the left (or "liberals"), who put confidence in our ability to use science and collective action to transcend our given circumstances and reshape our nature. Where conservatives seek to reform the individual, and through the individual society, liberals seek to reform society, and through it the individual.

In seeking to temper us, conservatives look unabashedly backward to a time when the wisdom of our ancestors, embodied in customary institutions, beliefs, and practices, was respected and followed. This looking backward means, of course, that we also must accept inequalities and even injustices. The conservative would have us expend more effort preserving what is good than changing what is bad. To the liberal's dismay, the conservative is more concerned to preserve our confidence in the goodness of our society than to constantly improve it, because he fears that constant criticism will make the people lose confidence in their society's basic decency. And when we lose this confidence civil, social, and moral disorders are sure to follow.

Conservatism is an anathema to many on the left precisely because it emphasizes our need for tradition and customary social arrangements. At least since the Swiss Intellectual Jean Jacques Rousseau wrote in the eighteenth century, many on the left have argued that our inherited institutions and customs are primary sources of human misery. Rousseau insisted that society spawns human conflict. Social pressures make men see themselves as others see them and so they begin competing with one another in pursuit of honors. Envy, hatred, and violence, Rousseau and his followers argue, are the natural results of this competition.

Marxists see virtue as an elaborate ruse intended to dupe losers in the race of life into quietly serving the winners. Religious standards in particular are "opiates" the powerful use to keep the poor from seizing their rightful share of the wealth. But the injustice of our economic system nonetheless spawns righteous indignation, anger, and hopelessness—and from these passions come crime and other social dysfunctions.

Liberals are overtly opposed to both of these analyses but nonetheless argue that the conservatives' attachment to tradition is too confining. According to this view, some combination of rational self-interest and inborn conscience makes most individuals moral, provided public institutions provide them with the proper incentives and disincentives. Sharing assumptions with Marx and Rousseau, this liberal vision sees self-seeking individuals producing public peace and prosperity—with the aid of public policy makers.

A Movement Beyond Ideology?

Not surprisingly, their differences have produced hostility between conservatives and liberals. Liberals, conservatives argue, reduce everything to politics and in the process destroy the social institutions (principally families, churches, and local associations) that alone can form decent character. Conservatives, liberals argue, ignore and even apologize for political, economic, and social injustice in the name of social peace and their own privileges.

Recently, a group of intellectuals closely allied with the Clinton administration has sought to transcend this debate. Taking for themselves the name "communitarian," these figures, including sociologists Amitai Etzioni and Robert Bellah, one-time Clinton presidential adviser William Galston, and Canadian philosopher Charles Taylor, seek to construct communities in which both common rules and individual rights are respected; in which the best of the old may be preserved as we progress to new heights of wealth, toleration and decency. In Etzioni's phrase, the goal is "a new moral, social, public order—without puritanism or oppression."[7] According to Etzioni we must have common moral values so that we may have moral order, but we must beware of "puritan" moral and religious absolutes.

Etzioni's formulation of the communitarian position raises a number of questions: Can one defeat "puritanism" while retaining vigorous standards of virtue? If we are to have a "new" social order, where will its standards of conduct come from—from tradition or the social scientist? Indeed, the central question raised by the rediscovery of virtue may be whether social scientists and policy analysts are up to the job of pointing out how to regain it, or we must return to older standards rooted in religious tradition.

In addressing these questions I will examine communitarianism as both a philosophy and a social movement. Today's communitarians are intellectuals; they work with ideas. But theirs is self-consciously a *movement*; they seek to affect public opinion and policy, to change the way Americans view and act toward their political community. Their success is measured in public statements and reforms proposed by powerful policymakers. Thus I will at times examine the acts and rhetoric of the Clinton administration which, despite its frequent shifts of policy and rhetoric and despite Galston's departure from the list of presidential advisers, shows the extent of communitarian influence as a political movement. Communitarians clearly are not responsible for every word and deed of the Clinton White House. But where that administration illustrates communitarian influence in important ways I will point out that fact.

Perhaps in part to foster public confidence in the moderation of their intentions, the "new communitarians" took their name from an earlier generation of "communitarian" conservatives like Robert Nisbet, without taking on Nisbet's philosophical or cultural vision. MacIntyre also is often called a communitarian, and he does share Nisbet's desire to resuscitate institutions, beliefs, and practices rooted in religious tradition. But MacIntyre's connection with the *new* communitarians rests solely in the eyes of some intellectual observers. In fact the new communitarians openly reject the reverence for tradition and transcendent standards on which the old communitarianism relied.[8]

But the new communitarians still claim to be nonpartisan. They claim to transcend and transform the traditional liberal-conservative debate by combating all forms of "selfishness" and promoting a form of virtue on which we all can agree. This virtue is based on tolerance and commitment to public service and democracy. As such it is intimately linked with politics and public policy.

The new communitarians ask prominent public figures from former Bush cabinet member Jack Kemp to socialist academics like Benjamin Barber to "sign" their founding document, the "communitarian platform." And the platform itself is phrased in nonpartisan terms. Rather than particular positions on most issues, it urges attention to the long-term effects of policy decisions on "the fragile economy of families and their supporting communities."[9] But the platform also outlines communitarian positions on those specific issues, such as public financing of elections and a national program of public service, which they believe are crucial to a civil public life.

Communitarians may or may not have a direct and significant impact on public policy in America. Clinton in particular has been an inconstant friend to the movement—displaying Etzioni's book on his desk one week, seemingly abandoning public virtue for pork barrel politics the next. But the widespread use of communitarian concepts and rhetoric convinces me that communitarianism already has had a vast impact on public discourse in America. It has changed the way we look at public policy issues and the very nature of our community.

Indeed, this is not just a book about the new communitarianism, because in an important sense we all are communitarians. Americans of all political stripes today wish, like communitarians, to resuscitate private and public virtue. New communitarians reject conservatism because they find it too confining. But they have been influential precisely because they do *not* represent a stunning new way of thinking. Communitarians do not seek to found a new school of thought on the ruins of liberalism. They seek to save liberalism from its own excessive hostility toward authority, to save liberalism from itself.

The new communitarians seek not to replace our existing structures with ones harkening back to a former, more virtuous existence. Neither do they wish to conduct a revolution, upending our society so that a new and improved one can take its place. They seek to control the society that exists already, shoring up its weak points—particularly its spiritual weak points—so that it may thrive still.

Communitarians want to construct a "new covenant" of rights and responsibilities. When Bill Clinton spoke of this new covenant at the 1992 Democratic National Convention he captured the spirit of the movement itself in calling for "a government that offers more empowerment and less entitlement." He promised less bureaucracy and more economic opportunity. Americans would produce both, working together on the basis of "a solemn agreement between the people and their government, based not simply on what each of us can take, but on what all of us must give to our nation."

The nation would become like a family, a natural group whose members seek the good of all, rather than merely of themselves. Only in this way, communitarians argue, can our society survive. Yet the pursuit of virtue, and the drive for the moral consensus on which virtue depends, could destroy the very society communitarians value. Communitarians worry not only that our society may disintegrate in a sea of selfishness, but also that it may be destroyed by men willing to institute their vision of the good society through authoritarian means.

Thus communitarians advocate only very basic, public virtues like tolerance, law-abidingness, and nondiscrimination, which they believe command support among all Americans.[10] They reject what Etzioni calls a "leave it to Beaver" fantasy of moral certitude, 1950s style. They particularly distrust religious principles because they feel that such principles can produce intolerance toward homosexuals and others pursuing alternative lifestyles. New communitarians seek to maintain a balance between the demands of individuality and the requirements of a society, such as ours, that fosters individual growth. They value individual choice and initiative but recognize that any society, even one dedicated to individuality, requires some minimum amount of selfless service from its citizens. We must choose to be virtuous, lest we destroy the society that allows us to choose our way of life.

Communitarians are convinced that our society's breakdown is due not to liberal attachment to the individual but to the lack of any countervailing loyalty among individuals for their society. They seek to balance individual choice with commitment to liberal democratic society. To succeed they must make us *choose* to serve our community.

But how can they do so if they eschew tradition and religion, the two most powerful teachers of respect for authority? How can they foster virtue without undermining individualism?

The key appears to be civil religion. All societies have a set of common beliefs and values that order their lives together. As Scottish philosopher David Hume observed, they are based on opinion. If the people, or at any rate those with the military and other means to keep the people in check, do not see their government as in some way legitimate, it will fall. Love of the king, belief in the sanctity of the monarchy, habitual attachment to an aristocratic class, faith in the goodness of democratic rule, all are shared opinions underlying political regimes. Peoples must believe in the basic goodness of both their political system and their given way of life—be it one characterized by military honor, humble faith, or a harmonious ordering of varied classes—if they are to survive.

Such belief is particularly difficult to inculcate in a society, such as ours, which is hostile to established standards of virtue, indeed established institutions and beliefs of all kinds. Thus new communitarians seek to construct a civil religion proclaiming democratic participation—engaging in public discussions over how to modify existing public institutions and standards—the key virtue. Their civil religion also will teach us that liberal democratic society embodies the virtue of public discussion and therefore is itself worthy of reverent service. So long as we decide in common what we shall deem good, communitarians argue, we have done our duty and should be satisfied that we have been done justice.

But to subject all our lives to democratic rule is no easy task. It requires that we reform our society and especially ourselves to conform with a public ethic that lauds individual self-direction but demands that all our choice meet with public approval. New communitarians deal with this seeming contradiction in part by pointing to the liberal virtue of tolerance, which demands that all personal choices not involving harm to others be respected. To put forward one's own views and choices while recognizing all others as equally valid requires a specific psychology, one that revels in choice-making, whether at the individual or the community level, for its own sake. Communitarians must foster this psychology through educational and other policies if their project is to succeed.

The philosophical bases for this psychology and the educational program meant to instill it in the citizenry are the subjects of this book. I first will examine the philosophical grounding of the communitarian movement in the thought of Charles Taylor and William Galston. Both men have extensive philosophical credentials, albeit of different sorts. Taylor is a Canadian socialist committed to reinfusing moral understanding into the drive for collective meaning. Galston, a student of political philosopher Leo Strauss (often termed a conservative) seeks to shore up the moral foundations of our society by convincing us that peace and prosperity require virtue, and that religious understandings, while false, are necessary to convince the masses of the need for selfless action.

Both Taylor and Galston call themselves liberals. They argue that we must serve our individualistic society so that it may continue to protect individuals. Both also argue that service to the community makes for a better life than selfish individualism. It is this seeming paradox—our need to protect an individualism that is inherently impoverished and destructive—that I will examine at greatest length. Throughout this book I will eschew questioning the details of each author's historical or sociological theory so that I may concentrate on explicating his project's nature and goals.

New communitarians are using a number of tools to change our characters—particularly theology and civil religion, rhetoric, practical politics, and social science. They use a distinctive language and tone of voice when using each of their tools. Each represents an important aspect of the communitarian vision, and each is used most forcefully by rather different communitarians.

Chapter 2 concerns the nature and uses of civil religion. The main focus of the chapter is sociologist Robert Bellah, whose *Habits of the Heart* did much to return questions of morality and religious consciousness to academic debate. Bellah's book was influential because it combined theological and sociological argument. He sought to bring religion down to earth by showing the ways in which religious ritual can be used to win the people's allegiance for communitarian political causes.

Chapter 3 discusses the communitarian use of history. I say "use" of history because communitarians seem convinced that actual historical knowledge—the ability to re-create the true meaning of important documents and events from our past—is beyond our reach. I focus in this chapter on the work of Garry Wills. Wills declined service as a speech writer in the Clinton asministration to continue his work as journalist and explorer in the realm of the history of ideas. Once a classical scholar, his work emphasizes the importance of rhetoric. His studies of the American Founding did much to spawn the "communitarian" reading of that era. They concentrate on the power of words and images to affect our views of our past and our nation's ideals. Much might be written concerning the nature and adequacy of his scholarship, but I am convinced that this would be beside the point. Wills's true goal, as a communitarian, is not to extricate "truth" from our past but rather to provide stories from which we can learn communitarian lessons. He uses history to convince us that we are free to reconstruct our society and that participating in such projects is the way to great glory.

At the end of Chapter 3 I turn to one pursuer of political glory, several term New York governor and almost Democratic presidential contender Mario Cuomo. Often termed a New Deal liberal, Cuomo in fact shows the broad influence of communitarianism—as well as its fundamental liberalism. As governor and now as elder statesman, Cuomo seeks to forge a national community, in effect a "family of America" that would make loyalty to the nation the center of our public life. All this while achieving greater economic equality and moral tolerance.

Chapter 4 concerns the standing of local communities in communitarian politics and theology. I focus again on Bellah because his conception of a community—a group tied together by a common sense of its past and committed to common goals to be put into action through public, political action—shows the communitarian vision at its most complete. I examine the means by which Bellah seeks to reorganize our private and local lives along communitarian lines. He and his colleagues wish to resuscitate local feelings of solidarity so that the institutions in which we learn to treat one another decently may again flourish, but this time along communitarian lines. He seeks not to bring back an older, more locally minded America but to forge new local ties that will further the cause of equality and moral tolerance.

In Chapter 5 I examine communitarians' attempt to reform politics and society through inculcation of the new liberal civil religion. Communitarians will not reinvent our government in any meaningful way. But their commitment to liberal ideology and the tools of social science renders their attempt to change our character problematic. Fearing anarchy, despotism, and especially traditional beliefs and norms, communitarians end by relying on the very psychological counseling and therapy that has encouraged Americans to become so distressingly shallow, self-satisfied, and self-serving.

In Chapter 6 I discuss the role communitarians seek to play in our society. Communitarians wish to interpret for us our past and the meaning of our fundamental documents and shared beliefs. Committed to economic equality, they nonetheless recognize that their project requires a group of individuals capable of using powerful rhetoric to convince the people that liberal democracy is worthy of their support, even in hard times. The question is whether such activity, and the civil religion at its heart, is itself consistent with liberal democratic ideology.

In Chapter 7 I sketch an earlier vision of the good life. This vision, rooted in American history, emphasized man's need for local attachments to foster virtue. The goal was neither a life of individualistic isolation nor a life of communal action. Instead the goal was a decent life lived as an independent individual bound by affection and duty to family, friends, and neighbors. What held this vision together was a commitment to following God's will through worship and moral conduct and a commitment to organizing society in a way that would encourage such pursuits. The result was less egalitarian and less insistent on individual rights than many today would like, but it rested on the conviction that man is truly free only when he follows God in leading a pious and moral life, and that only free men can maintain free societies.

America's Founding Fathers were aware of the difficult feat they were attempting when they broke with Great Britain. They sought to found a nation in which the people would rule but would not abuse their power. Such a government would be possible only if the people themselves were good, decent, and public-minded. As John Adams put it soon after the Constitution was ratified: "We have no government armed with power capable of contending with human passions unbridled by morality and religion. . . . Our Constitution was made only for a moral and religious people. It is wholly inadequate to the government of any other."[11] Only men of good character can maintain their freedom. And for the Founders, good character requires religion.

Communitarians seek to accomplish a noble goal: to restore the broken foundations of our way of life. They recognize that common feelings are necessary for such a restoration. They even argue that religious feeling has a role to play in this restoration. But whence will come the moral consensus on which community and virtue rely? Like it or not, Americans today face the questions posed by Adams and by our very form of government: Can a people be free without being moral? Can a people be moral without being religious?

This is a book about communitarianism. But, more fundamentally, it is a book about the relationship between religion and politics in American life. My analysis is based on the belief (which I hope to justify) that current debates over the proper form of virtue and over how we should go about teaching virtue are, at heart, religious. Current debates over virtue revolve around questions of the proper form, use, and goals of religious understanding—for it is only with such an understanding that we can address the fundamental question: Why should I do unto others as I would have them do unto me?

One cannot pursue virtue unless he sees himself as serving a higher good. There must be some source of standards above us, giving us rules to live by which we cannot change or discard at our whim. Otherwise everything is permissible—even the rule of promise-keeping would be out of order and no longer a rule.

To find the rules of life in revealed religion is, for communitarians, too unreflective and too restrictive of individual experimentation. But communitarians recognize that few of us will pursue virtue for its own sake. Thus they seek to convince us that democratic politics is the proper source of moral rules and values. The political community in which we participate, in which we create our own morality, is itself holy. Communitarians seek to instill in us a faith in civil or political rather than spiritual religion. They seek to convince us that our nation is the proper source of our morality; that love of nation is as natural as love of family, and that to fail to act on this more abstract love is impious.

In framing my analysis in this way I risk being dismissed as someone concerned solely or primarily with "winning" souls to my own religion. But my goals are neither so ambitious nor so partisan. I seek rather to understand the nature and possibilities of recent shifts in our public discourse. And it seems to me necessary, if one is to gain this understanding, to face questions that have been seething beneath the surface of public life in the United States, and indeed the

West, for more than two centuries: Is it possible to harness religious sentiments for political, economic, and even social gains? Or must we value the religious impulse, and religious practice, for its own sake if we are to enjoy even its secular benefits?

Historically, communities were held together in large part by a common understanding of their place in the order of the universe. Trials and disappointments in this life were explained, in part, as tests for entry into a better next life. Modern thought is based in large measure on a rejection of this tragic sense of life. Liberal democratic regimes in particular promise their citizens greater satisfaction here on earth. And they accomplish this in part by setting aside public consideration of the demands of the next life. But without the understanding of our duties that is provided by a shared vision of the relationship between this life and the next—between politics and religion—how are we to know how we should act and why? The question we face today may well be whether it is possible to have a good society that does not look for guidance, and ultimate fulfillment, to the next life.

Chapter One

A Liberal Community?

Socrates sought to teach the ancient Athenians the route to wisdom. They executed him for his trouble, having convicted him of religious heresy. Aristotle fled Athens to avoid the same fate. Niccolò Machiavelli in Florence (tortured), Algernon Sidney in England (beheaded), Thomas Hobbes and John Locke (voluntarily exiled from England), and Rousseau (exiled from Geneva)—all suffered for their teachings.

It seems ironic that Karl Marx, himself an exile because of his radical beliefs, thought it necessary to observe that "the philosophers have only *interpreted* the world, in various ways; the point, however, is to *change* it."[1] But then Marx wrote during a time in which people demanded more and more concrete benefits from their governments and their philosophers. Modern philosophers must constantly prove their "relevance" to the lives of the people. Considered "unworldly," those who seek wisdom risk mockery unless they can show that their knowledge is good for something tangible and pleasant. Nowhere is this more true than in modern liberal democracies. Here a philosopher who seeks to make his vision of the good life a reality must convince the people to act according to his will. And the people will obey only if they believe that to do so is in their self-interest.

Perhaps more than any philosophical movement before them, communitarians seek to convince the people to accept their vision of the good life and also to practice the virtues necessary to make it real. Thus communitarianism is self-consciously as much a political movement as a philosophical one. It is as much an attempt to change public policy and opinion as a search for wisdom. And today this requires attention to the art of persuasion as well as to the various "sciences of man"—whether sociology, history, or political science—to which modern philosophers turn in their quest for knowledge.

Ours is an era of public relations. Anyone seeking to influence public opinion and policy had best learn how to deal effectively with media elites (the producers, editors, and reporters who control access to television, radio, newspapers, and magazines) and how to communicate effectively through the media itself. Communitarians clearly have learned this lesson well. Gathering endorsements for their platform is only one means they use to convey their message. Etzioni appears on talk shows, publishes an academic journal called *The Responsive Community,* and runs a formidable public relations organization.

These efforts have borne some fruit. Founded in 1991, *The Responsive Community* had four thousand subscribers by 1994. Still dominated by academics, the communitarian movement nonetheless could boast by 1994 that it had five thousand members, with five hundred members actively involved in communitarian activities nationwide. As befits a primarily intellectual movement, these activities are broadly educational. Communitarians have convened several well publicized "teach-ins" in which academics, policy analysts, government workers, and community activists discuss major public policy issues and their effects on family and community life.

More important, communitarians have had a significant influence on Clinton administration rhetoric and policy proposals. Not only Clinton's call for a new covenant of American rights and responsibilities at the 1992 Democratic National Convention but also his welfare reform proposals, intended to put the new covenant into effect, were taken directly from an article written by communitarian Robert Shapiro.[2] Clinton had forged working relationships with a number of communitarian policy analysts while serving on the Democratic Leadership Council (a group of Democratic governors promoting "moderate" stances on issues like welfare reform) and working with the "new democrats" at a Washington think tank called the Progressive Policy Institute.

Clinton's new covenant speech, his 1993 Memphis speech lamenting our "crisis of the spirit," and his State of the Union Addresses all emphasized communitarian themes. In each case Clinton began by promising federal programs to help all Americans but went on to note, as he did in his 1994 State of the Union Address, that the American people have got to want to change from within if we're going to bring back work and family and community. We cannot renew our country when, within a decade, more than half of the children will be born into families where there has been no marriage. We cannot renew this country when 13-year-old boys get semiautomatic weapons to shoot 9-year-olds for kicks. We can't renew our country when children are having children . . . we can't renew our country until we realize that governments don't raise children; parents do. Parents who know their children's teachers and turn off the television and help with the homework and teach their kids right from wrong.

Clinton's arguments are communitarian. According to him violence and family breakdown constitute the core of our problems as a society, but neither can be solved by government alone. Only a renewed sense of family and social responsibility can help us rebuild our society on a firm basis. Virtue must replace, or at least augment, self-interest if we are to solve our nation's crisis of the spirit.

Thus, for Clinton our political and spiritual problems are intertwined. The people must be made more virtuous if the government is to do its job of providing them with safety, material well-being, and freedom. The issue then concerns what role government should play in fostering virtue, and whether this role is in keeping with liberal democratic politics and ideology.

The Pursuit of Liberalism

From its origins in the late seventeenth-century philosophy of John Locke and particularly since John Stuart Mill laid out its full implications in the mid-nineteenth century, liberalism has been seen as a political philosophy and movement that seeks to separate the private from the political realm. Mill's *On Liberty* is devoted to the proposition that politicians oppress us when they use government to do more than is absolutely necessary to protect our liberty. His argument, which has become an often unspoken liberal assumption, is that it is only by pursuing our *private* plans of life—in our professions and choices of lifestyle—that we develop our personalities and lead full lives. Mill did not seek to use politics to build utopia. He sought to remove political constraints on private action so that individuals could pursue their own visions of the good life.

But liberalism's true goal is not limited government per se; it is liberty. Liberalism seeks to free us from external constraints so that we may pursue our own, self-chosen goals unmolested. Mill worried at least as much about social restraints (including popular bias against "eccentrics" who act in unusual ways and bad material or educational conditions that might keep us from pursuing our goals) as about government repression. He argued, for example, that government must enforce the rights of children against their parents. According to Mill the state should punish parents who fail to properly educate and care for their offspring. Children cannot develop the capacity to pursue their own goals without proper care, and thus proper care must be guaranteed, as a right, by the state.[3]

Anything that prevents us from pursuing our goals is, in liberal terms, oppressive. At its inception liberalism sought to free individuals from the constraints of absolute rulers who used the powers of government to decree how we should lead our lives. Tyrants forced their subjects, among other things, to serve in their wars of conquest. But as individuals have come to reject absolute government as illegitimate, and as nations in the West have moved toward republican government, liberalism has evolved. It has become less concerned with keeping government out of our lives and more concerned with *using* government to free us from deprivations, such as poverty, which prevent us from achieving our goals and leading the fullest, most satisfying lives possible.

Mill argued that civilized societies would eventually move toward some form of socialism. According to him we should reconsider what forms of private property and consumption the government should allow. The form of property that promoted the most just distribution of wealth and work while providing all men with the means necessary to pursue their vision of the good life would be best, and would involve some form of government control over economic life. Indeed, socialism would "free" individuals by encouraging them to leave behind mere economic concerns so that they might concentrate on moral self-improvement.[4]

To be sure, some who consider themselves "classical liberals"— most prominently modern libertarians such as Milton Friedman— maintain that economic life must be protected from political interference. We need free markets, Friedman argues, because only they can produce prosperity and more importantly because a people that loses its economic liberty soon will lose all its liberties. According to Friedman no government has gained control over economics without going on to control its citizens' political and moral choices as well.[5]

Friedman actually makes two arguments in favor of economic liberty: one, economics is an important part of life, in which the freedom to follow our own reason to achieve our own goals is both morally and financially necessary, and two, economic liberty is intertwined so closely with other forms of liberty that we must defend each for the sake of the other. Friedman believes that all forms of liberty are valuable because they prevent the government from interfering with private conduct. What Friedman values most is the quintessential liberal good of individual autonomy. A society is good, for Friedman, to the extent that it allows individuals to make their own moral choices and follow their own life plans.

Communitarians also want us to pursue our own goals. But for them this first requires that we free our communities from crime and also from all forms of selfishness. Because the connection between selfishness and individualism is very close—because to seek one's own fulfillment typically requires that one value oneself above others—communitarians are in the awkward position of decrying liberalism's actual effects while lauding its theoretical goals. Criticizing selfishness they nonetheless praise the individual self-love at its base.

But then communitarians recognize this problem. They seek to solve the dilemma of selfishness by arguing that we can truly fulfill ourselves only through political action in the community. Communitarians see liberalism's failure to defend the role of virtue in public life as a crucial flaw. Without a sense of connectedness, of communal duty and belonging, they believe, our lives lose meaning and society degenerates into a battleground of competing interests.

Communitarians share the liberal vision of the good life. On this view each individual "flourishes," developing his own capacities to their fullest, by pursuing goals he has chosen for himself on the basis of his own independently constructed moral code. Communitarians do not seek to replace liberalism but to save it. Providing liberalism with an understanding of man's social nature and needs, communitarians hope to reinvigorate liberal society. They, like traditional liberals, seek to further our individual attempts to find fulfillment in the pursuits and attachments of our own choice.

Charles Taylor argues that the liberal-communitarian debate is actually one between liberals "who believe that the state should be neutral between the different conceptions of the good life espoused by individuals, on the one hand, and those who believe that a democratic society needs some commonly recognized definition of the good life, on the other."[6] Communitarians are liberals who want to reestablish a common sense among the people of what the nation is for, of what its people share in their history and what they should strive to accomplish.

Galston argues that

> every society is constituted by certain core principles and sustained by its members' active belief in them. Conversely, every society is weakened by the diminution of its members' belief in its legitimacy. Loyalty—the developed capacity to understand, to accept, and to act on the core principles of one's society—is thus a fundamental virtue. And it is particularly important in liberal communities, which tend to be organized around abstract principles rather than shared ethnicity, nationality, or history.[7]

We need a shared sense of identity and purpose—an "American way of life"—if we are to maintain the patriotism necessary to a free and democratic society. As Taylor puts it,

> every political society requires some sacrifices and demands some disciplines from its members: they have to pay taxes, or serve in the armed forces, and in general observe certain restraints. In a despotism, a regime where the mass of citizens are subject to the rule of a single master, or a clique, the requisite disciplines are maintained by coercion. In order to have a free society, one has to replace this coercion with something else. This can only be a willing identification with the polis on the part of the citizens, a sense that the political institutions in which they live are an expression of themselves.

According to Taylor free citizens will serve only what they themselves have created. Citizens must participate in government, shaping day-to-day policies, if they are to see it as their own and support it. But to govern responsibly the citizens must be loyal and productive. If it is to be free, then, the state must see to it that its citizens are capable of directing their own actions in a way that upholds rather than undermines the regime.[8]

Let me return to Mill here. He argued for authenticity—but only for those with the capacity to exercise it properly: "If a person possesses any tolerable amount of common sense and experience, his own mode of laying out his existence is the best, not because it is the best in itself, but because it is his own mode."[9] It would seem, then, that anyone *not* possessed of a tolerable amount of common sense and experience should not be allowed to lay out his own existence.

Mill argued in *On Liberty* that it is only if we have the right character that we can be free.

> Despotism is a legitimate mode of government in dealing with barbarians, provided the end be their improvement, and the means justified by actually effecting that end. Liberty, as a principle, has no application to any state of things anterior to the time when mankind have become capable of being improved by free and equal discussion. Until then, there is nothing for them but implicit obedience to an Akbar or a Charlemagne, if they are so fortunate as to find one.[10]

Civilizations that have not attained the heights of reason possessed by the Europe of Mill's day could only hope for a great leader to give them enough common sense to pursue their own ends. Political leaders—great legislators—must give their people the characters of free men if their people are to be free.

Communitarians do not decry liberalism's commitment to individual autonomy. They decry liberalism's confidence that individuals can govern themselves responsibly without the aid of a tutelary state—a government that teaches them virtue. Liberalism fails to provide even a coherent theory of virtue, leaving judgments concerning good and bad conduct to individuals and political and economic processes. The result, communitarians argue, is an inability to discuss, let alone foster, the kinds of behavior necessary if liberalism itself is to survive.

The Critique of Pure Liberalism

Communitarians are highly critical of America's liberal tradition. And they are not alone. Many have argued that liberalism, while it promises personal fulfillment, cannot provide a full, meaningful life for its citizens. And, having disappointed them, a liberal regime will find those citizens unwilling to provide it the support it needs to survive.

Because it focuses so much on the individual, liberalism provides no grounds on which to argue that we should act virtuously, in support of our community. Nor do liberal principles or assumptions readily yield such grounds. The Lockean emphasis on individual rights provides the basis only for the hedonistic pursuit of base pleasures. And base pleasures can provide no good life for either individuals or communities.

Communitarians blame liberal capitalism in particular for destroying families and towns, the training grounds of virtue, in the name of economic efficiency. Further, they blame the very basis of capitalist economics—the profit motive—for encouraging the selfishness at the heart of family and social breakdown. At least as damaging for communitarians, however, is the liberal vision of human nature and the faith this vision fosters in society's ability to turn private vice into public prosperity.

Liberalism assumes that individual selfishness can produce the common good. Through a combination of natural laws and political mechanisms, on this view society can benefit from individual self-interest and even greed. From Adam Smith in the eighteenth century to Friedreich von Hayek in the twentieth, liberal economists have insisted that individuals who pursue their own economic gain are led by an "invisible hand" to produce public prosperity. The merchant who wishes to make a profit, for example, must provide good products at good prices—thus benefiting society—or his competitors will put him out of business.

Liberal confidence rests on a vision of "spontaneous order," the belief that men's self-directed actions will produce social order because our interests are in fundamental harmony. My desire for a new coat and the merchant's desire to sell coats combine to produce mutually beneficial commerce. For some liberals this transaction rests purely on calculations of self-interest. Each party tries his best to take advantage of the other, held back only by fear of the law and perhaps the profit-killing public perception that he is a sharp dealer from whom one can expect only bad bargains.

Other liberals argue that each of us acts according to an internal guide or voice, our conscience. Our conscience naturally tells us to act honestly and with integrity. Only a few moral cripples lack this conscience and so must be held in check by laws. The rest of us, liberals argue, come to mutually beneficial agreements because in a voluntary market we can always refuse to close a deal. And liberals believe this same natural harmony of interests applies throughout public life.

So long as a few basic ground rules prohibiting force and fraud are maintained, each of us will promote the public good if left to his own devices. And because private whim produces public good, virtue and the demands of the community become matters of personal preference. We may even come to see the daily demands of family and community life as somehow oppressive and counterproductive because they interfere with both the individual's pursuit of self-fulfillment and the smooth working of nature's invisible hand. Binding marriage contracts and military service, for example, may be seen as unjust infringements on freedom of movement that also keep us from more profitable relationships and economic pursuits. Politics should provide protection against exactly these unjust infringements on the private conduct that in the end produces public prosperity.

Religion, too, comes to seem dangerous for liberty. Locke, arguably the philosophical founder of modern liberalism, based his argument for natural rights on God's creation and ownership of all mankind. Because God created us all, and because He has not given mankind any unmistakable sign that some should rule and use the rest for their own ends, we all have an equal right to our own lives, liberties, and property.

But Locke wrote in the seventeenth century, before liberal societies came to be. Once men became accustomed to enjoying their rights they forgot the need for any ultimate justification for them. Indeed, individualism became self-justifying because in theory it produced more happiness for more individuals than any other system.

Religious worship, while perhaps a pleasant private diversion, in this light is actually dangerous because it teaches us *not* to pursue our own interest, or at any rate our own earthly interest. Religion teaches us that service to one's neighbor is more important than increasing one's own enjoyment and so endangers the mechanism of self-interest on which liberal prosperity relies. Religion also denies the validity of liberalism's vision of the good life by claiming we should follow God's will rather than pursue our individual, self-chosen ends. Thus liberals progressively have pushed religion out of public discourse and failed to replace it with any other set of transcendent standards by which to judge our actions.

But without religion or some other putatively transcendent set of standards telling us to do unto others as we would have done unto us, society breaks down. Individuals come to see their community as a source of benefits to be exploited rather than the locus of a way of life they wish to protect. We lose our commitment to and our knowledge of virtue and commence lives of selfishness, irresponsibility, and even crime.

Unfortunately, according to communitarians, the liberal vision, with its corrupt and corrupting attachment to selfishness, has infected public life in America from the beginning. And in this at least they are not alone. Until recently, academics in general have seen America as a "liberal" nation, from the Revolutionary era to the present.

From the "progressive" Marxist historians of the early part of this century to Louis Hartz's highly influential *The Liberal Tradition in America* and to a large extent even today, commentators have argued that ours has been a liberal nation from the beginning. Our Constitution, in this view, enshrines the idea that self-interest can protect liberty and public peace and is the only proper basis for public life. And American public life and discourse have followed suit, glorifying the individual as the source of public good.

Liberalism rests on the belief that individual behavior naturally leads to social cooperation. Whether self-interest or an instinctive benevolence born of conscience, liberals believe there is something in our nature that produces spontaneous order from self-directed action. Even in politics, selfish conduct produces the public good or at least can be led to do so through mechanical means such as institutional checks and balances.

Thus, in interpreting constitutional ratification debates (and *The Federalist Papers* in particular), commentators emphasize the Founders' "new science of politics." On this reading, the Founders' Constitution is a mechanism intended to chain self-interest to the public good. As Madison, Hamilton, and Jay, writing under the joint nom de plume Publius, stated in *Federalist* 51, "ambition must be made to counteract ambition." By maintaining a separation of governmental powers and by checking and balancing one branch of government and one faction against another, the Constitution would prevent tyranny and promote public order.

Aspects of the Constitution seem to reflect the amoral political vision such commentators find in *The Federalist Papers.* The Constitution is a blueprint of governmental structures rather than a call for unity and public service. Unlike earlier state constitutions, the federal document does not refer to God. Nor does it refer, as had earlier constitutions, to the basis of individual rights in a common belief in God's sovereignty (and our equality in His eyes) and a long, shared tradition of public participation and local group rights.

Further, in *Federalist* 51, Publius explicitly argues that constitutional mechanisms can channel self-interest into productive avenues. Liberal government would protect all citizens by separating political powers among the branches of government, connecting the ambitions of particular politicians with particular competing political offices. In this way "the private interest of every individual may be a sentinel over the public rights."

A number of scholars have argued that the American Revolution sparked a rebirth of commitment to classical Greek and Roman virtues. On this view, service to the political community was a high good, the means to glory and the root of public spirit during the war for independence. Our nation was founded in an effort to save public-minded Americans from the political and economic corruptions of the British imperial king and Parliament. But these "civic humanist" scholars also argue that *liberalism* provides no theory connecting private and public morality. Indeed, they are attempting to "save" the Founding from liberalism by showing that nonliberal elements were active during that era.

And even civic humanist scholars deny the role of virtue in American public life beyond the early republic. J. G. A. Pocock proclaims the Revolution "the last great act" of a classical virtue that was given new life in Renaissance Italy and buried at the Constitutional Convention. Gordon Wood argues that virtue died in American public life in the course of the ratification debates, when Madison successfully reinterpreted the goals and proper mechanisms of republican government in liberal terms, substituting individual rights for public virtue.[11]

According to these commentators, classical virtue went underground either during or soon after our Founding. The ideal of a nation of public-interested citizens was replaced in public discourse by commitment to a commercial republic in which greed would produce liberty and prosperity. But this did not render virtue and communal life irrelevant to the American experience.

The Voices of Community

In seeking a virtuous tradition on which to build, Robert Bellah and his communitarian coauthors of *Habits of the Heart* claim to have found an underground "voice" in American politics competing with our dominant liberalism. This voice, according to Bellah, expresses Americans' yearning for a more democratic community. Americans want to decide as a community, in their local areas, how to allocate economic and social goods—from money to honor to housing arrangements.

Habitually losing out to liberal greed in the public realm, our communitarian or "republican" voice nonetheless affects public life to this day. It inspires political movements aimed at opening liberal politics to virtue and communal sentiments. But these movements, according to Bellah, always fail to "save" our public life from its liberal selfishness.

Communitarians do not seek to show that contemporary politics reflects the republican vision. They hope to show merely that our politics at one time was enriched by this vision, and that it can be so enriched again. As communitarian Michael Sandel puts it, "If the 'republican school' is right about our ideological origins, then perhaps there is hope for revitalizing our public life and restoring a sense of community."[12]

This does not alter the fact that for communitarians contemporary American politics belong, if not completely then in large measure, to liberalism and to Locke in particular. Locke, on this reading, was the philosopher of property and self interest, and his claim that we have a natural right to "life, liberty, and property" can properly be reduced to a defense of the pursuit and enjoyment of wealth. This defense rests on the belief that self-interested individuals will cooperate with one another for their mutual benefit if only government will prevent political oppression and violence.

Factions are a problem, on this liberal view, because they are combinations of individuals who pursue their own interests at public expense. As government must prevent self-interested actors from engaging in force or fraud in the private sphere, so it must guard against individuals who combine for bad purposes—such as securing government decrees eliminating private debt—in the public sphere. But government's role must be limited because government action is by nature coercive and corrupts the natural order of the private sphere. Checks and balances and separated powers, then, constituted the Founders' Lockean defense against those who would interfere with society's spontaneous order. That such a defense would in action protect those who already possessed great wealth (such as mortgage holders, afraid of debt-forgiveness schemes) does not alter the liberal character of this vision of factions.

But faction and fractionalized government did not constitute the whole of the Founders' vision. Publius argues in *Federalist* 10 that factions do not inevitably produce oppression. Factions become dangerous only when their members gain both the impulse and the opportunity to serve themselves at the public expense. Faced with such temptations, "neither moral nor religious motives can be relied on as an adequate control" over faction. That is, moral and religious motives by nature counteract bad motives, and may in fact be sufficient in many circumstances to protect the public good. But while "a dependence on the people is, no doubt, the primary control on the government . . . experience has taught mankind the necessity of auxiliary precautions."

We have come to know *Federalist* 51's "auxiliary precautions" as "the separation of powers" as we have come to know the precautions dealt with in *Federalist* 63 as "checks and balances." But Publius discussed a more primary precaution in *Federalist* 10: representative government. Rather than direct democracy, the Constitution would provide free government on the basis of electoral representation. Americans would elect a small group of governing citizens and thereby "refine and enlarge the public views by passing them through the medium of a chosen body . . . whose patriotism and love of justice will be least likely to sacrifice it to temporary or partial considerations." Americans would choose representatives with "fit characters," with "enlightened views and virtuous sentiments," who would guard the public good. In this way, Publius argued, they could sustain free government.

The Founders did not seek to construct free government on self-interest alone. They expected (or at least hoped) that Americans would elect good, unselfish, and public-spirited men to protect their liberty. The mass of Americans would have sufficient virtue to reject representatives concerned solely with advancing their own local interests. Instead they would choose men of higher virtue who would recognize and seek to serve the public interest. The Constitution would not produce virtue but would rely on virtues "spontaneously" produced in the associations making up its prized private sphere.

Our Constitution clearly is morally incomplete. But then it frames an incomplete government. As written, it gives only certain delegated powers to the central government. The bulk of power, activity, and attention was intended to remain in the states and localities. Character formation was not a federal issue because, as George W. Carey has argued, "the family, churches, schools, communities— would cultivate and nourish the virtue necessary not only for the perpetuation of the regime, but for the pursuit of the collective good."[13]

The Founders were not, then, wholly pessimistic about the possibility of virtue. Nor did they consciously reject virtue in favor of self-interest. Rather, they were confident that the institutions of local life would produce a reasonably virtuous people, whose excesses could be controlled by "auxiliary precautions." Because men are basically reasonable and our interests generally are in harmony, on this view self-interest is dangerous only when the temptation to do wrong is great and the defenses against it inadequate.

Nonliberal elements clearly were influential in the Founding. But the Founders need not be "saved" from the charge that they were liberals in order to account for their concern with virtue. Their confidence in human nature is well in keeping with Locke's (and many seventeenth- and eighteenth-century) "liberal" visions. Locke's discussion of the growth of political societies shows a confidence in men's ability to form peaceful associations on the basis of mutual self-interest. Not just commercial life but even family and political life for

Locke grows from self-interest, which naturally produces associations of mutual deference and peaceful cooperation.

Our natures incline us to love and revere our parents (mothers as well as fathers) and incline our parents to teach us the ways of virtue. Even in the state of nature, for Locke, there is a law to guide our actions, a natural law that dictates familial ties and demands respect for individual rights. Natural law tells us "that being all equal and independent, no one ought to harm another in his life, health, liberty, or possessions." We all naturally recognize this law and recognize that it requires us to treat one another with fairness.[14]

We require government only because we tend to favor our own cause too much when we are involved in any altercation. We need government to provide neutral judges to settle our private disputes. The agreement to form a political society—the "social contract" so often identified with Locke—was made necessary by human frailties. But it was made *possible* by mutual trust. Real contracts (as opposed to the Hobbesian pseudocontract of public peace secured only by the overwhelming force of the sovereign) require that each party trust the other, to some degree, to uphold his side of the bargain.

Trust that the sovereign's interests are in harmony with one's own is the basis of all government. Indeed, according to Locke, even monarchies arise from trusting consent. Monarchies originally came into being because "it was easy, and almost natural for children by a tacit, and scarce avoidable consent, to make way for the father's authority and government. They had been accustomed in their childhood to follow his direction, and to refer their little differences to him, and when they were men, who fitter to rule them?"[15] Through a series of small steps, paternal government became monarchy.

This is not to say that communitarians are wrong to see in American liberalism the roots of the individualism they abhor. Quite the contrary, given early American confidence in natural laws controlling human nature, it is not surprising that the invisible hand became the dominant metaphor for so much of public life. Because natural forces drove us to act virtuously and promote public happiness, it was thought that all government need do was control itself (through checks and balances) and prevent private violence. Given this, public prosperity would continue to increase forever.

The Breakdown of Liberalism

Theodore J. Lowi has argued that America's vision of itself as a self-regulating society gave way when it confronted the Great Depression. Liberalism decreed that government be limited, restricted by numerous checks and formalities. Liberal government could not, in Lowi's view, face the depression and win, particularly because Americans no longer knew why they should value it. Constitutional checks and balances produced gridlock—severely limited government that could not "solve" then-pressing economic problems. Because liberals felt that government existed to solve problems, liberal government's failure to solve the depression discredited their political vision.

But Americans did not, as in Europe, turn to a socialist, planned economy as a cure for their ills. Instead they replaced liberalism with "interest group liberalism." Instead of formalism, we now would depend on informal bargaining among groups organized to pursue their own interests to keep government in check and, more importantly, hammer out agreements concerning what government should do to help us. Checks and balances would be replaced by bargaining tables as the instrumentalities of politics.

Americans rejected "old" liberalism—limited government based on confidence in natural laws of human nature. They also rejected authoritarian socialism, with its confidence in man's "scientific" ability to map out the details of economic and political life. Instead Americans chose to *extend* the logic of liberalism into an expanded public sphere. As Lowi puts it, they founded a new liberalism, borrowing "from political science the pluralist notion that the pulling and hauling among competing interests is sufficient due process."[16] They assumed that fair bargaining naturally would produce mutually beneficial results in politics as they all along had assumed it would produce such results in economic life.

Americans rejected limited government, but they did not replace it with a government that would plan their economic and political lives for them. Instead they established a national government whose primary purpose according to Lowi was "to provide domestic tranquility by reducing risk. This risk may be physical or it may be fiscal. In order to fulfill this sacred obligation, the national government shall be deemed to have sufficient power to eliminate threats from the environment through regulation, and to eliminate threats from economic uncertainty through insurance."[17]

Interest group liberalism remained liberalism. It was based on the conviction that each of us should be left alone, wherever possible, to pursue his own private goals. Government would merely "protect" us from economic and physical uncertainty, in fact "freeing" us to lead fuller lives. Of course, this meant that power had to be concentrated in national bureaucratic organizations, eliminating traditional checks and balances that reduce executive efficiency.

On Lowi's view we dispensed with the rule of law in favor of bureaucratic discretion so that the government might help more individuals without having to "interfere" unduly with their lives. We no longer would pass laws directing particular individuals to do or not do specific things under specified circumstances. Instead we would have broad, vague legislation, for example establishing a new agency to create a "safe working environment." Instead of directing agency employees to take specified actions, the legislation would empower them to make ad hoc agreements with regulated industries concerning what the legislation means and how it should be implemented. These agreements would be "fair," it was assumed, because everyone would get a hearing—because everyone would have a right to form or join an interest group.

The new liberalism frees government to provide the people with many more material goods. But it has problems. To begin with, when the driving force of government is the desire to reduce risk, everything becomes a proper object of regulation. Because everything brings risks in this life, the government has a right, and even a duty, to regulate it to make the risk as low as possible.

In addition the new state is, in matters of regulation, literally lawless. It provides no coherent set of rules that prohibit specific kinds of conduct akin to criminal laws prohibiting murder in its varied forms. Instead the liberal regulatory state provides only rules governing bargaining among groups. The lawmaking authority demands a "safe working environment" but tells those involved nothing about how they should produce it. It provides only guidelines for bureaucrats to follow in determining what standards of "safety" (still undefined) to apply and to whom.

The resulting rules and regulatory actions are presumed just, whatever their content, because they are the result of "consultation" with various interest groups. But there is no claim that the rules so promulgated are inherently right, or even that the resulting actions will produce the desired results. The people must be content with a government that provides fair rules to govern their own self-interested bargaining over regulatory policy and the distribution of public goods such as tax breaks, subsidies and other forms of government largesse.

Unfortunately, such a liberalism cannot sustain even the limited virtue called for by the Founders. Because only those who are organized into interest groups can gain a hearing, and because the system assumes that the results of interest group lobbying will automatically be just, there is no call for public-minded service. Cynicism and a chaos of conflicting policies (government policies to discourage smoking co-existing with tobacco subsidies, for example) are the natural result.

Government risk minimization also poses problems for liberalism. Although it leaves us free to engage in the regulated pursuit of our self-chosen goals, risk minimization actually undermines a prime liberal virtue: self-reliance. In reducing our risks, government saps our desire and ability to take care of ourselves.

Liberal confidence in the private sphere's ability to produce virtue rests on the belief that individuals are naturally led to work, form families, and train their children in the ways of self-reliance. Only in this way will the "natural laws" of market forces produce public happiness from self-interested action. But government welfare programs create incentives for individuals to rely on government handouts rather than work; they encourage fathers to abandon their families, secure in the belief that government will see to the needs of mother and children.

Lowi has argued that liberalism undermines itself. Liberals believe that government should not be in the business of judging private morality. Government should instead insure us against the harmful effects of private actions.[18] But liberal insurance programs encourage the very behavior they are supposed to guard against. For decades Americans have been told that policymakers could "get at the root causes" of crime, illegitimacy and poverty. These root causes, we were told, are primarily economic. If the government would redistribute money and job opportunities sufficiently well, then families would form, people would take jobs, and criminals would choose to make an honest living.

Unfortunately, the antipoverty and regulatory programs instituted in the 1960s actually encourage the kinds of behavior that produce poverty, crime, and hopelessness. Communitarians recognize as much.[19] But the situation becomes dire when one notes that government's role as facilitator of personal choice has turned welfare into another "right." For contemporary liberals, government must support those without work so that they may continue to pursue their own self-chosen lifestyles without suffering from material want. This means that government must continue to support aberrant, unproductive behavior. What is more, because government cannot give us all the concrete goods to which we have a "right" as we pursue our own ends, its citizens always see it as a failure.

Liberal government cannot give the self-directed individual the absolute safety, financial security, and freedom to which he feels entitled. It cannot even maintain public order because individuals do not believe it legitimately can direct them to curb their appetites and desires. The dissatisfied, ambitious individual remains the center of concern but cannot be controlled. So public life breaks down into a chaos of competing "rights" asserted by competing interest groups in the legislative process, competing legal pressure groups in the judicial process, and competing lawyers in the "process" of private life. Local culture—the institutions, beliefs, and practices that make up a community's way of life—no longer serves as the spontaneous, self-perpetuating source of virtuous citizens. Instead the moral vacuousness of liberal politics invades our communities, replacing the moral and institutional ties that bind a people together with a destructive glorification of selfishness.

Saving Liberalism from Itself

William Galston observes that "the United States is in trouble because it has failed to attend to the dependence of sound politics on sound culture."[20] On this view liberals do not understand the proper connection between private conduct and public order because of their blind faith in the social utility of selfishness. Communitarians like Galston argue that we must open our eyes to the dangers of selfishness and reorient our policies, encouraging personal responsibility and concern for the good of one's local community. Only in this way can we reconstitute a viable culture and politics.

As a starting point, communitarians seek a number of reforms to America's current welfare system. These reforms, including increased day-care subsidies, nationalized health care, and public works jobs, are intended to make it more attractive for those on welfare to get job training and return to work. In this way individuals may regain control of their lives as well as the habits of responsibility that come with steady employment.

These habits are useful. But communitarians are more concerned to promote public spirit than utility. They want communities to work together to maintain public civility. They are willing to use public institutions and authorities to maintain order and develop regular habits in the people because they believe this is necessary for a worthwhile public life.

Unlike traditional liberals, communitarians are eager to discuss the kind of character and character-forming institutions they feel are necessary for a good life and a good society. Communitarians seem, then, to reject liberalism's emphasis on the primacy of the individual. But it would be wrong to claim that communitarians wish to construct an illiberal, let alone "undemocratic," society. Their platform observes, rather, that "the success of the democratic experiment in ordered liberty . . . depends . . . on building shared values, habits and practices that assure respect for one another's rights and regular fulfillment of personal, civic, and collective responsibilities."[21]

Liberty depends on proper character, which in turn depends on the maintenance of a healthy culture. As Galston puts it, "a healthy liberal democracy . . . requires . . . the right kinds of citizens possessing the virtues appropriate to a liberal democratic community." And cultural institutions, particularly "stable, intact families, make a vital contribution of such citizens."[22] According to Galston cultural ills such as crime, poverty, and hopelessness undermine liberty. Because they prevent these ills, we must support families, along with other local associations and institutions that help families survive. Families are good because they produce the kinds of citizens we need if we are to maintain a liberal democratic society.

Commitment to families and local communities is not new. Nor is the view that it is in these local associations that we learn the basics of decent behavior. Aristotle argued twenty-five hundred years ago that it is the community's duty to use both political and social means to instill proper habits in the citizens. Only in this way, he argued, could citizens learn how to lead good lives and learn to join together to help the community.

But virtue itself did not begin in the community as a whole. It began at home. Thinkers from Aristotle to the nineteenth-century French philosopher and statesman Alexis de Tocqueville—himself a favorite of communitarians—have argued that we begin to form habits of virtue in the intimacy of family life. Through the subtle rewards and punishments we all receive from the time we are infants we gain the ability to recognize what is expected of us in personal conduct—share, do not destroy the furniture, and so on. Through the often not so subtle punishments and rewards of the playground and our relations with family and neighbors we extend and develop habits such as honesty, politeness, and hard work as we reach adulthood.

Tocqueville argued we even gain a "taste" for doing unto others as we would have done unto us because this conduct makes life more pleasant. And such a view is in keeping with Aristotle's notion that in the end what holds a community together is friendship. Only if we can trust our neighbor, or merchant, or customer to abide by basic rules of decency and civility can we get on with daily life. Only if we can agree on standards of conduct and expect them to be followed (for the most part) can our community survive.

Liberalism rejects these standards of conduct. Customary standards are confining, binding us whether we wish to be bound or not. Standards to which we do not overtly consent keep us from exercising our individual will and following our individual desires and so are, for the liberal, unjust.

Conservatives, on the other hand, openly accept the authority of customary standards and ways of acting. For conservatives the point is not to free the individual from all constraints or construct the perfectly just and free political order. The point is to nurture proper conduct. As Russell Kirk, the father of modern American conservatism, observed:

It has been said by liberal intellectuals that the conservative believes all social questions, at heart, to be questions of private morality. Properly understood, this statement is quite true. A society in which men and women are governed by belief in an enduring moral order, by a strong sense of right and wrong, by personal convictions about justice and honor, will be a good society—whatever political machinery it may utilize; while a society in which men and women are morally adrift, ignorant of norms, and intent chiefly upon gratification of appetites, will be a bad society—no matter how many people vote and no matter how liberal its formal constitution may be.[23]

Conservatism rests on the conviction that our traditions, varied as they are, nonetheless embody essential elements of an immutable, universal natural law. The Roman jurist Cicero referred to natural law as the governing law of the world, which has its foundation in nature and not in mere opinion. Following Cicero, conservatives look to the consensus of mankind, found in history, for evidence of an eternal order that we reject or "improve upon" at our peril.

According to conservatives, we must look to the Golden Rule—the admonition found in some form in all cultures to love your neighbor as yourself—as an essential guide to our conduct. But we also must respect our local traditions. Traditions are accepted, preexisting practices, and they determine in large part what kind of treatment we expect from one another.

We come to know our traditions in the basic associations of local life. Robert A. Nisbet argues in *The Quest for Community* that

in earlier times, and even today in diminishing localities, there was an intimate relation between the local, kinship, and religious groups within which individuals consciously lived and the major economic, charitable, and protective functions which are indispensable to human existence. There was an intimate conjunction of larger institutional goals and the social groups small enough to infuse the individual's life with a sense of membership in society and the meaning of the basic moral values.

But the modern welfare state has made the fundamental institutions of life irrelevant. This state is committed to "social justice" and insists that we can achieve justice only by gathering everyone into large bureaucratically designed and integrated categories and organizations. It has destroyed the connections between private associations and public life and with them the bases of community and virtue.[24]

Our families, churches, and local associations all have customs that provide standards by which we can judge one another's conduct. If we dismiss these standards, conservatives argue, the institutions that formed them will fall into disrepute and die. Then the state will be the only institution left to teach us right from wrong, and the state is not up to this task. As a result, we will lose our ability to judge the morality of our actions as the state comes to regulate more and more of our lives.

Communitarians wish to dispense with notions of natural law and the authority of custom. They agree with traditional liberals that both are too confining and that they may protect inequalities of power and income many find unjust. But communitarians also wish to maintain the connection between private habituation—private *conduct*—and the public good. We must learn proper habits, or we will ignore our public and familial duties and society will disintegrate. As the communitarian platform asserts:

> the preservation of individual liberty depends on the active maintenance of the institutions of civil society where citizens learn respect for others as well as self-respect; where we acquire a lively sense of our personal and civic responsibilities, along with an appreciation of our own rights and the rights of others: where we develop the skills of self-government as well as the habit of governing ourselves and learn to serve others—not just self.

Only if we have the proper character can we preserve liberal democratic society, the only kind of society communitarians believe can respect and protect individual rights.

A community must train its children or it will disintegrate. Galston says "the core issue is a traditional one: the role of the family as a moral unit that transmits, or fails to transmit, the beliefs and dispositions needed to support oneself and to contribute to one's community."[25] These "beliefs and dispositions" are what communitarians seem to be after—the bases of personal responsibility, cooperation, and public spirit. Without them, communitarians believe, liberal society cannot survive.

Communitarians defend the family for a particular reason: because it produces the particular habits and virtues necessary for the maintenance of the liberal democratic society they value. As Galston argues, in a book significantly titled *Liberal Purposes,*

> the family is the critical arena in which independence and a host of other virtues must be engendered. The weakening of families is thus fraught with danger for liberal societies. In turn, strong families rest on specific virtues. Without fidelity, stable families cannot be maintained. Without a concern for children that extends well beyond the boundaries of adult self-regard, parents cannot effectively discharge their responsibility to help form secure, self-reliant young people. In short, the independence required for liberal social life rests on self-restraint and self-transcendence—the virtues of family solidarity.[26]

The family, then, must be valued and protected for the good things it produces. And some of its products are quite concrete. As Galston points out, "from the standpoint of economic well-being and sound psychological development, the evidence indicates that the intact two-parent family is generally preferable to the available alternatives."[27]

Because families are so crucial to the well-being of both individuals and society as a whole, Galston argues, government must see to it that they survive the economic and cultural trials of modern life. Financial aid and psychological counseling should be made available. And divorce, while not prohibited, should become more difficult and time-consuming than it is now.

We should protect families because they are necessary for turning children into responsible, well-adjusted adults. Thus we should institute waiting periods and other steps to make divorce and remarriage less common and less wrenching for children. For the same reasons, Galston argues, courts should put children's interests first in any divorce proceedings. Financial support from the noncustodial spouse should be far more generous and strictly enforced for the benefit of the children.[28]

Communitarians seek to save liberalism from itself by solving its core cultural problem. Liberalism cannot produce public spirit because it is based on the notion that self-interest produces the public good, easy enough since the public exists merely to serve the private aspirations of private citizens. Communitarians condemn such a formulation as "selfish." They seek to replace its individualistic assumptions with an understanding of man's social nature.

We all are who we are in large part because of our families and other local associations. These institutions trained us, over time, so that we developed our characteristic habits or ways of doing things. Therefore it is vitally important, even or perhaps especially in liberal democratic societies, to see to it that families and other associations survive and function properly. But to what end? Why do we want families to turn children into responsible adults? And why sacrifice our own desires to do it? Who is to say what a "well-adjusted" adult is in any event? The true character of communitarianism comes forth from its answers to these questions.

The Liberal Good

According to communitarians we seek, and should seek, to fulfill ourselves. Developing our own life plans and putting them into action, we exercise our faculties and our faculty for moral choice in particular. Acting on our spontaneous feelings and desires we create a unique life for ourselves. We follow the voice that is inside us, and the better we do this, the more fulfilled and more fully human we become.

Virtue, in the sense of abiding by community standards (if you will), is good for communitarians only *instrumentally,* only because we must habitually abide by liberal democratic rules and values if we are to have a liberal society. And why is a liberal society good? Precisely because it does not answer the question "how should we live?" Because it lets us answer *for ourselves* the most important questions of life, morality and good character.

Galston argues that

liberal societies rest . . . on the belief that the development of *individual* capacities is an important element of the good . . . liberal societies contend that their organization reflects . . . two fundamental truths of the human condition: the diversity of human types and the inherent incapacity of the public sphere to encompass more than a portion of human activity or to fulfill more than a part of human aspiration.[29]

Public life, for Galston, should be the servant of the more fundamental pursuits of private life. It provides us with *tools* with which to fulfill our own highly varied desires and our own visions of the good life.

According to Galston Americans constructed their liberal government to provide themselves with a number of good things. What are these good things? For a list Galston looks to the preamble of our Constitution—securing domestic tranquility, providing for the common defense, promoting the general welfare, and so on. He finds our liberal society worth defending because it does a relatively good job of providing these concrete goods.[30] But these goods are by nature instrumental. They cannot provide a good life for the citizens. And they can *help* us lead good lives only if we put them to good use.

But what good use? Authenticity. Taylor is most explicit, here. He notes we are living in a "culture of authenticity." In such a culture, being in touch with your instinctive "moral sense" is no longer good because it makes you treat others as you ought to—according to some transcendent set of standards such as the Golden Rule. Instead, in a culture of authenticity, being in touch with your internal instincts, being "true to yourself" is good for its own sake. It makes you a "true and full human being."[31]

Individual autonomy—following one's authentic or spontaneously generated desires and goals—is the good for which all other putative goods must serve as mere tools. Communitarians are liberal because they reject any formulation of the goals of life that transcends development of our individual talents and capacities—that, for example, sees loyalty to one's family, class, or God as imperative even if it means leading an impoverished life in terms of both material rewards and personal development. They do not wholly dismiss visions of the good, such as religious salvation. But communitarians such as Taylor insist that such visions are good only instrumentally. They should be used when and to the extent that they help individuals flourish.

Taylor lists a number of possible "backgrounds" against which we must "define our identities." These include religion, history, class solidarity and natural law. We each need one or more of these "things that matter" in order to develop our selves. Taylor does not, however, want us to join together as a community and *choose* among or order these "things that matter." The authentic self must define what matters by conversing with other selves. In the end each of us must decide for himself what matters.

We no longer have, or *should* have, a coherent set of shared, "supposedly sacred" beliefs. Beliefs like the early modern conception of a "Great Chain of Being," according to which man has a singular place in God's creation between beasts and angels and in which each of us also has a specific place or station in our society, no longer hold true. We no longer look to such beliefs to find our particular duties. And according to Taylor beliefs that do not order our lives are by nature false.

We lack any set of common beliefs to order our common life. We have no common set of principles that in and of themselves tell us what is right. Thus moral choice is and should be a matter of individual desires and dispositions.[32]

Galston at least recognizes the moral conflict inherent in this vision. We need communities to fulfill ourselves, and a people cannot have a real community without a *common* vision of the good. Thus Galston argues that we must reopen the public square to moral arguments; arguments concerning what it means and what it takes to lead a good life. We must, for example, pay greater respect to individuals' religious visions than we do now.

But Galston also argues that we cannot allow religious arguments into public debates unless they are phrased in instrumental terms. For example, religious folk may defend the family but should do so only on the grounds that it is a useful tool in promoting "the successful functioning of a liberal community"—because intact families produce more productive citizens. *Religious* arguments concerning the sanctity of marriage vows—let alone the sacred character of traditional sex-roles, sexual orientation, and so on—should not be allowed because they foster dissension and intolerance.[33]

This does not mean that private opinions concerning the relative worth of various ways of life cannot be strongly held. But for Galston they must be held in combination with the conviction that ways of life we consider inferior and even morally repellent must be tolerated.

Public discussion must be based on the view that coercion is to be eschewed in favor of persuasion.

What is more, public education must both maintain and teach "civic tolerance." Again, for Galston this does not necessarily mean that parents may not rear their children in a given way of life. Nor does it mean that the schools must teach that all ways of life are equally good. But it does mean that the state must guarantee that parents not impede "the normal physical, intellectual, and emotional development of their children. Nor may they impede the acquisition of civic competence and loyalty."[34] Parents must allow teachers to grade their children according to how well they learn and practice liberal values; values that go against and may even destroy small, traditional communities like the Old Order Amish.

The state must see to it that children are taught liberal virtues, and toleration in particular. It need not take over all functions of the family, however, because "every child will see that he or she is answerable to institutions other than the family—institutions whose substantive requirements may well cut across the grain of parental wishes and beliefs." In particular, the child will be given "critical distance" from his parents' way of life by a public school system that does not hold authority and faith sacred.[35]

Families are good because and to the extent that they complement and further the goals of liberal democratic society. To the extent that they teach intolerance, "the unexamined life," or any way of life that stifles individuality they are bad. Galston defends families precisely because their tendency to teach current liberal democratic values outweighs their occasionally excessive "parental brainwashing" into any one particular form of life.[36]

Taylor also argues that we must recognize the importance of families and other associations in forming our character, without granting them any unquestioned moral authority. He seeks to return "holistic individualism" to our public life. "Holistic individualism" holds that man is a primarily social animal. He acts in the context of his habituated loyalties (for example, to his ethnic group) and political sentiments "but at the same time prizes liberty and individual differences very highly."[37] Our social nature is a fact with which we must come to grips on this view. But our goal remains *individual* flourishing.

Taylor seeks to correct the mistake made by English-speaking heirs of John Stuart Mill. These heirs have forgotten that *On Liberty* did not merely sum up liberalism as that political community that tolerates maximum deviance. Mill also insisted that only societies at an advanced stage of civilization and education have the means at their disposal to make such a life possible.

Tolerance, for Mill and for Taylor, is the ultimate liberal virtue. But tolerance is not natural. It does not spring automatically from man's selfish desires. Tolerance must be *taught* as a democratic "value" or virtue.

What Shall We Value?

Communitarians add to liberalism the conviction that our desires and dispositions are formed in local institutions and associations, and that these desires and dispositions can undermine society if not properly formed. Society's job is to promote individual flourishing. But if it is to do its job it also must teach its citizens to defend, serve, and participate in its public life.

The liberal emphasis on individual rights frays the social fabric. It also keeps us, as individuals, from leading full lives. Individuals demand their "right" to be free from public standards and controls so that they may act as they wish. But the proper goal of life is not mere liberty, mere independence, or mere choice. The proper goal of life is individual fulfillment. And Taylor argues that we must find fulfillment "in something . . . which has significance independent of us or our desires." We cannot develop our authentic selves merely by satisfying our own appetites. We must serve something that transcends our wants of the moment. But this something can take many forms: "I can find fulfillment in God, or a political cause, or tending the earth."[38]

The communitarian goal is not mere choice. But neither is it service to any specific "higher" good. The goal is personal fulfillment, which communitarians believe requires both a sense that one belongs to a community and the ability to choose one's own lifestyle and life plan. But this raises a problem. It seems unclear how we can establish any common standards concerning what goals we want to encourage individuals to pursue. Without these common standards it remains unclear how we will judge conduct virtuous or unvirtuous.

We must choose as individuals, and without closing off future revision, what shall matter to us. But why commit to something that is
not important in and of itself? Why seek fulfillment by serving something that in reality is no more important than any other higher order
good (why serve God when we might just as well serve "the earth")?
Why serve a community or fulfill our duties to other people when fulfillment of our own desires, choices, and life plans is the final goal?

Taylor is aware of this problem. He addresses it by arguing that
relationships of mere utility, in which we use other people for the
wealth or pleasure we get from them, are by nature unfulfilling. Because we develop our characters by interacting with other individuals, "it would seem that having merely instrumental relationships is
to act in a self-stultifying way. The notion that one can pursue one's
fulfillment in this way seems illusory."[39] Using other people results in
a shallow, unfulfilled individual identity and life. We may satisfy our
desires for things such as money, fame and sex. But if we do not form
full relationships in which we share our lives with others we will not
become true and full human beings.

Self-fulfillment requires social commitment. As Taylor puts it, "if
the intense relations of self-exploration are going to be identity-form-
ing, then they can't be in principle tentative—though they can, alas,
in fact break up." The same goes for our "background understandings" or "things that matter." If we see God or the earth as merely
tentative goods, useful only so long as we find enjoyment in serving
them, we will not be able to use them to develop ourselves.

We should convince ourselves that our relations with others (and
with our "things that matter") are important in and of themselves because only in this way can they serve their instrumental purpose.
Only if we act as if we cannot cast off our spouse, God, or friend can
we develop ourselves as we ought. Yet it remains true that we may,
and often should, cast off marriage, religion, or friendship.

Apparently Taylor wants us to convince ourselves that people
and commitments are not tentative when in fact they are. Such a self-
imposed false consciousness seems unlikely to motivate unselfish
conduct for long. But Taylor believes that our natures allow for both
substantial commitment and significant autonomy. To begin with,
while engaged in committed action we do not stop to consider how
tentative our commitment really is; we act. As important, there are
certain commitments, for Taylor, that are deeply imbedded in our

identities and so become difficult to cast off and impossible to entirely expunge from our personalities.

Liberal tolerance actually provides the basis for communitarian
commitment. Tolerance requires us to recognize "the equal value of
different ways of being" and of the individuals who lead them. But if,
for example, "men and women are equal, it is not because they are
different, but because overriding the difference are some properties,
common or complementary, which are of value. They are beings capable of reason, or love, or memory, or dialogical recognition." To recognize our equality we first must recognize a commonly held standard of value. We must join with our fellows to construct a social
standard or "horizon of significance" according to which we can
value one another's differing lifestyles.[40]

We form communities by joining together to decide what is important to us. As the communitarian platform puts it, "communal
values must be judged by external and overriding criteria, based on
shared human experience." Somehow the "external and overriding
criteria" by which we judge our values must be based on the experience of the community. That is, it is not the voice of God that tells us
what is right, but the voice of the community as it ruminates on its
own experiences.

Even the standards of liberal procedural justice must bow, on occasion, to shared experience. Taylor argues that the Canadian prov-
ince of Quebec must protect its French culture and language "even if
this involves some restriction on individual freedoms." English
speakers must bow to the needs of Quebec's remaining French culture. Quebec society, with its shared French culture, language, and
history, must pursue a vision of the good based on its shared experience, even if its actions at times conflict with liberal democratic values.[41]

Taylor goes so far as to doubt our ability to condemn Islamic calls
for the assassination of Salman Rushdie, whose book *The Satanic
Verses* mocked that religion. We must accord the demands of Islamic
culture equal status with the demands of our own. We must hesitate
before condemning actions that violate liberal ethics. According to
one form of Islamic teaching, Rushdie's blasphemy calls out for the
ultimate punishment. Because this teaching is accepted by numerous
individuals, it constitutes their horizon of significance, defining what
is important for a given community, and so we must respect it. Taylor

does not, of course, go so far as to suggest we give up Rushdie for execution. That would violate our own commitment to free speech. Thus we have an unresolvable conflict among values, calling for mutual tolerance and forbearance. What we should do with Islamic gunmen who seek to carry out Rushdie's death sentence Taylor does not say.

Our only proper (liberal) recourse amid such conflict is to "fuse our horizons" with the other culture and so expand our idea of what is worthy. Beginning with the presumption of equal worth, we must study the other culture to determine how we may come to value its goals and conceptions of the good. Any other means of examination is based on our own standards of worth. Thus it involves condescension and should be avoided.[42]

Indeed, to fail to accord equal respect to other cultures is to commit the sin of "non-recognition." It is to cause a concrete harm to the "self-esteem" and identity of another. Denying the equality of another culture was not always a bad thing, but liberal society has reached the stage where nonrecognition is now on a par with physical assault.

Taylor argues that we already use his favored form of cultural analysis. In liberal democratic societies, at least, we have gone beyond cultural selfishness and prejudice and achieved "universal solidarity" or benevolence. We have come to value the well-being of others even if they do not share our history or values. Although we do not always live up to the ideal of universal benevolence, we attempt to aid foreigners in trouble and establish physical and financial security for all.[43]

At first this argument seems strange coming from Taylor. After all, he is committed to the notion that we are socially embedded beings who achieve personal fulfillment through service to those with whom we share significant values. Why, then, would he celebrate universal benevolence? The notion that we should love all men equally and seek equally to serve them all would seem to undermine the basis of any substantive community. We are imbedded in families and local associations, not mankind. Thus to call on us to love all men equally would loosen the local ties that foster virtue.

But Taylor wishes us to value all men equally. Our problem, in his view, is not that we have spread our affections too widely. Rather, we have become too enamored of the *mechanisms* of universal benevolence. We concentrate too much on the production and distribution of goods and so do not treat aid recipients as fully human.[44] Our commitment to the instruments of benevolence blinds us to the human needs (especially self-esteem) of our fellows and so exacerbates our slide into selfish individualism. If only we were truly committed to the principle of equality, and to the conviction that each individual is equal to all others, we would transcend selfishness and produce true community.

The Politics of Solidarity

Liberalism from its inception has stood for equality before the law. Whether in Locke's *Letter Concerning Toleration* or repeated arguments against broad readings of the British king's right to act outside the law, liberals have argued that punishments and rewards should be handed out according to known, universal rules. The sovereign's unbridled will was unjust because it might reward or punish for improper (or "unequal") reasons.

Further, the argument went, laws themselves should punish only those activities that cause actual harm to the commonwealth. Such convictions easily led to a liberal hostility toward unearned power and privilege, most prominently inherited aristocracy. In subsequent years it has produced the demand that government guarantee through various "civil rights" measures, that career advancement in even the private sphere be based solely on economic value or merit. Because it is by nature impossible for the government to define and dictate, let alone ensure, this "fairness," men came to demand affirmative action, quotas, and other policies designed to "compensate" individuals for unequal abilities that policymakers blamed on past injustices.

In the end the very idea of merit became problematic. Determinations of merit require that we judge the wisdom and virtue of private choices. And this is most unliberal.

To believe that we all should follow our own "authentic" or spontaneous feelings and convictions one must believe that all individuals are equally capable of leading moral lives. To allow for unequal distributions of income, to allow people to become rich and poor, then, is to reward and punish individuals unjustly. It is to value one choice of lifestyle above another. Thus Taylor worries about "the ways the demands of economic growth are used to justify very unequal distributions of wealth and income."[45]

Even old conceptions of honor must be destroyed in favor of "a universalist and egalitarian sense, where we talk of the inherent 'dignity of human beings.'" No longer can we allow one's place in society—one's profession or family for example—to determine his status, let alone his identity. Indeed, the failure to recognize someone as an equal, whether on the basis of race, sex, or choice of lifestyle, now is for Taylor a very concrete attack on that person. It harms his sense of self-worth and personal identity and so should be avoided.[46]

Equality is good for its own sake and because it shows and reinforces our commitment to authenticity. But if even equality serves the cause of individual authenticity the question becomes how we can come together as a true community. Tempted by selfishness and instrumentalism, how can we forge a common conception of the good? How can we put this conception into practice in a manner that will promote individual flourishing? Taylor, and communitarians in general, find the answer in politics. Taylor argues that the "only effective counter to the drift towards atomism and instrumentalism . . . is the formation of an effective common purpose through democratic action, . . . fragmentation grows to the extent that people no longer identify with their political community."

Taylor's emphasis on the political community causes him to deem "partial groupings" like ethnic minorities, adherents of particular religions, and special interests as dangerous. These local groups "fragment" citizens' allegiance to the community. And "a fragmented society is one whose members find it harder and harder to identify with their political society as a community."

We must see our political society as our primary community, as the proper focus of our individual allegiance. Adherence to religious or other "fragmented" groups "comes about partly through a weakening of the bonds of sympathy" among citizens, which in turn comes about when democratic participation degenerates into interest group liberalism. When our family, locality, or interest group becomes more important to us than our political community, we have become individualists; we have sunk into selfishness, forgetting the high virtue of patriotism.[47]

According to Taylor, patriotism has been and will continue to be an important bulwark of liberal democracy because "pure enlightened self-interest will never move enough people strongly enough to constitute a real threat to potential despots and putschists." For evidence Taylor turns to the Watergate scandal. The only basis for public outrage at such a seemingly petty series of events, he argues, was the widespread belief that President Nixon and his aides had acted against "the American way."[48]

Our history and experience have produced a particular set of habits and beliefs by which we expect our public officials to abide. Openness, honesty in public dealings, and respect for the democratic process form key parts of this "civil religion." Because Nixon betrayed the people's trust that he would abide by the tenets of their public system of beliefs and habits, he fell from public favor and power.

The communitarian project is tied intimately to the liberal democratic civil religion. Communitarianism builds on liberal individuals' belief in democratic values. It seeks to foster communal action and a communitarian personality through democratic participation. As the communitarian platform states, its adherents

> seek to make government more representative, more participatory, and more responsible to all members of the community. We seek to find ways to accord citizens more information and more say, more often. We seek to curb the role of private money, special interests, and corruption in government. Similarly, we ask how 'private governments,' whether corporations, labor unions, or voluntary associations, can become more responsible to their members and to the needs of the community.[49]

Private or public, economic, social, or political, all associations must be opened up to greater participation. Only in this way will they respond to the needs and desires of their members. Only in this way will society again provide its citizens with a sense of belongingness, with the belief that their lives have meaning.

According to communitarians individuals develop their identities by participating in various groups. But the principles according to which all citizens of a liberal democratic nation must live are fundamentally political rather than social or economic. It is to the political community that we must look first in ordering our loyalties. And it is to the political principles of equality and democracy that we must look in judging even private associations. Associations that exclude (for example, on the basis of sex) violate these prime liberal directives.

Communitarians argue that local associations, at least in our liberal democratic society, must be reconstructed along liberal democratic lines. But this is not to say that we must eliminate them. Taylor argues that it is best for a society if its political power is decentralized, particularly "if the units to which power is devolved already figure as communities in the lives of their members." Individuals may share a history more narrow in scope than that of the nation. They may, for example, share a regional or ethnic culture. "Regional societies" such as the provinces of Canada have their own common culture and history and so constitute communities. They can be trusted to involve their people in common projects and a common commitment to the good of the whole. Such regional societies even have the right to violate some liberal precepts in order to maintain their character. But a liberal democratic nation also requires "a common understanding that can hold these regional societies together."[50]

Communitarians do indeed call for commitment to local communities. We form our identities principally through interaction with family and neighbors, not with the nation as a whole. And local associations can add to the public discourse concerning how we ought to act as a nation. The communitarian platform says that "America's diverse communities of memory and mutual aid are rich resources of moral voices—voices that ought to be heeded in a society that increasingly threatens to become normless, self-centered, and driven by greed, special interests, and an unabashed quest for power."[51] According to that platform our society has lost its moral bases and can regain them only if we, as individuals, learn the "voices" in which moral language is spoken. And we learn to recognize and imitate these voices in local communities.

But communitarians believe that our moral language must be tied to and serve the national community. It must bind us together as a people. Only in this way will it give us a shared conception of the good. Only in this way can we pursue self-fulfillment within a common "horizon of significance." We need a national morality that is rich enough that we can fulfill ourselves by deliberating over and serving it but not so authoritative and comprehensive that it makes individual or local choices irrelevant.

New Ties to Bind Us

Patriotism and authenticity must be made to coexist and even support one another. Only if we value our nation for its own sake, only if we commit ourselves to our way of life, can we defend liberal democracy and individual flourishing. But why defend our way of life? Surely many Americans defend the American way because it is American, because they have lived with it and so become attached to it out of habit. But communitarians do not highly value such habitual loyalty. Indeed, it goes against the liberal attachment to individual flourishing.

As Galston defines it, individual flourishing requires rational self-direction. We must formulate rational rules telling us our duties and telling us to maximize our individual powers. Having made these rules we then must act in accordance with them.[52] To value a way of life out of mere habit, or from appeal to the authority of tradition, is self-stultifying on this view. To follow habit or tradition is to put aspects of our way of life beyond the reach of independent rational inquiry—beyond our ability to question whether they are good. Habit and tradition fail to call on, let alone develop, our individual rational powers.

But then we do not begin life as fully rational agents. Further, as Galston notes, all societies must give their citizens a "civic education" aimed at "the formation of individuals who can effectively conduct their lives within, and support, their political community." Liberal democracies, no less than any other societies, must form the characters of their young. According to Galston, character formation must be "more rhetorical than rational." It must produce "a pantheon of heroes who confer legitimacy on central institutions and are worthy of emulation." Men do not go to their deaths in defense of abstract principles, save to the extent these principles represent the institutions, individuals, and way of life they love. Even a liberal nation must engage its people's passions if it is to garner their loyalty and affection.[53]

Government must recognize that public morality itself has religious roots. According to Galston the American Founders, including religious skeptics such as Thomas Jefferson, held that "only a relatively small number of citizens can be expected to understand and embrace liberal principles on the basis of purely philosophic considerations. For most Americans, religion provides both the *reasons* for believing liberal principles to be correct and the *incentives* for honoring them in practice."[54]

Concepts of divine creation, order, and judgment, along with a short list of moral commandments, taught Americans tolerance and the need for calm participation in public life. Based on a false faith in God, Galston indicates, such beliefs were nonetheless necessary for the establishment of American liberal democracy. Indeed, "by Tocqueville's time, a distinctively American political culture had been forged. Its major elements were three: the essentially secular principles of democratic liberalism; the moral maxims derived from Christianity; and the mores of Protestant Americans."[55] The American combination of political ideals and religious beliefs and habits constituted the American culture for many generations. American mores, or "habits of the heart," thus derived in large measure from religious sources.

Despite its deep roots in historical belief and practice, however, American culture spawned severe and perhaps fatal opposition. In the twentieth century Americans increasingly came to question the fairness of their culture. According to Galston, this culture tended to penalize and cast out entire groups—including blacks—on the grounds that their "lifestyle" was not in keeping with American norms.

The civil rights movement corrected much of this unfairness, Galston argues, by establishing a "neutral state." Unlike previous American governments the neutral state established by civil rights laws would not make or act on judgments concerning the lifestyles of its citizens. Further, the state now would prohibit citizens themselves from discriminating against individuals or groups on the basis of such judgments. "Private" moral codes condemning choices like unmarried cohabitation no longer would be allowed to influence public laws or even private decisions, such as whether to rent an apartment to a particular couple.

Overall Galston believes the civil rights movement in America was a success. It increased equality and decreased the costs of individual lifestyle choices. In this way it enhanced individual and group autonomy. Unfortunately, construction of a "neutral" state hostile to all value judgments also undermined the cultural bases of liberal democracy.

Galston's goal is neither to reconstitute nor to destroy traditional American culture. As a communitarian, he seeks to *use* our culture to serve liberal ends. He seeks a "functionalist traditionalism" that would maintain and use religion and traditional morality to the extent they are necessary to promote liberal virtues—much as he seeks to use liberal virtues to promote the liberal goods of authenticity and individual flourishing.

According to Galston, religion can undergird liberal virtues and liberalism can protect religious freedom. If we allow religion and liberal politics to conflict, partisans of each will attack the very "diversity" that is liberalism's goal.[56] Religious believers will seek to stifle diversity while believers in liberal politics will come to denigrate religion and all its cultural products. We must, then, balance these two forces, emphasizing the need for mutual toleration in a liberal state. We must found a civil religion that will make us teach virtue to our young, not in the name of God but in the name of the nation and its people.

But how are we to inculcate this toleration and belief in the goods provided by liberal democracy? It is here that we turn to the thrust of communitarian argument today. It is here that we return to the question, and the uses, of civil religion. It is here that we must examine more closely the way communitarians would use the liberal state to teach us how to be good liberals.

Chapter Two

From Social Cohesion to Radical Reform: The Politics of Civil Religion

> In truth, there never was any remarkable lawgiver amongst any people who did not resort to divine authority, as otherwise his laws would not have been accepted by the people; for there are many good laws, the importance of which is known to the sagacious lawgiver, but the reasons for which are not sufficiently evident to enable him to persuade others to submit to them; and therefore do wise men, for the purpose of removing this difficulty resort to divine authority.
>
> —*Machiavelli,* Discourses

Long before William Galston reflected on the political uses of religion, Renaissance philosopher Niccolò Machiavelli sought to transform Christianity so that it might aid in reuniting his native Italy. The church, in Machiavelli's view, had helped destroy Italy by rendering its people passive and effeminate. Unlike ancient Roman paganism, Christianity exalted piety and humility above strength and audacity, sapping the thirst for worldly glory on which all great civilizations rely.[1]

Religion clearly was a powerful force in the world, Machiavelli reasoned, because our notions of right and wrong, our determination of what is glorious and what inglorious, derive from our notions of what God (or the gods) demand of us. Thus ancient Roman leaders were wise to use religion to support their collective goals. They manipulated pagan fortune-tellers to give confidence to their troops, but they also maintained a public illusion of piety so as to safeguard the people's faith and fear of the gods.[2]

According to Machiavelli the people are incapable of reasoning properly. They must be manipulated. They must be given religious symbols and reasons for doing what wise men know is simply necessary. Particularly when great change is needed, the lawgiver must use religion to awe the people into serving the public interest.

The political use of religion was not new, even in Machiavelli's time, and later, Galston's teacher, Leo Strauss, held that politics rests on the wise manipulation of religion. Strauss argued that all states, from the ancient Greek city-states to modern America, have been held together by some myth of a common founding and a common belief that the gods favor their people. The philosopher has a particular duty to uphold such myths: he knows they are false, but knows also that they are necessary to maintain political unity and the possibility of philosophy. If the philosopher is to be left alone to pursue his calling, he must convince the uninitiated masses that laws protecting public peace (and the philosopher) are divinely sanctioned.[3]

But how can one or a few philosophers convince a people to believe something, however useful, if it is not true? Surely part of the answer lies in the understandable faith those who work with language have in the power of words. Machiavelli, an out of work diplomat, could not hope to affect public policy save through his rhetoric. Intellectuals in general make their living and hope to have a wider effect on the world by convincing others, through force of argument, to follow their advice.[4]

Yet the religious force Machiavelli sought to harness was very concrete. His examples from ancient history were of blood sacrifice and war. He sought to tap into what he saw as a primordial drive for immortality (whether in heaven or in the annals of history) as well as the awe-inspiring force of traditional beliefs and fears. Only by capitalizing on such hopes and fears could he make the people again love Italy enough to die for her.

Communitarians would reject Machiavelli's reinvigorated Italy. The glories of conquest and the politically and morally useful terrors of the executioner's block play no role in their vision of human flourishing. But communitarians share Machiavelli's revulsion at the selfishness of contemporary society and echo his call for radical reform in the name of the common good. They also share Machiavelli's conviction that political reformers must use religious symbols to convince the people to follow their lead.

Communitarians do not seek to reestablish pagan Rome or even

Machiavelli's paganized Christianity. Their goal is not to found an empire but to shore up liberal democracy. They seek to make use of religious symbols while rendering religion itself even more passive and tractable than it already is.

Selfish liberalism has severed the bonds of our community, thereby impoverishing our lives. We must construct a new civil religion—a set of political symbols, ceremonies, and beliefs that the people will hold sacred—so that we may forge a new sense of commitment to a new, national community. Like all civil religious reformers communitarians seek to convince us that it is cowardly and wrong to live in preparation for a future life, accepting the tragedies of this life and seeking to enrich our souls through personal interaction with God, man, and society. Instead we must fight to recast the earth as much as possible in the mold of a heaven we ourselves invent through common action, deliberation, and worship.

Individualism Versus the Common Good

Communitarians clearly detest much of our contemporary society. They find it overwhelmingly selfish and materialistic. Robert Bellah argues that capitalism has destroyed communities in the name of money and leisure. Americans now leave hometowns, old friends, and even family to pursue their own material well-being. Adrift from community, Americans have become mere consumers who can only "express their identity through shared patterns of appearance, consumption, and leisure activities. . . . They are not interdependent, do not act together politically, and do not share a history."[5]

Our communities have degenerated into "lifestyle enclaves" in which individual Americans consume the same products without coming together to forge a common purpose and identity. Preoccupied with our private lives, we have endangered the public roles of our families, religions, and local democratic politics. These institutions once told us what actions and personality traits were legitimate. They once taught us the habits we need to participate in a just public life.[6] They have been all but destroyed by the pulls of the market and our consumer society.

Individualism—selfish concern for our own well-being—has become a cancer infecting the body politic. It has eroded our commitment to the common good. But in Bellah's view selfishness itself, ironically, is self-defeating because we can become full human beings only by working for the common good or "social justice." By working for social justice good citizens exercise and maintain community control over the distribution of goods, services, and opportunities. And only through such local democratic action can we achieve what Bellah calls "human dignity."

Human dignity, for Bellah, is by nature political. He cites one local political activist:

> People's political development—their capacity to organize their common life—is both an end and a means. It fundamentally conditions their ability to participate in other development, including economic development. Job creation should take place through locally based, cooperative organizations such as community development corporations . . . to create jobs to meet the neighborhood's needs and to help neighborhoods to meet society's needs. It is a matter of justice.

Work itself, in this view, "should be seen as 'a calling, contributing to the common good and responding to the needs of others as these needs become understood.' " We become fully human by participating in a political process, distributing jobs and other economic goods in equal and therefore just proportions throughout the community.[7]

We instinctively desire community. We know in our hearts that capitalism destroys community, that it is unhealthy and unjust because it encourages greed, selfishness, and material inequality. But our selfish individualism keeps us from recognizing with Bellah that "a life of material austerity, of pride and pleasure in the quality of workmanship rather than in the amount consumed . . . would be far healthier for our society, ecologically and sociologically, than our present dominant pattern of ever-accelerating consumption."[8]

Bellah offers democratic socialism as the cure for our society's woes. Unfortunately, too many socialists are avowed atheists, and this is a "great stumbling block" to socialism's progress. The people will not accept soulless socialism. But there is a more "humanistic" socialism available to Americans, one that speaks to man's spirit as well as his intellect, showing him what is just and right in his nation.[9]

The Character of Spirituality

President Clinton gained praise early in his administration by frequently expressing religious sentiments. In a meeting with religious leaders in August 1993 he decried public disparagement of religion. He went on to argue that "each of us has a ministry in some way that we must play out in life, and with a certain humility, but also with deep determination." We should treat our respective callings, whether religious or secular, as holy. We must be committed to the civil religion of democratic authenticity. We must commit ourselves to our self-chosen calling and to the democratic community that makes such pursuit possible.

Bellah argues that religion is a crucial element of public life. This is particularly true of the life of radical reform he demands. He wants us to join in the process of "communal re-creation through public worship." He insists that only a "public church" making "calls for sweeping cultural and institutional transformation" and embodying egalitarian values can foster community and spiritual fulfillment. Luckily, we have many such public churches available. From Zen Buddhism to New Age religion to feminist theology, many good religions join in seeking to displace America's economic individualism.[10]

A religion is good in Bellah's eyes to the extent that it promotes egalitarian community here in this world. He praises mainline, liberal Protestant churches "able to combine a sense of continuity with the past and an engagement with the public world of the present." Continuity with the past consists of public religious ceremony. Engagement with the public world of the present consists of community work, involvement with organizations such as Amnesty International, attempts to work out "family patterns" among homosexuals, and hiding illegal aliens from chosen nations.[11]

Religion, properly speaking, is political. Bellah asked one clergyman "whether the Episcopal church, which has traditionally stood close to the centers of power in our society and attempted to influence the power structure from within, should continue that policy or perhaps take a position closer to the margins of society, protesting against it." In response the clergyman pointed to his political activities on behalf of Central American peasants and against South African apartheid. Neither Bellah nor the clergyman thought to question whether a clergyman's primary duty really is "to influence the power structure" in a particular, political direction.[12]

The proper role of religion, then, is to bring the individual out of his isolation by involving him in public ritual and political action. Belief in God and an immortal soul have necessarily and properly declined with man's "enlightenment." But religion, according to Bellah, remains powerful because it remains true, because it is "inherent in the structure of human experience."[13]

Man is a (civil) religious animal. He need not believe in a transcendent God, but he must believe that his experience, his life, has meaning. Thus a good religion, in Bellah's view, will make sacred those experiences that are in keeping with the proper ideals. A good religion will promote radical reforms aimed at achieving social justice. Note, for example, Bellah's praise for the egalitarian religious "tradition" of the 1960s:

> Unlike the religions of the sky father this tradition celebrates Nature as a mother. The sky religions emphasize the paternal, hierarchical, legalistic and ascetic, whereas the earth tradition emphasizes the maternal, communal, expressive and joyful aspects of existence. Whereas the sky religions see fathers, teachers, rulers and gods exercising external control through laws, manipulation or force, the earth tradition is tuned to cosmic harmonies, vibrations and astrological influences. Socially the [earth tradition] expresses itself not through impersonal bureaucracy or the isolated nuclear family but through collectives, communes, tribes and large extended families.[14]

According to Bellah the religions produced by the 1960s—pastiches of oriental mysticism, Marxist politics, psychoanalysis, and remnants of the Western tradition—themselves constituted a "tradition." In only a few years, these new religions somehow formed a "community of memory" opposed to "sky father" religions like traditional Christianity. Bellah found hope in the experimental communities of the hippie movement because they presented moral values hostile to American individualism. After all, what makes a religion valuable, for Bellah, is the shared moral values it produces.

Bellah defines God himself as a "relational symbol . . . intended to . . . bring together the coherence of the whole of experience."[15] Because our reason is limited, we cannot directly understand how all the various activities of life, from politics to cooking to poetry, relate to one another. We must create a God (or some form of divine will) so that we may explain to ourselves how human action, taken as a whole and in our individual lives, makes sense.[16]

As to those who believe in the more traditional notion that God's will is revealed in the Bible, they must recognize that "the Bible is the collection of texts that Jews and Christians have used through history to make meaning."[17] Religion is a means by which we create our morality. And for Bellah we "make" morality through participation in democratic political life. We formulate religious beliefs and practices to help us integrate our lives into meaningful wholes. Religion provides the means by which we create common values and communities.

Echoing and occasionally citing Bellah, Charles Taylor argues that free societies in particular require "spontaneous cohesion" on the part of their citizens. If the people are to order their own lives they must, of their own accord, accept and obey common laws and standards of behavior. And "spontaneous cohesion requires common values." It requires that the people share a core set of beliefs and an attachment to common institutions, including the institutions that constitute the political system.[18] It requires a civil religion.

The Politics of Civil Religion

Bellah argues that religion is an "indispensable prerequisite for government."[19] Self-consciously following sociologist Emile Durkheim, he further asserts that "every nation and every people come to some form of religious self-understanding."[20] And the basis of this self-understanding is at least as political as it is religious.

> It is one of the oldest of sociological generalizations that any coherent and viable society rests on a common set of moral understandings about good and bad, right and wrong, in the realm of individual and social action. It is almost as widely held that these common moral understandings must also in turn rest upon a common set of religious understandings that provide a picture of the universe in terms of which the moral understandings make

sense. Such moral and religious understandings produce both a basic cultural legitimation for a society which is viewed as at least approximately in accord with them and a standard of judgment for the criticism of a society that is seen as deviating too far from them.[21]

Religion provides moral consensus for the community. A people uses its religion to legitimate its society and to help measure and correct deviant practices. Civil religion—religion that holds the political community together—is a tool; it is the means by which we make sacred our fundamental political ideals. To carry out this function it also must make sacred the men who first put these ideals into action and those who saved them from ruin in time of crisis. It must make sacred the founders and heroes of our history, men against whose mythical standard of conduct we may judge current practice.

No one who visits Washington, D.C., can escape the powerful presence of American civil religion. Massive monuments and statues are inscribed with bold words of idealism and sacrifice, all in the name of America. No one familiar with the art and rhetoric of our revolutionary and Founding eras can doubt that civil religious symbolism has deep roots in America. George Washington, the nation's "father," was a favorite object of adoration. He was sculpted in Roman splendor and regalia. After his death painters portrayed him being escorted to heaven by great heroes from the past.

Bellah argues that our monuments, patriotic holiday observances, and political rhetoric serve "as a genuine vehicle of national religious self-understanding."[22] Our "sacred" images, along with our national holiday observances, constitute a national religion. These national symbols and celebrations order our lives; they tell us what we ought to value as a nation and how we should honor those who have served us.

But our "national religion" is not religious in the traditional sense. It has more to do with what is required of us by the nation than by God. Its observances are concerned with glory in this life rather than bliss in the next. It is a distinctly secular religion.

Religion serves its communitarian purpose by helping the individual order his own values and place patriotism at the top. Catherine Albanese, a student of American civil religion, argues that men act religiously whenever "structuring their world in terms of a preconceived vision of the meaning of life and the significance of human endeavor."[23] On this view we act "religiously" any time we act according to a preexisting set of beliefs concerning how we ought to act and why.

We act religiously by attempting to live up to our nation's ideals. Albanese argues that the American Revolution formed "structures of consciousness," especially patriotism, which have motivated Americans' actions ever since. The Revolution "was an inner myth out of which [Americans] lived and operated."[24]

On this view Americans were more self-conscious than most peoples in constructing their myth of free and noble origins—we engaged in public arguments as much as we accepted the work of great poets and rhetoricians. But our myth is as subjective as any other. We created our American "religion" out of materials at hand, including the ideology of liberty, older (especially Roman) myths, and poetic readings of our own history. And we shaped these materials to suit our own wants and desires.[25]

We tend to accept our subjective religious vision as if it were true always and everywhere, rather than merely useful to us in the here and now. Apparently we fool ourselves into believing that our values and commitments are righteous rather than convenient, so that they may give meaning to our lives. Religion, like class solidarity or environmentalism, has no ultimate value but must be believed in so that it may motivate and shape our conduct. What is important is that we maintain a well accepted civil religion so that we may maintain our society's cohesion.

Albanese argues that as traditional religion fades, we are becoming more like primitive peoples. Luckily for us, she believes, we no longer limit our view of what is sacred to God and the things of the next life. On the contrary, like primitive peoples we increasingly make all aspects of our lives sacred. As she puts it, "the American penchant for teeth-brushing or flag-waving may have as much or more to do with religious orientation than church and synagogue attendance."[26] Rituals as seemingly meaningless as teeth-brushing and as seemingly secular as patriotic observances have more effect on our lives, Albanese argues, than does attendance at church. These practical customs ritualize our lives; they integrate us into the nation by allowing us to act on common values—including cleanliness but emphasizing patriotism.

Political life is central to communitarians because it forms the nexus within which we create and order our values. Just as we require common values to hold our society together, so we require society to help us form common values. Thus it is not surprising that civil religion should come to the fore in communitarianism; civil religion combines political and religious concerns. For communitarians we need symbols and ideals that transcend the particular interests of particular actors—we require common values that apply to everyone in our society. But we also require politics; we require a mechanism by which to motivate the people and put our ideals into action.

Civil religion is equivalent to Galston's "functional traditionalism." It combines "religious" idealism with practical politics. Bellah argues that American civil religion, because it "was never anticlerical or militantly secular," managed to form a truce with the various church religions and even to borrow "selectively from the religious tradition." In this way, "the civil religion was able to build up . . . powerful symbols of national solidarity and to mobilize deep levels of personal motivation for the attainment of national goals."[27]

The civil religion has its own God, albeit one "on the austere side, much more related to order, law, and right than to salvation and love." This God, the creation of public debates concerning America's national purpose and role in the world, is the source of principles Americans must follow if they are to secure "political prosperity." But it is not merely by living up to these principles that Americans show their piety. They also observe numerous rituals making up the liturgy of their religion.

> Memorial Day observance, especially in the towns and smaller cities of America, is a major event for the whole community involving a rededication to the martyred dead, to the spirit of sacrifice, and to the American vision. Just as Thanksgiving Day, . . . serves to integrate the family into the civil religion, so Memorial Day has acted to integrate the local community into the national cult. Together with the less overtly religious Fourth of July and the more minor celebrations of Veterans Day and the birthdays of Washington and Lincoln, these two holidays provide an annual ritual calendar for the civil religion. The public school system serves as a particularly important context for the cultic celebration of the civil rituals.[28]

According to Bellah American civil religious values are inculcated to this day, if increasingly fitfully, through public exhortations to do God's will on earth and through "cultic celebrations" of national holidays. Such celebrations serve to convince Americans of the goodness of themselves, their nation, and their causes. "Rededicating" themselves to the nation's martyrs, Americans come to believe that it is good to die for their community's values. Civil religion integrates the political with the religious and so motivates citizens to act for the one as if it were the other.

But what of the costs of patriotism? Do men not die for their nation? Is such "commitment," entailing the ultimate sacrifice, based on nothing deeper than the supposed need for some, any, ordering of our values? Not for communitarians. On this view, the creation and ordering of values is so important, so primordial and deeply embedded in our nature, that it constitutes the purpose of life.

Civil religion fulfills the communitarian individual. It allows him, through political action, to help posit communal values. Further, our civil religion holds us together as a community by giving us a moral consensus. But this does not mean that civil religion should be used merely as a support for existing institutions and practices. Indeed, given the inevitability of each society's religious dimension, the responsible course of action is "to seek within the civil religious tradition for those critical principles which undercut the ever present danger of national self-idolization."[29]

There are two sides to any civil religion properly so-called. On one side are beliefs and practices that sanctify the existing order and bind us to our community. On the other side, however, are principles calling on us to make ourselves and our communities more just and virtuous.

Given what Bellah deems the constant danger of self-idolatry, civil religion must downplay its laudatory side. Particularly in liberal America, civil religion must laud, in essence, the tradition of social and political criticism and reform. In effect, Bellah posits two civil religions—one that binds us to the liberal institutions, beliefs, and practices he abhors and one that criticizes existing structures in the name of solidarity and authenticity. Thus we have a bad liberal civil religion and a good republican civil religion. The first sanctifies current practice, the second, embattled as it is, points us to a better life.

The ideals Bellah claims inform our "good" civil religion are radically opposed to the actual way of life Americans lead. This is why civil religion is so useful to communitarians: it provides a set of criteria they can claim is based in our history and experience but which supports their own vision of the good life rather than that of the American "individualism" they loathe. And the very fact that the "good" civil religion has no significant basis in current practice frees it from the charge that it idolizes any existing, confining and possibly unauthentic set of institutions. We can be virtuous without serving the supposedly outmoded, authoritarian structures that actually developed over the course of our history. We need only adopt the proper politics and appropriate sacred symbols to support it.

Religion, Politics, and Virtue

According to Bellah, America's Founders supported religion because they understood that it was "the indispensable underpinning of a republican political order." Like Galston and other communitarians, Bellah and the Founders believe that only a religious people will have the social cohesion, public spirit, and self-discipline to remain free. Thus responsible leaders should publicly support religion, even if they do not believe in God.[30]

Borrowing from scholars of republicanism or "civic humanism," Bellah argues that the Founders sought to use religion to promote virtue. Virtue was "zeal for the public good." Corruption, the opposite of virtue, was an "exclusive concern for one's own good," the pursuit of private enjoyments and the accumulation of wealth. Religion was a necessary support for virtue because it provided common values and attachments, bringing the individual out of himself and into the community. The civil religion made virtue possible because it glorified public service in its cultic rituals.[31]

Bellah does not claim that America's early years were purely virtuous and republican. Rather he seeks to show that there was a republican "voice" that once was heard in American politics along with the individualistic voice so dominant today. He argues that Americans have interpreted their common values from either a biblical/republican or a utilitarian perspective. Indeed, "the meaning of every key term in the civil religion—certainly liberty and the pursuit of happiness, but also equality and even life—differs in those two perspectives."[32] And this difference in perspectives has far-reaching consequences.

According to Bellah the biblical or republican tradition of interpretation, with its roots in Puritan theology and local, communal political practice, urges us toward virtue. The more powerful utilitarian tradition, with its roots in the philosophy of Locke and the economics of the market, has led us toward selfish individualism.

> One can read the great tenets of the civil religion in either of the two perspectives—as [Puritan leader John] Winthrop would have read them, or as Locke would have read them. Is equality a condition for the fulfillment of our humanity in covenant with God or is it a condition for the competitive struggle to attain our own interests? Is freedom almost identical with virtue—the freedom to fulfill lovingly our obligations to God and our fellow men—or is it the right to do whatever we please so long as we do not harm our fellow men too flagrantly? Is the pursuit of happiness the realization of our true humanity in love of Being and all beings, as Jonathan Edwards would have put it or is it, as Locke would contend, the pursuit of those things—notably wealth and power—which are means to future happiness, in Leo Strauss's words, "the joyless quest for joy?" Does life mean biological survival in our animal functions or does it mean the good life in which our spiritual nature and our animal nature are both fulfilled?[33]

True freedom, in Bellah's biblical/republican perspective, is found through work. And our work on earth is to follow God. But we must not follow God merely by living our private lives in a godly way; that would be selfish. Instead we must answer John F. Kennedy's call to "struggle against the common enemies of man: tyranny, poverty, disease and war itself."[34] We must strive to make this world more like what our civil religious God intended; that is, we must strive to make this world more like what we ourselves intended when we created a God to embody and explain our ideals to ourselves.

Americans see themselves as God's chosen people, like ancient Israel bound by covenant to do God's bidding on earth and shine as a beacon to all nations. And this picture of ourselves as God's chosen lies behind, and morally *demands*, great projects of political transformation. "The American Israel theme is clearly behind both Kennedy's New Frontier and Johnson's Great Society."[35]

America was built "centrally on utopian millennial expectations."[36] Americans sought to bring the reign of God down to earth through their own political actions. In this effort they constructed a civil religion promising glory to those who do good for their nation. Civil religion rewards not the humility of the saint but the audacity of the reformer who seeks to defeat all enemies of the state—from foreign powers to internal problems such as poverty.

The biblical/republican perspective is difficult to sustain because it rests on virtue. Only those whose God demands public service will discern its dictates. Only those who see political participation as an essential part of their being will put these dictates into practice. Only those who identify their own will with the will of their community will promote the common good.

Unfortunately, those who reject the republican perspective have used our civil religion as a "cloak for petty interests and ugly passions." According to Bellah "the civil religion has not always been invoked in favor of worthy causes. . . . An American-Legion type of ideology that fuses God, country, and flag has been used to attack non-conformist and liberal ideas and groups of all kinds."[37] American civil religion has a dark side. It may be used against progressive ideas and groups and in favor of a patriotic "ideology." Indeed, as essential a notion as the

> theme of the American Israel was used, almost from the beginning, as a justification for the shameful treatment of the Indians so characteristic of our history. It can be overtly or implicitly linked to the idea of manifest destiny that has been used to legitimate several adventures in imperialism since the early nineteenth century. . . . [And w]hen our soldiers are actually dying, it becomes possible to consecrate the struggle further by invoking the great theme of sacrifice.[38]

Our civil religious myths have produced moral triumphs and moral tragedies—great projects of social and economic reform and programs of racism and genocide. And our good and bad actions can be traced to the good and bad formulations of our civil religion. The republican tradition, critical of established orders, promotes equality and virtue. The utilitarian tradition cloaks self-interest behind a facile and corrupting patriotism.

The tension between the republican and utilitarian perspectives, between virtue and vice, has dominated American public life. Bellah argues that American history is replete with waves of revivals, of "conversions" to republican ideals that have been followed by new covenants enshrining those ideals in documents, institutions, and practices. But utilitarian opposition keeps us from fulfilling our millenarian ideals. We seek to build the kingdom of God on earth, but the selfish side of our tradition keeps undermining the attempt. And each betrayal of our better selves in turn cries out for yet more national "conversions" and so continues the cycle of American politics.

Bellah believes, for example, that the Thirteenth, Fourteenth, and Fifteenth Amendments to the Constitution (and in particular the clause of the Fourteenth Amendment guaranteeing equal protection of the laws) show the promise of millenarianism to help us "progress" as a community. These amendments, enacted soon after the Civil War, were the products of a "renewed experience of divine salvation [which] led to a heightened sense of the imperfections of the national covenant and demanded a nation purged and renewed after the long travail of slavery."[39] If we put the radical reforms Bellah believes were promised by these Amendments into practice, we may yet remake our society in the form our God would intend.

> Even though the radical meaning of these clauses was undermined for many decades by narrow court interpretations and a regressive political situation, their meaning can hardly be exaggerated. They are the charter under which many of the advances of the last 20 years have been made. They are the mandate for many more. They altered the role of the national government from one of largely passive observation in the field of individual rights to one of active intervention and responsibility. They give the constitutional legitimation for much that is still to be realized politically.[40]

The post–Civil War amendments embodied a "conversion" of the American spirit. They revived and strengthened American commitment to radical political, economic, and social equality. The extreme egalitarian ideals Bellah claims are inherent in these amendments were not put into practice immediately, prevented by our utilitarian tradition. But our ideals have guided us as we have "discovered" the amendments' full implications.[41]

According to Bellah the implications of these amendments are extensive. They demand, in his view, that the national government guarantee "civil rights" defined as equal educational, employment, and other outcomes. The national government must see to it that jobs, diplomas, housing, and other goods are distributed in equal numbers according to race so that we will have a more equal, and therefore just, society. Sex- and sexual preference–based programs of distribution, although not mentioned in the amendments, also embody their spirit and so must be enacted as well.

According to Bellah the American covenant and therefore the post–Civil War amendments sought to establish not only freedom from slavery but also freedom from material inequality. The men who enacted these amendments must have intended to enact affirmative action and other national programs to distribute economic, social, and political opportunity according to race, sex, and so on. These programs fit the spirit of the republican civil religion and so must inhere in all good public acts.[42]

Unfortunately, Bellah argues, our republican impulses consistently lose out to utilitarian forces. Our "regressive political situation" remains with us and is deteriorating. Increasingly since the rise of industrial capitalism in the early twentieth century, we have become a nation of selfish individualists.

We have undermined our republican tradition, leaving only biblical and republican "second languages." Each second language is a way of speaking and thinking left over from more virtuous times. The religious and political elements of our biblical tradition no longer cohere. Thus each is more easily manipulated by selfish interests. But together they still hold the proper alternatives to our individualistic dilemma.

We once had a civil religion that called us to virtue. We once had a society in which our highest ideals and aspirations could gain a hearing in the public square. We once had local communities in which status and even some material goods were distributed through democratic means, according to a shared conception of the public good. We often acted wrongly, but the very fact that we discussed how best to make this world as close to perfect as possible made us a better society.

This is not to say that Bellah sees our early townships as perfect embodiments of the communitarian ideal. Quite the contrary, he often condemns them for religious, racial, and sexual intolerance. But Bellah wants us to look at his reading of the republican tradition to see what those communities might and should have been. He seeks to convince us that America once had a tradition in which true community, defined as democratic control of a dominant public life, was the rule. He also seeks to convince us that these communities, flawed as they were, looked toward an ideal of equality that would have produced, in time, the kind of local democratic socialism he values.

It is not utopia but the communal striving for utopia that communitarians value. Bellah saves his highest praise for the "movement organizer" who once attempted to forge Americans into a community devoted to millenarian change. The movement organizer made public life possible by bringing men together in pursuit of great projects. He sought communitarian ends through communitarian means.

As Bellah argues, "perhaps the only alternative we as a nation have ever had, or are likely to discover, to the dominance of business leaders or the rule of technical experts" is "the tradition of democratic reform that arose in response to the emerging industrial capitalist order." Bellah continues:

This reforming impulse flourished in various embodiments during the great transitional period at the beginning of the century. The motive force of these movements of democratic reform was a fundamentally similar political understanding. It animated the agrarian populism of the Midwest and Southeast, the socialism of eastern industrial workers and western labor, some aspects of Progressivism, and the upsurge of industrial unionism in the 1930s. Suspicious both of the massive private power that was undercutting the basis for independent citizenship and of government without popular control, these movements sought to use government at all levels to bring a degree of public responsibility to the new technologies and the wealth they generated. They strove to adapt the old Jeffersonian republican sense of democratic citizenship to twentieth-century conditions. Politically, of course, the movements failed to do more than place limits, often fragile, on the exercise of private power. But they left a considerable legacy of experience, symbols, and the exemplary type of the movement organizer.[43]

Early twentieth-century movement organizers did not defeat capitalism or the individualism it spawns. But they created symbols, heroes, and myths we can use to reinvigorate our republican tradition. Their commitment to social justice and the tools of solidarity make them proper models for us today. They sought to establish a community in which the common good would be recognized both in and through collective control of a dominant public life. Communitarians wish to convince us to follow the movement organizer's lead. But first they must convince us that he indeed furthered the public good. They must make us remember our history as a grand struggle between good biblical republicans and bad utilitarian capitalists.

Communitarians believe that peoples come to share values only when they come to share a common memory. Only a shared myth of their origins and purpose as a people can provide the kind of cohesion necessary for that people to attain virtue. Communitarians seek to construct useful myths of America's origins and continuing purpose to convince us that we should support their program for change. Because communitarians propose radical change, they present us with a history in which radical change is valued. In this way change itself becomes a shared value. The difficult part is convincing the people that all this is true.

Chapter Three

Rhetorical Foundings and the Great Leader: Garry Wills and America's Principles

Bellah stopped using the term "civil religion" because some observers accused him of promoting national self-worship. But he continues to recommend religious rhetoric and ceremony as a source of republican ideals and practices. Garry Wills also criticizes religious understandings of American politics that praise more than criticize existing institutions. But he himself seeks to create civil religious myths spurring us to communitarian reform.

Wills shares Bellah's conviction that religions should be judged by their political consequences. The truth of religion is unreachable or nonexistent. What we are left with are social structures that may help or hinder us as we reconstruct society along communitarian lines.

This is why communitarians seek to reconstruct our past to make it more useful for their ends. We currently are in the grips of a bad civil religion, one that sanctifies selfishness and undermines public service. Eventually it will undermine liberalism itself. Bellah responds to this seeming predicament by pointing to elements of a second civil religion more conducive to communitarian action. He uses his sociological training to try to reconstruct religion, making it a more useful tool to help us achieve our earthly goals.

But the construction of a civil religion involves more history than sociology. A "community of memory" rests on shared beliefs about its past. Thus Wills plays an important role in the communitarian project by using religious language to sanctify a new, communitarian interpretation of our past. He writes historical works to construct a past that can make us virtuous in the communitarian sense.

Bellah also tells useful stories concerning our history. Like Wills he urges us to look to the Declaration of Independence and the Gettysburg Address as founding statements or sacred texts of a religion of equality, authenticity, and political participation.[1] But it is Wills who seeks to tell a systematic communitarian story of our origins. Particularly in his work on the American Founding, Wills aims to convince us that we can be true to our tradition only by coming together as a community to rethink our values and institutions, re-creating (or refounding) our society on a regular basis. He seeks to convince us that our very tradition is both communitarian and antitraditional.

Ironically, Wills once described himself as a conservative. A regular contributor to the magazine *National Review,* he persistently criticized liberals and "free market" conservatives for failing to recognize that freedom, properly understood, requires authority. According to Wills a people can govern itself without falling prey to tyranny or anarchy only by accepting common practices and institutions.[2]

Early in his career Wills defended tradition and family loyalties. He argued that societies can survive only if they sustain ties of familiarity and affection among the people. Such ties require moral consensus; they can exist only if the people believe that their parents and their inherited institutions and practices are basically good. Moral consensus and authority go hand in hand, and both depend on the social calm fostered by political compromise and respect for tradition.

Even after he joined the radical New Left movement in the late 1960s, Wills labeled himself conservative because of his commitment to moral and political consensus. He claimed in *Confessions of a Conservative* that he always had praised politicians and bureaucrats who were willing to compromise in the name of social continuity. Even Abraham Lincoln, probably the most powerful deity in Wills's civil religious pantheon, had to compromise with his supporters. "His leadership was a matter of *mutually* determinative activity, on the part of the leader *and* the followers. Followers 'have a say' in what they are being led to."[3]

This is not to say that a true leader is merely a poll watcher who gives his constituents what they want. Far from it. Although Wills is hostile to personal charisma, he demands from his heroes a political and spiritual rhetoric that creates rather than merely rationalizes consensus. Lincoln "had to *elicit* the program he wanted to serve, and that always involves *affecting* the views one is consulting."[4]

Wills's leader, like Machiavelli's legislator, molds the people's opinions. The true leader speaks to the souls of his constituents through mythical language, by recalling to them the heroes and great deeds of their past, and calling them to live up to their nation's highest ideals. And we need these leaders—"prophets" such as Martin Luther King, Jr.—to force us to change and enliven our communal conscience.[5]

The successful leader, the one who will make significant change, will raise the people's consciousness through his command of moral and political language. Wills, by training a scholar of classical languages, shares the communitarian emphasis on language's power to change men's minds, behavior, and very character. He argues that rhetoric, the art of persuasion, lies at the core of all leadership. Even business leaders, committed solely to their own profits, in Wills's view depend on rhetoric to motivate their employees, who in turn use rhetoric to motivate their own workers and/or customers. In one form or another, the sales pitch rules our lives.[6]

We use images and poetry as well as logical reasoning to persuade. *Cincinnatus,* Wills's book on George Washington, contains as much art and literary criticism as political and philosophical history. The book's eighty-five illustrations intend to show how artists and sculptors as well as poets, historians, and men of letters helped create a heroic image of our first president. Washington himself, according to Wills, self-consciously re-created the role of the classical Roman hero Cincinnatus, a poor Roman farmer who was made dictator in time of trouble, then returned to his plow after saving his nation.

But even Cincinnatus will fail if the times are corrupt. Calls to public-spirited action will not be heeded if the times are not right and if the people are not virtuous. "A corrupt people is not responsive to virtuous leadership."[7]

A virtuous leader will come to grief in vicious times. What, then, shall we do with a corrupt people? Convince them to be virtuous.

A Myth of Virtue

John F. Kennedy's inaugural address, telling Americans to "ask not what your country can do for you" but rather "what you can do for your country," caused great civil religious fervor. It encouraged Americans to join the Peace Corps and other organizations dedicated to spreading "the American Way" around the globe. Wills, however, has only contempt for Kennedy and the trappings of that presidency's mythical Camelot. Kennedy's charismatic leadership spawned an American self-confidence that Wills blames for national blunders such as our intervention in Vietnam.[8] Leaders like Kennedy can and have used religious myth to justify great wrongs which, according to Wills means that religion itself has been at least partly to blame for these wrongs. Our essentially Protestant tradition has been, in Wills's view, anti-Semitic, anti-Catholic, antiblack, and anti–American Indian. It justified mass murder and oppression in service to our "Christian nation."

According to Wills we must reject overtly religious influences on our public life if we are to progress as a people. Indeed, "it is our task, . . . to complete the effort of . . . removing religion from state ceremony and proclamations." Today we can appreciate better than earlier generations the need to use religion as a tool to make clear our weaknesses, rather than a banner under which we should march to national glory.[9] We must not allow the state to use religious symbols and rhetoric to support its nationalistic programs. We must eliminate what remains of religion's presence in our schools, public buildings, and public functions.

Wills does not, however, wish to erase every last vestige of religion from our politics. Indeed, he criticizes 1988 Democratic presidential candidate Michael Dukakis for being "the first truly secular candidate we had ever had for the presidency." Dukakis disdained personal political interaction as he disdained serious concern for religious dogma, ceremony, or sentiment. Rejecting religion, Dukakis also rejected personalities and compromise in favor of detailed, mechanistic public administration. In this way he dehumanized his politics and himself.

Dukakis proved too cold to lead America. He doomed himself to electoral failure when he blithely told a reporter that the rape and murder of his wife would not change his position on capital punishment because "statistics show" that it is not a deterrent.[10] Lacking religious sensibility, a politician also will lose appreciation for things spiritual and become emotionally flat. And one cannot lead the people without empathy for their spiritual needs and desires.

Although it may be misused for patriotic reasons, religion remains central to American political life. "The civil rights and antiwar movements of the sixties and seventies show how effective religious leadership remains—continuing a tradition of 'conscience politics' that made the churches strong in the abolition, women's rights, and temperance movements." Like Bellah, religion for Wills shows both its power and its capacity for good through its influence on political reform movements. Similarly, complicity in bad acts such as defense of slavery and "religious complicity in war symbolized by the military chaplain system" show religion's capacity for harm.[11]

According to Wills, religion often has helped the state oppress the people, violating their rights and deadening their lives in the name of eternal truths. But religion also can help the people understand and fulfill their needs through political discussion. We must choose this second course, integrating religious consciousness and argument into our political rhetoric.

The forces of history, in Wills's view, are producing religious/political integration. Free market economics, technology, and the women's movement have combined to destroy the male-centered public life of the nineteenth-century. Far from natural, Wills argues, the division of life into a male-dominated public sphere and a private sphere of home and hearth theoretically ruled by wives and priests was a creation of nineteenth-century popular revolt. Enraged by public discussion of sexual morality and the excesses of liturgical elites, the masses in effect splintered Americans' worlds. Women and priests were relegated to a "private" sphere, through which they supposedly controlled sexual morality. Men, meanwhile, went about the economic and political business that make up the bulk of public life. Today, however, women refuse to be subjugated as they once were, and economic necessity renders such subjugation impossible in any event. Thus the private sphere of morality has disappeared. Sexual materials in particular flood our homes; in Wills's view mothers and priests quite properly can no longer stop or effectively censor them.[12]

But none of this, for Wills, need dampen our enthusiasm or respect for proper religious understandings. Instead it means that "women and priests can participate in public life *only* as citizens, with no special preserve of their own to make people fall silent. . . . If they want to influence public life, it must be with argument and persuasion."[13] All of us, regardless of training, sex, or status, must be equal participants in the political debates in which Americans structure their morality as a people.

We should not be frightened by this politicization of religion, according to Wills. Nor should we see it as something revolutionary or new. Religion always has been primarily political. Even the apostle Saint Paul was at base a savvy politician, whose compromises with "perfectionists" and "fundamentalists" we should emulate. In this feminist age, Wills argues, the Catholic church in particular must compromise with its rebellious clergy and church members, ordaining women, blessing artificial birth control, and dropping its opposition for abortion and sexually active priests. The church has caused pain to its clergy and laity by condemning practices many think morally sound. It must better please its constituents if it is to lead them; if it is to play its proper role in public life.[14]

The church must abandon its commitment to moral absolutes. Indeed, there are no moral absolutes because a moral rule's unpopularity renders it invalid. Of course, this raises public opinion to the status of a moral absolute. It makes it morally wrong to enforce an unpopular rule. By enforcing rules its members do not like, in Wills's view, the church rejects political compromise (and good leadership) with its constituents in favor of prideful insistence on unobtainable goals.

Today, according to Wills, we should look to religious leaders such as Mary Baker Eddy, founder of Christian Scientism. Eddy abandoned her child when he was six years old so that she could tend her real child, her church. She "took what was a general mood in the America of the last century and turned it into a body of teachable knowledge that could serve as the basis of spiritual discipline for a body of believers." Her work continues to inspire many, not the least feminists who praise her rejection of the trinity and her transformation of God into "Our Father-Mother."

Because Eddy left a body of thought that helps many order their lives and that serves the interests of sexual equality, she was a great leader. Rather than retiring into private life, she stormed the public world and changed a part of it for good. She provided a belief system that her followers continue to find therapeutic and helpful in organizing their moral lives. She also pursued egalitarian political goals. Together these deeds made her a good religious leader.[15]

We need common beliefs if we are to remain a viable, free people. But these beliefs cannot be so demanding that they cause us personal discomfort, let alone significant public disagreement. Therefore we must have a civil religion. We must construct a set of beliefs that will bind us together as a people. In this context, Wills praises Thomas Jefferson for finding in our religion a kind of lowest common denominator.

Jefferson believed in God but dispensed with any hierarchical priesthood or religious ceremony in favor of democratic principles and practices. Jefferson's deism also dispensed with the Christian belief in Christ's divinity, instead putting faith in man's reason and goodness and in the ability of Jesus' philosophy to lead us toward virtue. Jefferson's religion, on Wills's reading, calls for virtue without making any divisive claims about religious truth or the nature of the divine. By concentrating on the proper *use* of religion, Jefferson's beliefs provide the basis for community.[16]

There is much room for religion in our public life, according to Wills. But it must be a distinctly political religion, one addressed to citizens by citizens and in the interest of citizenship. Good religion makes sense of the community's public life. It binds us to common beliefs but also subjects these beliefs, and the moral rules we derive from them, to political bargaining. Only with such a religion can democratic politics and consensus combine to form a community of shared values and virtuous public service.

Civil Religion, Civic Humanism, and the American Founding

Civil religion and civic humanism (or "republicanism") are intimately linked. Indeed, civil religion is the means by which leaders attempt to foster republican virtue. Civil religion consists of rhetoric and myth intended to win the people over, to make them believe that the cause they are fighting for is holy. It also is used to foster public service by making the people see the institutions, beliefs, and practices in which they learn virtue as themselves holy. It fosters loyalty and service to the nation by teaching men that to serve the community's values and institutions is worthy of glory.

Leaders not only must use civil religion but also abide by their civil religion's rules if they are to retain the citizens' loyalty. Thus, according to Taylor, Nixon fell from power because his dishonesty violated the American way valued by the people. Only by living up to the peoples' expectations can the leader maintain moral cohesion and lead the people where he wants them to go.

George Washington was a great political leader, according to Wills, because he both shaped and fulfilled the people's expectations. Wills argues that Washington's emulation of Cincinnatus was a premeditated ploy intended to increase his own power and his ability to lead America. Washington ostentatiously resigned his commission from the Continental Congress in person after the Revolutionary War and repeatedly declined office so that he would be seen as taking power as Cincinnatus would have done—reluctantly and at the command of the people. In this way he gained the people's trust, in himself and in the national government he institutionalized.

Our rules of conduct come from myth. They grow out of the stories we construct about our own past and about earlier peoples we wish to emulate. Roman heroes like Cincinnatus were deeply important to our Founding generation, Wills insists that the Founding era was one of virtue, in which Americans looked to the past for models they might follow in establishing a great new nation.[17] Washington continued and enriched the Roman myth of Cincinnatus through his own actions. But it was not Washington's actions so much as the cult that grew up around him that, in Wills's view, made Washington's public service the source of continuing mythical power.

Through rhetoric, through the skilled use of words and images, we create myths. Not so much the actual events, but rather the way we remember them controls how and whether we will emulate our ancestors. The historian, then, comes to hold extensive power because he can manipulate and in effect create men's memories and thereby control their beliefs and conduct.

In his study of communitarianism, Derek Phillips argues that all communitarians look backward to some golden age. Their critique of American individualism rests, he argues, on their insistence that a better community than ours once existed. Whether in ancient Athens, medieval Europe, or early America, communitarians argue that we may find in history a model by which to order our own actions. Thus, according to Phillips, communitarians must show us that their reading of history is factually correct—that men formed a close-knit, sharing community devoted to the public good in some golden age. Otherwise both their program of action and their critique of modern individualism fail.

Phillips proceeds to argue that no communitarian "golden age" actually lived up to their vision of the good society.[18] But this entirely misses the point of communitarianism. Communitarians need not "prove" that the golden ages they describe literally fulfilled their demands of a good society. They need only convince us that the myths they are constructing of our past are attractive and that we should seek to fulfill the ideals they present to us. They need only a successful rhetoric in order to institute their program of reform. (Whether they are correct in believing that this rhetoric also will be sufficient to render their program successful I examine later in this book.)

Wills argues that the factual events of our revolution and Founding are almost entirely irrelevant to current politics. In the prologue to *Inventing America: Jefferson's Declaration of Independence,* Wills presents himself as the skeptical historian, out to destroy the myths that have grown up around the Declaration. Myths, such as that of America's "virgin birth" as a nation, distort our view of our own past. They make us believe that we created our own nation at the Revolution, forgetting that the Founders built on more than a century of self-government in the new world.

We view our Founding as an object of worship and so have distorted our history. We have used the Founding for our own purposes and in the process have lost its original meaning. According to Wills:

The Declaration is not only part of our history; we are part of its history. We have cited it, over the years, for many purposes, including the purpose of deceiving ourselves; and it has become a misshapen thing in our minds. Jefferson never intended it for a spiritual Covenant; but it has traveled in an Ark that got itself more revered the more it was battered.

Also according to Wills it is up to him to correct our overly reverential vision. It is up to him to bring back the true spirit of the Founding, for he recognizes that "the best way to honor the spirit of Jefferson is to use his doubting intelligence again on his own text. Only skepticism can save him from his devotees, return us to the drier air of his scientific maxims, all drawn with the same precision that went into his architectural sketches."[19]

But Wills does not seek to make us more aware of the Declaration of Independence's true nature so that we may better live up to its

ideals. Instead he ridicules the very attempt to recapture the truth of
the Founding as impossible and counterproductive. In 1976 Pennsylvania's lieutenant governor wished to reenact the (in any event fictitious) mass signing of the Declaration. "The man was asking for the
impossible, for a resurrection of the dead. Most of those brought in
for such a ceremony would not know what on earth they were admit-
ting to. And those who might know, and still wanted to sign, would
have to justify their act in ways so devious as to defeat speculation on
their motives."[20]

Wills asks incredulously, "Do we really think we can find people,
running around alive in the street, who believe in the psychology of
Louis de Jaucourt, the contract theory of David Hume, the mechanics
of benevolence as elaborated by Francis Hutcheson? And, if not, how
can we ask people in good conscience to endorse a document of eighteenth-century science based on such beliefs?"[21]

Wills does not want us to blindly follow the Declaration's dictates. Neither does he want to teach us about it so that we might follow them knowingly. He seeks to show us that the Declaration of Independence and our Founding as a whole are, and can be, important
to us only as a fountain of civil religious myths; myths that we may
use in the never ending process of re-creating our nation and ourselves.

Inventing a Past

Wills devotes the bulk of *Inventing America* to re-creating the
mind of Thomas Jefferson. His stated goal is to illuminate Jefferson's
original draft of the Declaration of Independence. He relates stories
of Jefferson's participation in the Continental Congress, his many
mathematical formulations and their relationship to some rather odd
notions of legal and institutional reform, and his lifelong passion for
reconstructing his home. He also relates stories of famous eighteenth-century scientists and philosophers and makes a number of
assertions concerning the origins of their ideas. Understanding all of
this, Wills claims, will make us better able to grasp Jefferson's intent
in penning phrases such as "our sacred honor" and the "course of
human events."

But Wills himself indicates that these stories are largely irrelevant. He argues that the views he ascribes to Jefferson, most fundamentally that societies are held together by affection rather than contract or force, were largely rooted out of the final draft of the Declaration. Indeed, the ostensible purpose of Wills's book is to present to the world Jefferson's original draft so that we might see how radically the final version strayed from Jefferson's vision and intent.[22] Jefferson's Declaration is of interest to Wills precisely because it has had so little effect on American public life.

According to Wills, not only Jefferson's draft but the final, adopted Declaration was essentially irrelevant when written and for years afterward. This is not surprising because it was not intended to be very important: "Its issuance was a propaganda adjunct to the act of declaring independence." It was written to win French favor, money, and assistance in the war with Great Britain. The actual treaty with France, along with the state constitutions and the Articles of Confederation, had much more practical import and in that very practical age were seen as far more important than the Continental Congress's sales pitch for French aid.[23]

The Declaration became relevant to American life only years after the Founding of our nation, and then only through "accidents" of history and faulty memory. Wills makes much of the fact that the colonies declared independence on July 2 and not July 4, the date the Continental Congress adopted the Declaration. Even the Founders came to misremember their own role in the events of 1776. Jefferson believed, against overwhelming evidence, that he and all the other delegates had signed the document on July 4, 1776. In fact, delegates did not even begin signing it until August 2 of that year.[24]

These historical accidents established July 4 in Americans' minds as the date their nation was founded. But Wills argues that it was John Trumbull's painting of the fictitious July 4 signing that made the Declaration our key Founding document. Wills spends pages detailing the painting's content and tone, as well as noting its historical inaccuracies.[25] Inaccurate or not, Trumbull's painting came to define our Founding moment.

Thanks to Trumbull's powerful vision, the Declaration became mythical. As years went by celebrations of its "signing" became more ornate and enthusiastic. Eventually Americans came to venerate the Declaration and its irrelevant philosophical sales pitch.

The Declaration's very irrelevance rendered it a powerful source of myth in American politics. The Founders deemed the Constitution the most important document of their era. Through the Constitution's detailed provisions they sought to establish a self-regulating political machine that would provide peace, prosperity and tranquility. In their view its strength lay in its specificity and relevance to political practice.

> But that first strength became a later liability. When things did not work well, or did not work as expected, the Constitution could be blamed for causing things it merely countenanced. The problem of slavery, for instance, had to be deferred to accomplish any kind of Constitution. But then it was used as a bulwark for state authority to enslave. Its powerlessness looked like complicity.
> The Declaration did not labor under those particular disadvantages. It did not (any more than the Constitution would) express a desire or form a plan to end slavery in America. . . . But the Declaration did say "all men are created equal," and that could be used as a pledge of future actions.[26]

The Declaration was a source of abstract philosophical language, and its provisions could be made to serve many masters. Later generations could use the Declaration for purposes alien to the Founders' intent but still see themselves as fulfilling its ideals. For example, most of the Declaration's authors did not contemplate freeing the slaves, let alone establishing racial equality, but the document's language could be made to appear as if it called for both. And therein lay its power.

The bulk of Wills's prologue to *Inventing America* does not deal with Jefferson; it deals with Abraham Lincoln. In it Wills argues that Lincoln accomplished "the recontracting of our society on the basis of the Declaration as our fundamental charter." Through the power of his rhetoric, indeed in the single act of the Gettysburg Address, Lincoln refounded our nation and dedicated it to the proposition that all men are created equal.[27]

Lincoln's refounding was not without its faults. Its myth of a virgin nation, created by a single document in order to "become a sign for the nations, a pledge that 'government of the people, by the people, and for the people shall not perish from the earth,'" gave

Americans a dangerous confidence in their own special status and mission. And

> there are subtler and more important results of the myth. A belief in our extraordinary birth, outside the processes of time, has led us to think of ourselves as a nation apart, with a special destiny, the hope of all those outside America's shores. This feeling, of course, antedated Lincoln. It was part of the Puritan ideal, of the city set on a hilltop. . . . It arose from Protestant America's strong feeling of kinship with the chosen people of its Old Testament. It returned in visions of manifest destiny at the beginning of this century. But Lincoln's was the most profound statement of this belief in a special American fate. His version of it was not pinned to a narrow Puritanism or imperialism, but simply to the Declaration itself. Its power is mythic, not sectarian. Lincoln did not join a separate religion to politics; he made his politics religious. And that is why his politics has survived the attack on less totally fused forms of "civil religion."[28]

Through his biblical rhetoric, Lincoln created a mythical, religious politics that remains powerful today. Based on the simple assertion that all men are created equal, it continues to charge our imagination and call us to action. It was vague enough, as was the Declaration itself, to lend itself to retellings that fit new circumstances and so continue to reflect our values and affect our politics.

Americans' belief that they had a special mission as a nation in Wills's view led to imperialism and the excesses of the Cold War. It dedicated America to an abstract proposition, and such dedication leads, for Wills, to intolerance. In refounding our society Lincoln dedicated us to a single proposition rather than to moral consensus. In this way he promoted a dangerous drive to achieve perfection. Jefferson the empirical scientist would not read his own document in such theological terms, Wills asserts, and neither should we. Jefferson thought "the highest test of a thing was its immediate practicality to the living generation." And this is how we should approach our Founding documents.[29]

Lincoln made the Declaration the central document of our public life. He deserves praise for his leadership, particularly because Lincoln's Declaration was all about equality, and for Wills equality is a great ideal. But the status of central, Founding document properly belongs to the Constitution, "the actual charter that gives us our law." The myth of our special status and Founding has taken attention away from the actual contract under which we live.[30] But what is this contract? What does it tell us about how we should live?

Irrelevant Law, Relevant Myth

Wills's book on the Constitution, *Explaining America*, shares much in common with *Inventing America*, his book on the Declaration. Most fundamentally, Wills attempts in both books to re-create the mind of the author of an important Founding document. But whereas he sought in *Inventing America* to recreate the mind behind Jefferson's early, unadopted draft of the Declaration, in *Explaining America* he seeks to illuminate the shared mind of the two men most responsible for our understanding of the Constitution: the principle authors of *The Federalist Papers*, James Madison and Alexander Hamilton.

Wills seeks to show that our Constitution is more of a republican than a liberal charter. He relates stories intended to convince us that the philosophy and morality of the Founders owed more to the supposedly communitarian common sense philosophers of the Scottish Enlightenment than to John Locke. But once again his deeper purpose is to convince us that we cannot and should not be tied to the language and intent of our Founding documents. According to Wills we should seek in our past not a specific vision of the proper nature and extent of government but rather examples of heroic conduct we can follow as we continually redefine our nation.

The bulk of *Explaining America* concerns Madison's thought, and *Federalist* 10 in particular. Madison, Wills argues, owes more to the Scottish philosopher David Hume than to Locke. Hume argued that a society can only exist if the people believe the rulers have a right to their power. Further, Hume argued, the right to rule comes from "opinion," from habitual attachments such as affection for an established royal family. Habitual attachments for Hume grow from the affectionate relations of family life. Locke, on the other hand, felt that societies begin and function solely by and through contracts. Self-interest, not affection, is the basis of Lockean society.

That this is an incorrect reading of Locke need not detain us here (see Chapter 1). The point is that Wills's Madison followed Hume (and agreed with Wills) in seeking to found a virtuous nation on public opinion. Under Madison's Constitution, the people would choose wise and virtuous rulers who would serve the public interest. Public opinion would keep public actors virtuous because politicians would seek glory and try to avoid the public humiliation accompanying failure and bad faith.[31]

According to Wills, "Madison expected a great deal from the people, from central power, and from their rulers. The people, since *they* were virtuous, would choose wise and virtuous rulers who would exercise power benignly—so long as America remained a republic."[32] The central government would hold the country together because the people of the various states would have the virtue and common sense to choose able patriots to lead them.

Wills's view of Madison is reminiscent of Bellah's vision of an underground republican tradition. Both see American virtue as real but beleaguered, losing out to selfish individualism while constantly reminding us of the need for and possibility of public service. Such a view might produce arguments over the true meaning of our Constitution and its corruption by selfish innovators. But Wills and Bellah do not want to tie our republican tradition to our Founding documents.

Wills argues that Madison's theories are not very relevant to the text of the document, let alone today's society. The Constitution was the result, he argues, of numerous state ratifying conventions that compromised and modified Madison's original plan. Rather than the philosophy of Madison or any one man, the Constitution was the product of compromise and the group consciousness of the American people.[33]

Most observers consider Madison's arguments in *The Federalist Papers* the best available justifications for our Constitution's plan of government. Even the theoretically minded Jefferson called *The Federalist Papers* the best "practical" treatise on government.[34] Nonetheless, Wills argues, we should not look to Madison for the Constitution's true meaning. More than this, according to Wills the Constitution itself is largely irrelevant to American public life. The world of the Founders is gone, their "deferential" society based on glory and prestige, the class system they took for granted, their virtue and confidence in the powers of reason, all have been swept away by democracy, industrialization, and the party system.[35]

Further, although Madison drew up the first draft of our Constitution, he did not believe even the final, adopted version was authoritative. No constitution could give a complete, final and fully coherent set of rules for governing. "The complexity of the matter to be dealt with, the fallibility of man's perceptions, and the unreliability of his verbal tools" made constitution drafting as much guesswork as political or moral science. The result could not embody hard and fast rules, let alone the spirit of a people: "The result is bound to lack final clarity, abstract symmetry, and 'artificial structure.' . . . The ability of the men at the Convention to resolve their differences is a pledge of future adjudications in the spirit of compromise."[36]

According to Wills's Madison, "future adjudications"—changes to the Constitution's meaning—need not await the formalities of the formal, constitutional amending process. In a society held together by social affections and the power of public opinion, informal compromise would be the rule. The public opinion of the moment must trump the supposed wisdom of the drafters.

> If the distinctions in the Constitution remain, of necessity, uncertain; if they await future 'liquidation'; if the ratifiers are to trust each other that differences can be *worked out* within the framework offered; if these future discussions and adjudications are to be guided by a large spirit of compromise, not a niggling regard to the letter of this first attempt at legislation; if considerations like these are the starting point and norm of constitutional discussion—then Madison is arguing for a very adaptable and flexible instrument reflecting the needs of social man. This test of utility . . . constitutes . . . one of the most extensive and ingenious arguments for the idea of the Constitution as a "living document" responding to society's needs, not as a text frozen in the first approximations of those who compromised it into being.

At first this reading of Madison's view of the Constitution seems quite curious. To begin with it goes against Madison's statement that those seeking to interpret the Constitution should look to the state ratifying conventions to find the document's full meaning. It would be odd to say the least for Madison to point inquisitors anywhere to any source if there existed no full meaning for them to find.[37]

Just as odd, Wills's interpretation seems to go against his own view of Madison's Humean tendencies. He identifies Hume, and through him Madison, with the notion that governments must hold the people in awe if they are to survive. If the people come to believe that only their active consent (given most likely through voting) can render political institutions and acts legitimate, the government will be weak and ineffective. The regime's legitimacy will be tied to the ever-changing popularity of current policies and officeholders. Thus, for Wills's Madison, the people must be trained to accept and even be in awe of their government at all times—unless they suffer under actual tyranny.[38]

Wills's interpretation seems to create a needless contradiction in Madison's thought. Wills appears to accuse Madison of lying either when he says the people should awe their government or when he claims they may change that government at will. The contradiction would be needless because Madison clearly believed problems could be worked out through the formal amendment process. Widely unpopular policies or institutions could be overturned through constitutional amendment as constitutionally, though not as readily, as unpopular officeholders could be defeated at the polls.

But Wills does not wish to be hemmed in by constitutional formalities. Nor does he wish us to see Madison's "awe" as a bar to democratic action. Wills's interpretation makes sense if one sees "awe" as a kind of summation of public approval. The people are in awe of their government if they see its basic structures and its fundamental ideals as holy. The document actually detailing the government's structure is of only secondary importance. It is merely, as Wills calls it, a "utilitarian division of labor within a generally benevolent set of social ties."[39] For a communitarian two things are important: the current consensus and authentic commitment to some ideal. And neither a nation's ideals nor its current consensus can be encapsulated in any document or era.

Madison's references to civility and the spirit of compromise must be taken as an invitation to constantly rewrite the Constitution because for Wills that is the only sensible thing to do. The point, for Wills, is not what the Constitution or Madison said, but what can be made of it. After all, what was said cannot be fully understood today and in any event bears little relation to current circumstances.

According to Wills our government and society have changed greatly, and largely for the better, since the Founding, and so the language and reasoning of our Founding documents no longer can guide us. But why, then, should we study them at all? Why retain an antiquated document? Not to regain a lost understanding of politics, let alone a lost structure of government, to be sure. Rather, we must look to Madison, as to Washington and Jefferson, as models of civic virtue. We must look to them, or at any rate to Wills's picture of them, to discover how we ought to act today. Only in this way will we learn that we must put public opinion into action as well as how we may accomplish this great end.

> If nothing else, Madison explains himself in the *Federalist*—not a minor thing. Without him and his like, without their ideals, their virtuous labors for the common good, there would have been no America to be preserved and passed on through the necessary changes of the centuries. In that sense, he does explain America—in explaining himself he tells us what Washington meant to his peers and friends and followers, what Jefferson meant. America has to be explained, historically, in terms of the Enlightenment, of the code of public virtue espoused without embarrassment by its most distinguished leaders. And the place to begin that effort is, indeed, with "Publius," the man of the people, the public man.[40]

Not Madison's theory of government but his choice of nom de plume is important. Madison's desire to gain public approbation by serving the public good and his great efforts in this endeavor show how we should act and what we should desire. Wills's stories of our first Founding seek not to promote a specific form of government but rather a specific form of virtue—one ruled by public opinion.

Our Constitution and Founding are good only because they provide useful myths. The Founding can be read in such a way that it gives us a myth of progress embodied in the idea of a living Constitution. We may create our own values and render them "constitutional" by declaring that the Constitution has no set meaning. We may look to changing circumstances and changing public opinion as the source of the true and the good, secure in the notion that our civil religious myths will motivate us to do what is right. We must, in fact, change the structure of morality on which our society rests on a periodic basis so that we may live up to the model of proper conduct Wills finds in our past.

The past itself is unrecoverable. And that is a good thing, because a mythical past allows the historian and the statesman to shape public opinion and lead the people in the proper direction—toward greater authenticity, greater adherence to the dictates of public opinion, and greater equality. It is to this last great value, Wills argues, that contemporary America's true founder, Lincoln, turned when he used myth to remold America.

Old Myths, New Founding

The subtitle to Wills's *Lincoln at Gettysburg* is "The Words That Remade America." Authors, or their publishers, often seek to increase sales by exaggerating a book's claims. Not so with this book. Wills claims nothing less than that Lincoln remade America with the *words* he uttered at Gettysburg.

As with all Wills's historical studies, *Lincoln at Gettysburg* includes a great deal of storytelling intended to reveal the context and mind of a great founder. But in this case perhaps more than any other Wills concentrates specifically on the rhetoric of a "founding" document. He focuses closely on the language of Lincoln's speech at the dedication of the Gettysburg battlefield cemetery.

The book begins with a chapter on the oratory of the Greek Revival. In it Wills puts Lincoln's speech into the context of the other speeches delivered at Gettysburg and, more importantly, of the "democratic" style of building, speaking, and so on popular in the mid-nineteenth century. He attributes the Greek Revival style to a rebirth of interest in ideas and things Greek, much as he had attributed myths from the Constitutional era, and George Washington's life in particular, to an earlier rebirth of interest in things Roman. The Greek democratic age had succeeded the Roman heroic age in America and had found its own rhetoric and historically based symbols.

The body of Wills's book ends, after a scant 175 pages, with a chapter on Lincoln's "Revolution in Style." This final chapter ends with the claim that Lincoln's style made possible a new American founding. Particularly in the Gettysburg Address,

> words were weapons, for [Lincoln], even though he meant them to be weapons of peace in the midst of war.
>
> This was the perfect medium for changing the way most Americans thought about the nation's founding acts. Lincoln does not argue law or history, as Daniel Webster did. He *makes* history. He does not come to present a theory, but to impose a symbol, one tested in experience and appealing to national values, with an emotional urgency entirely expressed in calm abstractions (fire in ice). He came to change the world, to effect an intellectual revolution. No other words could have done it. The miracle is that these words did. In his brief time before the crowd at Gettysburg he wove a spell that has not, yet, been broken—he called up a new nation out of the blood and trauma.[41]

Wills's Lincoln made history by changing his people's past. He convinced the people that his reading of their history was morally correct. He made Americans see their history as one properly dedicated to the pursuit of equality of human condition. In this way he convinced them to dedicate themselves to the pursuit of ever greater equality.

According to Wills Lincoln's weapon or tool in capturing America's heart and mind was his cunning rhetoric. He used biblical-sounding phrasing such as "four score and seven years ago" to set a reverential mood. He employed double meanings to make hidden points ("of the people, by the people, for the people" was intended in Wills's view to convince us both that the people should rule and that America was a single nation, with a single people, unaffected by regional history). He was a master craftsman of repetitive sentences (for example, "of," "by," and "for *the people*") that drove his points home.[42] With these tools Lincoln broke through the people's preexisting beliefs and shaped new ones. He imposed the symbol of equality on their minds through the power of his rhetoric and in the process transformed the ever-impressionable American Founding into one dedicated to the national pursuit of equality.

From the Civil War's blood and trauma Lincoln called up, through the force of his words, a *new* nation. He "had revolutionized the Revolution, giving people a new past to live with that would change their future indefinitely." He launched a "verbal coup" that refounded America on a single, abstract proposition: that all men are created equal.[43]

Equality as Wills understands it was not a part of America's first, late eighteenth-century, Founding. Slavery and the class system show the Founders' lack of commitment to equality of condition. Thus it may well be (one might argue that it is beyond doubt true) that the Founders would disapprove of contemporary programs like affirmative action and mandatory busing that aim to make Americans more equal.

But according to Wills we cannot return to our pre–Civil War ideals and practices. The past, as always, remains a reservoir of collective myth that can be tapped but not possessed. Those who would go back to the original Founding are doomed to fail, not because they are wrong about what the Constitution originally said or intended. Rather, "their job would be comparatively easy if they did not have to work against the values created by the Gettysburg Address."[44] We live in a different America because Lincoln's rhetoric *created* egalitarian values. Lincoln took the Declaration's statement that "all men are created equal" and turned it into a national commitment. He consecrated the battlefield at Gettysburg as the ground on which men died to protect human equality. He shaped the nation and the people into one defined by its commitment to equality.

According to Wills commitment to equality of condition was not a part of our original Founding. But the fact that Lincoln got his history wrong is irrelevant.

The Gettysburg Address has become an authoritative expression of the American spirit—as authoritative as the Declaration itself, and perhaps even more influential, since it determines how we read the Declaration. For most people now, the Declaration means what Lincoln told us it means, as a way of correcting the Constitution itself without overthrowing it. It is this correction of the spirit, this intellectual revolution, that makes attempts to go back beyond Lincoln to some earlier version so feckless.[45]

Our opinion about our past is what is real. Not the facts of the case but the myths constructed by the skilled rhetorician shape our values and acts. And these shared values and acts constitute the only reality we may know. The Gettysburg Address's powerful rhetoric shaped the mind of the people and so made it *the* authority on the American spirit and our proper commitment to equality.

But how can someone "correct" a constitution through a verbal coup? If he ignores democratic forms (such as the amending process) and instead reshapes the mind of the people with his rhetoric, is he not acting unconstitutionally, antidemocratically, and with moral turpitude? And what is left of a constitution whose limited purposes (essentially the protection of semisovereign states) have been transformed into a national commitment to equality of condition?

It is perhaps unsurprising at this point that Wills has no problem with these seeming dilemmas. Because what is important is not the contents or intent of a particular document or group of men, we should not place too much stock in our original Founding. Rather, Wills argues, for Lincoln as for Madison the Constitution was only a starting point for later collective discussion and compromise.

But Lincoln managed to *create* a starting point out of the Declaration. He created a mythical origin for his egalitarian ideal. Our actions and the institutions we build (such as our constitutional republic) inevitably fail to live up to this ideal. But in Lincoln's hand the Declaration nonetheless served as the font of our values. It provided the great rhetorician Lincoln with the opportunity to commit us as a nation to equality of condition. The Constitution, a "living" document with no set meaning, was changed as needed to make it a better embodiment of the Declaration's egalitarian ideal.

> The very author of the Declaration continued to own slaves. Moreover, the Constitution countenanced slavery, and the Constitution, not the Declaration, is the working law of the land.
>
> It was at this point in the argument that Lincoln distinguished between the Declaration as the statement of a permanent ideal and the Constitution as an early and provisional embodiment of that ideal, to be tested against it, kept in motion toward it.[46]

Lincoln argued strenuously throughout his career that the Constitution must be respected and enforced. He upheld the fugitive slave laws that forced Northerners to return escaped slaves. He argued that the Constitution forbade federal interference with slavery in the several states. He insisted that his opposition to slavery in the territories was supported by the language of the Constitution.[47]

Wills mentions none of this. He does, however, note Lincoln's insistence that "we see, the plain unmistakable spirit of that [Founding] age, towards slavery, was hostility in the PRINCIPLE, and toleration ONLY BY NECESSITY."[48] Lincoln also argued that any program to end slavery must be rejected if it contradicted the Constitution's plain meaning. But Wills dismisses this argument as a necessary concession to Lincoln's followers. Lincoln's actual intent, which he brought to fruition at Gettysburg, in Wills's view was to "correct" the Constitution itself through extraconstitutional means—by the power of presidential rhetoric.

Lincoln's "corrected" reading of the Declaration fundamentally changed our nation. This reading, one not in keeping with the Founders' vision, fundamentally altered the nation's Founding document, the Constitution. The abstract language of the Declaration, for Wills's Lincoln, must be read in such a way that it produces an absolute commitment to equality. This commitment then must be read into the Constitution, delegitimizing every phrase in the Constitution that contradicts it. Only the Declaration could transcend the spirit of the age and serve as a standard by which to judge our progress as a people. Only the Declaration—pure rhetoric unfettered by concrete considerations or circumstances—could be used by Lincoln as a mythical source of egalitarian values, the sole source transcending even public opinion.

We ought to refound our nation as often as necessary to live up to its fundamental principle. Wills's position seems, then, to create a paradox: we must replace our nation in order to live up to its values. But for Wills the nation's structure will change; federalism, for example, may be destroyed. The call to public service, on the other hand, remains constant and continual calls for leaders who will reform the nation and its people.

The highest political glory, for the republican, belongs to the founder. He who establishes a new regime, or reestablishes an old one on firmer foundations, provides the greatest possible public service. He is the father of his country.

Wills sees Lincoln as just such a father, and thus Wills, the student of rhetoric, dismisses as mere rhetoric Lincoln's warnings against those who would usurp power under the guise of public service. In his speech to the Young Men's Lyceum of Springfield, Lincoln urged opposition to the glory-seeking tyrant. He called for "the people to be united with each other, attached to the government and laws, and generally intelligent, to successfully frustrate his designs."[49]

Lincoln urged the people to unite in loyalty (awe?) to their legal government so that they might preserve their liberty. He called for intelligent, informed consent to laws that would prevent glory-seekers from undermining constitutional government. But for Wills such arguments must constitute mere youthful indiscretions, mere reflections of an overblown rhetoric with no basis in reality because what must count is the power of the statesman/orator. Thus even Lincoln's repeated attempts to save the union by denying that he would act against slavery in any state, along with his refusal to call for social equality for blacks, were mere tactics aimed at placating those less progressive than he. A great statesman must tell the occasional lie to keep his people on the right track.

Mythical Authenticity

Wills wants us to believe that we can create anew ideals, values, and institutions every time we join together in the presence of a great rhetorical mind. We shape meaning through our words, and our shared meanings shape our actions and our society. We must not be tied down by any one particular meaning, any one particular constitutional interpretation or set of laws. This would stifle our collective creativity and impoverish our lives. We must refound our nation and ourselves as we, with the aid of great leaders, see fit.

This is not to say that Wills sees Lincoln as the perfect statesman, or even that he sees Lincoln's refounding as entirely a good thing. Wills has never retracted his view that Americans are too enamored of abstract principle, that we should not be tied to *any* proposition, including equality, that is not subject to constant revision. But equality certainly is a good to which Wills would have us aspire, one that he feels need not interfere with our projects of collective value creation.

Equality itself is an abstract and malleable concept. Wills argues that, for the Founders, equality meant that Americans as a people were as civilized and worthy of respect as the English. For most of Lincoln's progressive contemporaries equality meant moral equality—the natural right not to be enslaved. The values Wills's Lincoln created have made equality mean equality of condition—the natural right to fairness of treatment and a "fair" distribution of jobs, education, and material goods.

Equality is an essential element of the communitarian faith. Beginning from the assumption that we all are equal in moral worth, communitarians go on to assume that none of us is better than any other, whatever our chosen form of personal conduct or lifestyle. Thus a fair society will be one in which material goods are distributed roughly equally among the populace.

The communitarian faith in equality rests on the notion that we all have a moral vision. All of us are equal members of the conversation of our society, except that certain powerful rhetoricians lead us. All of us have an innate moral sense that will lead us to act properly if not corrupted by social structures that are unequal and therefore unjust.

Wills goes to great lengths to present the Scottish "common sense" school of philosophy as the true source of our Founding. He further emphasizes that common sense, which guides us in our moral as well as practical conduct, is egalitarian and communal. We learn our morality, to borrow from Taylor, "dialogically." Rather than a transcendent set of standards or truths according to which we should order our actions, Wills maintains that the common sense philosophers saw morality as an outgrowth of social interaction.

God created morality only in the sense that he made men social creatures. It is from society that we learn good and evil. Common sense, for Wills's Scots, meant "*communal* sense, the shared wisdom of the community." The wisdom or, in effect, the voice of the community was in fact "the voice of God."[50]

Thus God is reduced to that which speaks through the people. For Wills's Scots God's lowered status would not endanger public morality because men were by nature good and moral creatures. Wills argues that for Scots such as Frances Hutcheson we act virtuously because we have a natural appetite for benevolence and naturally delight in seeing acts of benevolence (the giving of charity and so on). We copy the acts of benevolence we witness in our daily lives so that we may prolong the pleasure we receive from seeing them.[51]

By nature we all are inclined to treat others well; thus all of us should be treated as equally good creatures. We all should have a sufficient and equal amount of material goods and an equal chance to fulfill ourselves in liberal fashion—by shaping our own individual lifestyles in combination with our chosen partners of the moment.

But ironically authenticity does not come spontaneously. According to Wills authenticity is the product of training and leadership. Benevolence rests on shared feelings and unfortunately most of us are too ignorant even to express our feelings to close friends and relatives: "When deeply felt moments arrive—a death, a birth, a national catastrophe—we can only say 'I don't know what to say.' "[52]

This is why we need orators. The orator "uses artifice to reach the truth, to be adequate to the situation, to respond to and elevate the audience's feelings." Wills's great orator fulfills the function of Mill's great leader, be he Akbar or Charlemagne, who makes a people capable of positing its own values. He molds individuals into a greater whole. He is a great leader. His "first test is his ability to create heroes in response to his call. The orator's final test is his ability to create heroism in himself to match what he has been preaching. Here the artificial *becomes* the true in the most complete way. Leaders and followers prod *each other* toward their shared goal."

In a kind of dialogic relationship, leader and followers create virtue. Called out of myth and rhetorical technique, heroism takes on a life of its own and transforms those who created it. By manipulating myths and mythical language, the great leader shapes our minds. He creates new values and ideals for us and so makes possible our public moral life. The statesman, like the historian, creates history with his words; words that have the power to change our views, our values, and our very consciousness of our past and present duties.

The Authentic Leader: Mario Cuomo

Former New York governor Mario Cuomo does not cite Wills when he interprets Lincoln's life and thought. But he uses Lincoln in a way Wills would understand and appreciate, arguing that "Lincoln . . . not only led us, he *created* us. His personal mythology became our national mythology."[53] The great leader, for Cuomo as for Wills, binds a people together, making a nation into a family. He uses religion and other myths to make the people look on their nation as something familiar, important, and sacred enough to be worthy of the loyalty normally reserved for one's parents or siblings.

Like Wills, Cuomo molds Lincoln's legacy to create a useful myth of our heroic origins and national duties. An accomplished rhetorician himself, Cuomo seeks to harness Lincoln's image and poetic writings to convince us to enlist in his own political programs. "I use [Lincoln] to inspire us and to remind us that we are still in the process of perfecting the union," says Cuomo unabashedly. And the inspiration need not have any specific textual basis. Cuomo uses Lincoln's name, but no quotations, to support policies from open immigration to expanded welfare programs to government actions aimed at discouraging corporate buyouts.

Often called a "New Deal liberal" Cuomo certainly has the markings of an old-fashioned Democrat. He unabashedly prescribes government programs to solve social and economic ills from racism to poverty. But this shows not just Cuomo's liberalism, but also communitarianism's. Cuomo uses clearly communitarian rhetoric, particularly when speaking of the nation as family. He also fights for communitarian programs and policies. Indeed, Cuomo shows the extent and limits of communitarianism because his own failure at the polls rested not on discomfort with his rhetoric, but rather on the continuing conviction that his policies were too state-centered to meet contemporary challenges. Whatever one thinks of communitarian policies (or "old" liberal ones for that matter), New Yorkers rejected Cuomo's last bid for governor because they found his rhetoric of community insufficient reason to reelect him.

Yet Cuomo is the communitarian statesman par excellence. He insists that he governs "the family of New York," and he seeks to make us all serve "the family of America." His goal is to bind us to our political community by convincing us that we can act morally only if we support government programs to equalize wealth and minimize risk. And he does so in religious language intended to sanctify not any particular institutions or practices, but the communitarian goal of constantly redefining the norms of our community, making them ever more tolerant and egalitarian.

But Cuomo does not seek merely to convince us in liberal fashion that government can make us individually more free and secure by playing a greater role in our lives. He urges us to think of ourselves as members of a great, political family, whether of our state or of our nation. He seeks to bind us in civil religious fashion to the programs of the liberal state. His claim is that familial commitment will make us better human beings. We will act morally by supporting our siblings through government programs, and still be left free to create our own lifestyles and make our own moral choices on issues like abortion.

The Politician's Role

Ours is a time of mass democracy and popular demands for "progress." Recent political changes (including the Republican landslide of 1994) may indicate a shift in the public's views, but in recent decades the public has judged politicians' success according to whether they have produced concrete benefits—money, jobs, new public facilities, and so on. The politician who does not literally deliver the goods will soon fall from power. And to earn a reputation as a "strong" leader the politician, be he president, legislative leader, or governor, must make great changes. He must wage a "war on poverty" or "make the world safe for democracy" or institute vast social programs like Social Security.

Scholars as well as politicians may resort to useful myths (or "noble" lies) to sway the masses. This makes civil religion a helpful tool for all reforms, whether in the classroom or in the governor's office. But the politician ties his useful myth more closely to specific policy goals than does the scholar. Wills the scholar uses our history to paint pictures of political heroism and convince us that national service should be our highest goal. Cuomo the politician and self-described "progressive pragmatist" uses Lincoln to argue that only Cuomo's specific vision of an expansive, centralized government committed to equality of condition lives up to our national ideals.[54]

According to Cuomo, "Lincoln was the president who argued that government has a responsibility 'to do for the people what . . . they cannot . . . do at all, or do so well, for themselves.'"[55] Cuomo cites this famous passage from Lincoln many times. In the text from which he draws, Lincoln lists instances where the government should act in the people's interest. They include building and maintaining public roads, bridges, and schools, supporting charitable orphanages and hospitals, and using public courts and facilities to see that dead men's estates are divided as they wished. "But a far larger class of objects," Lincoln argued, "springs from the injustice of men." According to Lincoln, fighting enemies abroad and bringing wrongdoers at home to justice constitute the main business of government.[56]

Cuomo's vision of the federal government's proper role is not so limited as Lincoln's. Limited government is not communitarian. It requires that we see the government as something less than a national family, something that can provide only certain, circumscribed goods and services. We must ignore Lincoln's actual policy proposals so that we may fulfill the promise we ourselves have found (in reality created) in his words. According to Cuomo our government must do all things necessary to continue "Lincoln's work," which is the "struggle for inclusion."

We must include all Americans in the life of prosperity and opportunity. Otherwise we abandon Lincoln and the reality he shaped for us. "Our identity as a people is hostage to the grim facts of more than 33 million Americans for whom equality and opportunity is not yet an attainable reality, but only an illusion."[57]

Equality and opportunity, Cuomo insists, must be our goals. Not merely equality *of* opportunity but substantive equality—of income and material enjoyment—coupled with the opportunity to mold our own lifestyle—are our right and we must use government to achieve them.[58] Lincoln would want us to use government to eliminate material inequality, and thus refusing to use government in this way is a sin; in so refusing we go against the wishes of our national creator.

Lincoln created us when he created our values. He refounded our nation on the idea of equality, which makes us a special, chosen people. Cuomo asks, "What other people on earth have ever claimed a quality of character that resided not in a way of speaking, dressing, dancing, praying, but in an idea?"[59] Not our culture or our religion but our commitment to the idea of equality makes us American. To disagree with the American idea, the idea of equality, is to be un-American.

Cuomo's Lincoln did not bequeath to us a particular form of limited government and federalism. He bequeathed to us the idea of equality. We must show our respect for him by attempting to fulfill the task he gave us: to include everyone in the life of equal prosperity. We must reform our nation in ways Lincoln would have found pleasing—or rather ways Lincoln *should* have found pleasing. Lincoln's actual policies are not as important as the vision great rhetorical leaders like Cuomo can create from his words and images to spur us on to greater reforms. We must not set our creator Lincoln out of reach. Not the man but the idea we find in him must be holy to us.

Unfortunately, Lincoln often is made the object of an unhealthy worship. "We have chiseled his face on the side of a mountain, making him appear as a voice in the heavens." Mount Rushmore and the worship it inspires are dangerous because they strain "the sense of connection between [the objects of our worship] and the palpable, fleshy, sometimes mean concerns of our own lives."[60]

Cuomo maintains that we should look on Lincoln as a great hero, as our creator even, because he shaped our consciousness; he used his great rhetoric to commit us to equality. But we must not worship our creator Lincoln as a force somehow above ourselves. We must not look to him as a source of constant principles or any concrete set of policies and moral values that must bind us for all time. Setting Lincoln above ourselves would go against the idea of equality.

Our commitment to equality means that we cannot set up any one man, or any one idea, as a perpetual, unchanging standard against which to judge our actions. Not even our national idea should be unchanging. Luckily for us, the idea of equality (like the true meaning of our Founding documents) is sufficiently vague that we may infuse it with our own meanings, which may change over time.

Lincoln fought the unequal and therefore unfair treatment of blacks inherent in slavery. We must fight the unequal and therefore unfair treatment Cuomo finds inherent in poverty. The institutions and other means we use to carry on this task are mere tools, to be constructed or discarded as we wish. It is our commitment to equality, not to any particular structure of government or society, that makes us Americans.

That the Constitution the Founders drafted was not intended to establish a central authority capable of imposing material equality is irrelevant. We cannot tie ourselves to a historical document if that would interfere with current needs. "The original blueprint of our national unity would be tested—and shaped—by being stretched and configured on the Procrustean bed of reality."[61] "Reality"—changing economic circumstances and our progressive intolerance for social woes such as slavery, discrimination, and poverty—has changed the Constitution fundamentally. And this is good.

The "Procrustean bed" on which we have placed the Constitution has allowed us to lop off portions of the original blueprint that stood in the way of progress. When the legendary Procrustes placed unfortunate travelers on his bed and cut off the parts that did not fit, his victims died. But our Procrustean bed has improved the work of the Founding Fathers. The Founders must have wanted a richer, more open, and egalitarian nation. Government grew as our nation grew more equal and prosperous, and so must have produced these changes. It carried the family of America out of the Depression, "to new levels of comfort, security, dignity, even affluence." And because our Procrustean bed—the experience of expansive government—has produced progressive wealth and equality it must fit with the Founders' wishes.[62]

The point for Cuomo, as for Wills and for communitarians in general, is not to commit oneself entirely to any single political structure. One must instead commit oneself to the ever-expanding idea of equality. All institutions must give way before the goal of equality.

But why value equality? Cuomo does not see equality as life's ultimate goal. Instead he sees it as a necessary reinforcement of society's commitment to authenticity.

In a speech to graduating seniors, Cuomo opined that "the most important thing in their lives will be their ability to believe in believing"—otherwise the graduates would be doomed to despair.[63] It is through commitment to beliefs, and through action aimed at fulfilling those beliefs, that we fulfill ourselves as individuals and as a people. But for Cuomo as for Taylor and other communitarians it is believing itself—our commitment and not the thing to which we are committed—that gives life meaning.

According to Cuomo we should serve the democratic mechanisms that allow us constantly to reconstruct our political life. No single vision even of equality should become our goal because this would entail casting aspersions on others' views of what form equality should take. No one interpretation of the Constitution should rule because this would bind us to a past that was less just than today's society, which in turn is less just than tomorrow's no doubt will be. We must re-create our politics and our morality on an almost daily basis, secure in the knowledge that we will become progressively more just and moral as time goes on.

The moral life, for Cuomo, is neither lived nor taught through any specific, concrete political institution. Standards of behavior are taught by example. We learn how to be moral in the intimate relations of family life.

And it is to the image of the family, the primordial social institution, that Cuomo consistently recurs in his political speeches when he lays out his vision of our moral duties. As he put it in his 1984 Democratic National Convention keynote address, "We believe in a single fundamental idea that describes better than most textbooks and any speech what a proper government should be. The idea of family. Mutuality. The sharing of benefits and burdens for the good of all. Feeling one another's pain. Sharing one another's blessings."

We must "feel one another's pain." But how is government to act on this feeling? What standards of public and political conduct does this notion of the nation as family give to us? For Cuomo the answer seems clear: "A society as blessed as ours should be able to find room at the table—shelter for the homeless, work for the idle, care for the elderly and infirm, and hope for the destitute. To demand less of our government or ourselves would be to evade our proper responsibility."[64] We have a moral responsibility, according to Cuomo, to use government to ensure that all Americans share equally in an abundant material prosperity.

But we must not use government to impose any moral vision on other individuals or society as a whole. Cuomo seeks to use government to ensure that all of us have the means to pursue our own authentic visions of the good life. We must fight against those who believe "that government's only collective responsibility is to insist on a governmentally imposed mode of private behavior."[65]

Cuomo meshes the religious with the political to form a characteristically liberal civil religion. He proclaims at the same time our moral duty to support government welfare programs and to oppose any infusion of government into the moral realm. He invokes Jesus Christ in arguing that we have a collective moral duty to construct government programs that show our compassion while rejecting moral stances, such as opposition to abortion, that might limit individual autonomy.[66] In true communitarian fashion, Cuomo uses religious rhetoric to convince us that we should use government to fund authentic private lifestyles.

Moral Politics and Political Morality

Families depend on government funding, according to Cuomo. To fail to continually increase this funding is to deny Americans what is rightfully theirs; it is to write into American history "A Tale of Two Cities"—of self-indulgent affluence and poverty, of discrimination and despair. We must erase this tale and put in its place a palpable City Upon a Hill—"one city, indivisible, shining for *all* its people."[67]

Politics for Cuomo is a struggle between champions of the rich and champions of the poor. On the side of the poor, and thus the angels, are "progressive pragmatists" such as himself who understand that "by our own volition, freely, out of our Christian commitment, we can will not only to profess the faith, but to live it, to make our faith matter in this world, not just in the churches, but in the mean streets where people go hungry and homeless, without hope or love." Such sentiments must be willed, according to Cuomo, in both our private lives and our politics.[68]

According to Cuomo all of us

> are presented with a choice. Either we swim with the tide and accept the notion that the best way to improve the world is for government to help the fortunate, and then hope that personal charity will induce them to take care of the rest of us. Or we resist, by affirming that *as we hear God,* he tells us it is our moral obligation to be our brother's keeper, all of us, as a people, as a government.[69]

Cuomo's God tells us to use government to help our fellow Americans; to serve as champions of the poor by redistributing wealth and opportunity. Opposing him are "social Darwinists" who believe that government, because it cannot do everything, "should settle for taking care of the strong and hope that economic ambition and charity will do the rest. Make the rich richer and what falls from their table will be enough for the middle class and those trying to make it into the middle class."[70]

Perhaps Cuomo sums up his own political vision best with his commandment, "Thou shalt not sin against equality." He turns inequality itself into a sin. The robber barons with whom he equates members of the Republican party, the pro-life educators and legislators he decries as sexual oppressors, and anyone who opposes racial quotas—all are sinners against equality.[71]

Government must solve our problems by equalizing our wealth. But this is not to say that Cuomo ignores or dismisses the institutions and affections of private life. Quite the contrary, he wishes to use our natural affections toward our families to further his political program. This is why he constantly refers to "the family" of New York, of America, or of any number of political bodies. He wishes to invoke the imagery and sentiments of family life so that we will approach political and economic issues in the same way we would any other family crisis. Instead of distrusting our government's use of our money and constantly arguing for our own positions and interests, Cuomo would have us seek to help government more wisely and generously aid our worse off brothers and sisters.

Religious sentiments also are crucial. Cuomo would have us reason that, because we are morally bound to be our brother's keeper, we also should feel morally bound to support government programs that supposedly will benefit all members of the "family" of America. Indeed, Cuomo goes beyond even the nation, praising environmental regulation as "the ultimate selfless act" because through it we sacrifice our own welfare in the hope that we will benefit future generations, individuals we don't know because they do not yet exist.[72]

Family and Polity

Aristotle argued that the family is the essential building block of society. But he also recognized a fundamental distinction between familial and political attachments. A father is attached to his son as if to a piece of himself. His progeny is in a real sense his chance for immortality. The political community, on the other hand, depends on relations that are less natural and less intimate.

The form of friendship on which political life relies is more utilitarian, more likely to fade away or break altogether under the stress of conflicting interests, than is the blood tie. Indeed, blood ties often subvert political stability by draining loyalty away from the community as a whole in favor of family members. Political leaders often give favors to their relatives, seeking to found dynasties and/or improve the family name. Nonrelatives, not so well favored, often unite behind a different family head. And the result is tribal warfare that can destroy a nation.

To bridge the gap between family and political community always has been difficult. Particularly in modern times, men have sought to foster intermediate associations that can tie families to the larger community. Local associations, whether centered in the neighborhood, the church, or a particular profession, taught the habits of association—of friendship and mutual action—on which public virtue relies.

In particular, Cuomo's Catholic church long has recognized the principle of "subsidiarity"—that the functions of life, and even of charity, should be carried out at the most local level possible. Thus the central government should not take on any task of which the local government is capable. Most importantly, the greatest possible responsibility should be left with families, churches, and local associations. These local institutions form and maintain intimate ties of local life that teach us our responsibility to our fellows. Acting on this knowledge we develop, over time, the habits that make us virtuous.

Tocqueville praised the United States of his nineteenth century precisely because it avoided nationalizing matters of local concern. By keeping the local township at the center of the people's public lives, the United States allowed them to develop the bonds of interest and affection on which public service depends. As Tocqueville put it: "The general business of a country keeps only the leading citizens occupied. It is only occasionally that they come together in the same places, and since they often lose sight of one another, no lasting bonds form between them. But when the people who live there have to look after the particular affairs of a district, the same people are always meeting, and they are forced, in a manner, to know and adapt themselves to one another."[73]

We all want to be held in high esteem by those we must deal with regularly; "to gain the affection and respect of your immediate neighbors, a long succession of little services rendered and of obscure good deeds, a constant habit of kindness and an established reputation for disinterestedness, are required." We act virtuously at first because it is in our interest to do so—it gets us the respect we desire. We continue acting virtuously out of habit and because it makes life more pleasant for everyone involved.[74]

Cuomo also praises families, churches, and local associations. But he seems to value these institutions only to the extent that they help carry on the state's work of producing ever-greater material equality. He judges the state of our morality not on its own terms (by how virtuously we behave) but by the material conditions of our people. In this way he ties religious to material values. He seeks moral and spiritual fulfillment only as a reward for providing the people with material goods.

Thus does Cuomo's religious vision, his insistence that politics is the realm in which we act morally or immorally, not make him "unliberal?" To the contrary, the very purpose of Cuomo's politics (and the civil religion that serves it) is to make authentic lifestyle choices easier and more financially secure. Religious sentiment is important to him. It should guide us toward what he deems a moral politics. But for Cuomo politics is moral only to the extent that it promotes material well-being. Moral principles should not be allowed to produce political actions that would intrude on private moral choices. Rather, we should use religious sentiment to construct a public order that will shape all of us into citizens who insist on material security and the right of each individual to create his own morality.

Cuomo dubs immoral anyone who would "dictate a woman's choice on abortion, and how and where children should pray." To oppose abortion or support voluntary prayer in schools (let alone to support "moral" legislation on issues such as pornography) is for Cuomo to "insist on a governmentally imposed mode of private behavior." Such attempts to put religious principle into practice are, for Cuomo, frightening. By comparison, he seeks merely to serve the people, to give them "all the government they need, but only the government they need," and to do God's will by providing the people with the material security to pursue their own visions of the good life.[75]

Of course for Cuomo the state plays a significant role in any good life. He urges us to use families and churches, but especially public schools to teach children the nature and requirements of the moral life. We must, he argues, "convince youngsters to live *for* something, to believe in themselves, in the significance of their own lives."

And what is to make these lives significant? In what code of ethics are children to find a basis for believing in themselves? Cuomo sums up the virtues of any good life as *"equality, individual rights, the common good* (or *community,* what I prefer to call 'family'), *the rule of law, and love of country."*[76]

We all are equal in that we are human beings worthy of respect. Our equality gives us rights, which themselves are limited by the rights of others, including their right to the tax-funded public services Cuomo defines as the common good. In order to protect our rights we must respect the law. For all our blessings we must thank and love the nation that nourishes and protects us. Thus Cuomo paints a picture of personal virtue in which supporting the public servants who protect us combines with faith in equality to promote a communitarian ethos. We must foster a tolerant and egalitarian community in which each of us is as free as possible to pursue his own ends, secure in the knowledge that his choices will be supported with public approval and money so long as they do not impinge on the lifestyles of others.

Authentic Leadership

In nominating Bill Clinton for president, Cuomo praised him for adhering to the politics of inclusion, in which people "of whatever color, of whatever creed, of whatever sex, of whatever sexual orientation, all [are] equal members of the American family." Clinton, according to Cuomo, would "make the whole nation stronger by bringing people together, showing us our commonality, instructing us in cooperation, making us not a collection of competing special interests, but one great, special family—the family of America."[77]

The president must be a rhetorical leader. He must make us better by teaching us to cooperate and that we can cooperate because we all are essentially alike. Politics is and should be the focus of public life. But politicians must not insist on a particular code of moral conduct. Rather, they must insist that differences in moral conduct be ignored so that the nation as family can concentrate on providing everincreasing security and material equality.

This stance has brought Cuomo both praise and blame as a leader on moral issues. As a Catholic politician who openly supports abortion rights, including the public funding of abortions, he has come under fire from the church even as he has garnered praise in the media. He also has produced his most self-consciously intellectual work in response to this issue: a speech delivered at the Notre Dame Law School that later appeared in a law journal as well as in a collection of his speeches.

In this speech Cuomo defends his pro-abortion policies on explicitly political grounds. He believes in the church's teachings, he says. He believes that abortion is "to be avoided." But this is merely a private, personal opinion in keeping with the private practice of religion that cannot properly be acted on in public life. Why not? Because it is not sufficiently popular.

"Our public morality . . . the moral standards we maintain for everyone, not just the ones we insist on in our private lives—depends on a consensus view of right and wrong. The values derived from religious belief will not—and should not—be accepted as part of the public morality unless they are shared by the pluralistic community at large, by consensus."[78] To Cuomo, the very fact that abortions occur shows that we cannot "impose" pro-life policies. To do so would be positively sinful because it would constitute a frightening use of religion to forward a given "political" program.

It would be easy to fit Cuomo's position into a communitarian mold by claiming his Catholicism is just another useful myth, that he actually believes in no fundamental moral truths that transcend popular opinion except the need for democratic participation. But Cuomo is willing to take a stand even *against* a democratic majority when he believes his morality requires it. Despite overwhelming support in his own state for capital punishment, while governor Cuomo steadfastly refused to implement it. He repeatedly vetoed legislation providing for capital punishment and even entered into constitutional conflict with another state by refusing to extradite a convicted murderer serving time in a New York jail to Oklahoma where he was under sentence of death.

More recently, Cuomo suggested a state referendum on capital punishment. He expressed confidence that the people of New York would surprise everyone by rejecting the death penalty. Some might consider this new position an attempt to find moral consensus on the death penalty issue. But Cuomo would learn nothing about the moral consensus if the measure should fail and (given that he would be serving his last term as governor) lose little should it succeed. A mere 50 percent of voting New Yorkers could defeat capital punishment, and half the voters hardly constitutes a consensus of all residents or even of all voters. Consensus, after all, denotes broad, overwhelming agreement. If all consensus meant was that a policy had the support of a democratic majority, then Cuomo would be in favor of a number of restrictions on abortion.

Surely it cannot be the case that Cuomo believes that capital punishment is a political issue, on which he may fight for his own opinion, while abortion is not. The very premise of his Notre Dame speech is that abortion is *too political* an issue for religious morality to guide his public conduct. According to Cuomo, his economic "Christian ethic" should become law. But his Catholic church calls on government to recognize religion's importance and to protect the sanctity of marriage and unborn human life. Indeed, in Catholic thought government's primary purpose is to protect religious values, institutions, and practices. But according to Cuomo religious values are improper subjects for *any* legislation or even public support from an avowedly Catholic governor. When we leave the sphere of economic "morality" and enter that of social and private virtues, Cuomo vigorously argues for the separation of church from state, and even of religion from politics.

A number of religious thinkers, including Tocqueville and American Catholic John Courtney Murray, have praised the constitutional principle of church/state separation. They have seen the separation of church and state as an important practical basis for public forbearance and civility and thus for the promulgation of faith in a pluralistic society. Tocqueville praised the American system, not least because he thought it fostered moral teaching.[79] Freed (until recently) from both the crushing hand of state interference and the corrupting practice of state power, priests could concentrate on instructing their flocks in the fundamentals of religious and moral life.

But, as Murray argued, our nation is founded on a moral consensus concerning not just political rights but also the need for government to respect religion. And to banish religious morality from public life altogether—to ban prayer from the schools or to condemn the pro-life movement as oppressive because it would infuse morality into the public sphere—is to turn the church into just another club, a private group with no proper call on the public's attention, let alone on its moral imagination.[80]

Cuomo raises the prudent tool of church/state separation to the level of theological truth. Where Murray argued for civility and a recognition that certain sins cannot be punished if we are to enjoy the benefits accruing to religious life in a free society, Cuomo rejects religion's moral authority altogether: Cuomo's God demands equality but not life.

If Cuomo is not openly hypocritical, it would appear that he believes material equality is more important than "private" morality or unborn life. An essential element of his pro-abortion argument is frankly materialistic. For example, according to Cuomo, to cut off Medicaid funding for abortions "would burden only the already disadvantaged."[81] Because removing Medicaid funding of abortions would not keep rich women from having them, fairness requires that taxpayers provide for poor women's abortions. After all, *thou shalt not sin against equality.*

In Cuomo's view even pro-life forces should look to government funding as the answer to their concerns. We should, in Cuomo's view, use government programs to make it financially easier for women to "choose" not to abort. Without making truly moral (or "judgmental") arguments, we can make the individual's private and independent choice more authentic by taking away the financial burdens of pregnancy. In this way we might, perhaps, reduce the number of abortions. Once again, in other words, government redistribution of wealth will make life more "just" and allow all of us to make our own authentic, utterly private moral choices.

But this first requires that Cuomo, the rhetorical leader, change our political and moral vision. He must convince us that government must be used (and must only be used) to equalize wealth. He also must convince us that all authentic moral choices—even ones that go against our most deeply held religious beliefs—are equally valid and worthy of respect.

Political/Religious Vision

Whenever addressing the young, Cuomo waxes humble. He laments the failings of his own generation and proclaims that it has little to teach while at the same time praising the young for their un-spoiled idealism. This is not surprising because Cuomo effectively re-jects his own Catholic tradition and heritage. He also rejects the tragic view of life at the heart of Catholicism and traditional life every-where.

Cuomo finds the traditional Catholic vision of his childhood sad and morally unsatisfying. As he puts it, "The simple folk of South Ja-maica [New York] . . . perceived the world then as a sort of cosmic ba-sic-training course, filled by God with obstacles and traps to weed out the recruits unfit for eventual service in the heavenly host." For these people, suffering in this world was to be accepted as God's will and lived with in the attempt to be worthy of future grace.[82] Such a vision allowed for charity, for an intimate solidarity in the families, churches, and neighborhood groups still active during Cuomo's youth. But to accept life's tragic quality is, for Cuomo, to commit the sin of accepting material insecurity and inequality—a sin he will not abide.

One who accepts the tragic view recognizes that this life is im-perfect, and that he cannot perfect or even come close to perfecting God's creation. He recognizes that prideful attempts to act the part of God destroy the local communities and bonds of habitual affection that make virtue possible. He seeks not to save the world from all want and injustice but to do his best to help his neighbors—spiritu-ally as well as physically, indeed, spiritually more than physically. He entertains no dream of a world without poverty. Instead he strives with his fellows to form a community in which the poor are treated as full human beings, with dignity and virtue; in which people strive in their families, churches, and local associations to help others on a personal basis and develop their own virtue as they seek to treat oth-ers as they would wish to be treated.

There is a place for politics in the tragic view of life. But govern-mental activity properly is subservient to social activity. The proper focus of life is on the sharing of pain and happiness in the local groups in which intimate contact allows us to treat one another well and to learn one another's real needs. Government, on this view, can destroy virtue by taking away the functions of local associations—by separating us from one another in the name of a public compassion exercised through soulless bureaucratic mechanisms that feed the belly but starve the heart.

Despite his protestations, politics clearly plays a dominant role in Cuomo's life and thought. A lawyer before he entered politics, he often speaks of his early years providing "public service" by applying moral principles to his private life in family and community.[83] But his "application" of principle consisted of suing the state to make it spend more or better utilize its money for social programs. And Cuomo was no reluctant political competitor. He lost bids for both New York City mayor and lieutenant governor. Electoral success came only when then-governor Hugh Carey picked him as a running mate in Carey's successful run for reelection in 1978.

Politics constitutes the center of Cuomo's life and vision. It pervades his writings, even on as "private" and moral an issue as abortion. His public career has been a great crusade to use government to accomplish what society cannot: to eliminate all want and all substantive inequality.

The families, churches, and local associations that once dominated public life shrink in importance beside Cuomo's "progressive pragmatic" goals. His vision of a wealthy, equal community in which each of us pursues his own wants and desires is far afield from the traditional, tragic vision of his upbringing. Yet communitarians, the inheritors and would-be saviors of liberalism, base their arguments on the view that we must resuscitate the institutions of local life; the institutions in which we learn the virtues necessary to sustain the liberal state. Does anything substantive remain of this vision?

Chapter Four

The Politics of Community Life

> We form institutions and they form us every time we engage in
> a conversation that matters, and certainly every time we act as
> parent or child, student or teacher, citizen or official, in each
> case calling on models and metaphors for the rightness and
> wrongness of action. Institutions are not only constraining but
> also enabling. They are the substantial forms through which
> we understand our own identity and the identity of others as
> we seek cooperatively to achieve a decent society.
> —*Robert Bellah et al.*, The Good Society

The introduction to Bellah and his coauthors' latest work, *The Good Society*, is titled "We Live Through Institutions." In this most overtly prescriptive of their joint works, Bellah and his coauthors seek to teach us our need to commit ourselves to public institutions; to participate in the life of our community. But we participate in our communities by participating in the more limited institutions that comprise them.

We do not live primarily in our town or nation but in the families, churches, and other associations of our local lives. We lead our lives as members of various institutions, so to withdraw from our community's public life is to withdraw from life altogether.

Bellah argues that institutions are products of human interaction. They cannot merely be imposed on a people by some outside force, nor can people manipulate and reshape institutions to suit their current desires. In particular Bellah criticizes the classical liberal view that government is merely an instrument to be shaped and

formed to help solve specific and concrete problems such as a dearth
of passable public roads and bridges.

We cannot step outside our institutions and reshape them because we become who we are only by participating in them. We must
cooperate with others in order to survive. In cooperating we develop
the mutually accepted, customary rules and sanctions we need so
that we can act together. Our customs tell us what to expect from one
another and also what to expect from ourselves. We know at a minimum that we must not violate our society's central, fundamental customs or we will and should be punished.

Institutions form our character, according to Bellah, because they
are all around us. "For example, institutions may be such simple customs as the confirming handshake in a social situation, where the refusal to respond to an outstretched hand might cause embarrassment
and some need for an explanation; or they may be highly formal institutions such as taxation upon which social services depend, where
refusal to pay may be punished by fines and imprisonment."[1]

Our behavior is shaped every day by the social expectations we
encounter. One who refuses to shake hands will meet with constant
disapproval, or at least the need to constantly explain his reasons for
refusing. One who refuses to pay his taxes most likely will find himself in jail. Each is faced with the choice of changing his behavior to
meet public expectations or feeling the pain of public or official disapproval.

But Bellah does not want us to see only the punitive side of institutions. They are not only constraining but also enabling. By participating in a conversation that matters, by acting as a mother, father,
citizen, or government official, we adapt to the expectations of our
role. We share our views and experiences with other individuals
while learning to behave as the public expects. In this way we learn
the habits necessary to cooperate productively with those around us.

Civil religion is important for Bellah and other communitarians
precisely because it provides the models and metaphors we need if
we are to learn how we should act. Civil religious beliefs and heroes
provide patterns we can follow as we shape our daily lives. Historical
myths such as Washington's Cincinnatus-like behavior and Lincoln's
"creation" of our nation on the idea of equality become powerful,
prescriptive guides to human conduct. The public punishes or re-

wards us according to how well we live up to the virtuous ideals they provide.

Our civil religious models teach us how to act as individuals and, more importantly, as members of the community. Indeed, the purpose of our models and metaphors is to form us into a community, which will in turn constrain and enable us. In their earlier work, *Habits of the Heart*, Bellah and his coauthors cited Tocqueville in arguing that the American town was and should be a "moral grid" channeling "the energies of its enterprising citizens and their families into collective well-being."[2]

The title *Habits of the Heart* is a literal translation of Tocqueville's term "mores." In this earlier work Bellah claimed he was presenting a Tocquevillean analysis of the habits of belief and action constituting our current, sadly disjointed way of life. I have argued elsewhere that Bellah's analysis is remarkably un-Tocquevillean.[3] But the question here is not whether Bellah appropriates Tocqueville's name and reputation for un-Tocquevillean ends, creating another useful myth, but what kind of analysis Bellah actually provides.

Tocqueville was a natural choice as a vehicle for Bellah's views because the French philosopher emphasized the central role of the local township in American life. According to Tocqueville Americans learned the habits of virtue in their churches, neighborhoods, and local associations. And it was these habits that made well-ordered liberty possible in America because they fostered civility, respect for authority and a mix of independence and solidarity that made free and friendly cooperation possible.[4] Bellah also looks to local associations to teach us how to act. But he uses Tocqueville to present a distinctly communitarian vision of local life. In his view, local associations and the habits they foster must not be centered on local activity and the production of local good deeds. Rather, we must transcend local concerns and attachments so that we may participate in universal political programs. We learn the habits of virtue only if we commit ourselves to broad principles like equality and try to put them into action the world over.

We need local institutions because we live through them. But this makes it all the more important, for communitarians, that we join together *as a nation* to ensure that local institutions are just and that they teach us to be virtuous. Local institutions are a tool by which to achieve social justice and must be remade to suit their purpose.

One might argue that for communitarians we must treat institutions as tools so that we may build communities in which institutions are not treated as mere tools. But Bellah would disagree with this characterization because he would have us use democratic means to decide how to shape and use our institutions. And for Bellah democratic means are inherently humanizing; the democratic process makes even the most utilitarian decisions promote human dignity.

Social Justice and Local Politics

In *The Good Society* Bellah stops claiming that he is carrying on Tocqueville's work. Instead he emphasizes his intellectual debt to American philosopher John Dewey. Dewey provides a better model for Bellah because unlike Tocqueville he felt it was possible to maintain a good and virtuous community with and through large-scale institutions, particularly centralized government.

According to Bellah we now live in what Graham Wallas called "the Great Society," by which Wallas meant the "invisible environment" linking the modern world through new forms of communication and economic exchange. Dewey argued that this invisible environment was affecting men's lives "in ever more coercive ways but was almost beyond human capacity to understand, much less to manage." This meant that "the central problem of modernity" was that "'the machine age in developing the Great Society has invaded and partially disintegrated the small communities of former times without generating a Great Community.'"

Dewey did not, however, reject or seek to destroy the new Great Society. "Dewey had no nostalgia for the old small communities, too enthralled by custom as they were to release the energies of individual and social growth." Rather, Dewey wisely sought to "infuse public spirit and public consciousness into those now largely invisible structures characterized by the Great Society. For Dewey, hope lay in the enlargement and enhancement of democracy throughout our institutional life."[5]

Bellah follows Dewey in arguing that we must accept that our lives now are controlled by distant, centralized structures. He also accepts Dewey's view that this centralization makes it possible for us to construct a better life for everyone by reconstructing local institutions to make them more just. We need only make certain that we control these distant structures through democratic means. Institutions vary from the handshake to the multinational corporation, and it is only through democratic control over all of these institutions that we can restore decency to our public life. We must participate as equals in shaping even our most local and seemingly unimportant institutions.

But Bellah emphasizes our need to control the larger, more distant institutions that constrain our lives. "It is our sense that only greater citizen participation in the large structures of the economy and the state will enable us to surmount the deepening problems of contemporary social life." In part Bellah seeks to bring corporations and the central government under democratic control so that he may protect our more local institutions. For example, Bellah notes that corporate takeovers often harm small communities. When investors buy a small company that employs a large percentage of a town's residents, they gain power over that town. If the investors choose to close down the local plant or office, they will throw large numbers of local residents out of work, and the cost to the town in lost revenue and lost business for other local enterprises may literally kill it. A community may be destroyed so that faceless investors can make a quick profit.[6]

Bellah emphasizes society's larger structures because he recognizes the limits of private action. Concerned about poverty and material inequality, he reports with approval the view of one homeless shelter's leaders: "Our little crumbs are not enough. What the poor and the downtrodden need is not our piecemeal charity but justice." The shelter's leaders seek to make government do more for the homeless and establish greater material equality for all Americans. They lobby government because, in their view God demands social justice, and social justice means an equal sharing of material goods. Only government action can fulfill God's will because only it can produce material equality.[7]

Private charity cannot solve the problem of poverty. It cannot see to it that each of us has his material wants provided for. Thus we must act through government, and through government control of the economy, to establish what we cannot establish on our own. In part, then, politics is a necessary tool to achieve Bellah's goal of material equality.

But politics is not merely an economic tool. It also is a means to establish the kind of personal character and community life Bellah values most. Indeed, a central reason for Bellah's concern to free individuals from local attachments and link them to society's larger structures is his feeling that provincial communities spawn the wrong values. He argues that "a dangerously narrow conception of social justice can result from committing oneself to small town values,"[8] which for Bellah are too narrow and confining. "Too enthralled by custom," small towns stifle personal and communal flourishing.

Small town values stifle us economically. They tie us to old arrangements and to an outdated vision of how we should respond to new economic challenges. The belief that "charity begins at home," for example, leads individuals to care for family and neighbors more than for strangers. Focus on the local community leads individuals to reject the notion that we are a national (or global) family. We fail to learn that, as Cuomo put it, "the problems of a retired schoolteacher in Duluth are *our* problems. That the future of the child in Buffalo is *our* future. The struggle of a disabled man in Boston to survive, to live decently, is *our* struggle. The hunger of a woman in Little Rock *our* hunger. The failure anywhere to provide what reasonably we might, to avoid pain, is *our* failure."[9]

Small town values fail to teach us universal benevolence. They tend to focus attention and affection on those closest to us and so blind us to the essential equality of all human beings. Bellah, meanwhile, seeks to point us to "the urgent necessity—for transforming our national and international institutions so as to bring about a new, more democratic, more peaceful world order under the leadership of the United Nations."[10] We must leave behind even the family of America as we seek to integrate ourselves into a global family overseen by the UN.

We can achieve peace, equality, and prosperity—the essentials of communitarian social justice—only by transcending local attachments. Bellah is calling for the kind of virtue Cuomo praises in environmentalism, by which we sacrifice our own well-being in the hope that future generations will inherit a recognizably better environment. This is the virtue Taylor also praises when he lauds the increasing willingness of citizens of well-off nations to contribute goods and services to distant victims of famine and other natural disasters. Virtue does not mean serving those you know and love, to whom you feel a habitual loyalty and attachment. Virtue means serving strangers, whose suffering is a blot on our honor because it denies the necessity of universal equality.

Bellah wants to further develop our sentiment of universal benevolence. He seeks to render our new commitment to universal
well-being stronger and more concrete. Thus he urges us to create
new institutions and a new ethic that will fit the new Great Society.

Bellah dismisses the "moral language of the town father [that]
was the dominant language of the era Tocqueville described" because
it is obsolete in our era of "urbanization and industrialization." The
"town father" identifies his own interests with those of his community. He generally is a small businessman who has spent most of his
life in his hometown. He participates in local charitable associations
and tries to foster economic growth and social stability in his community. He serves his community not out of a sense of duty but out of an
enlightened self-interest. He identifies his own interest with that of
his community because he knows so many of his neighbors that he
would "feel their pain" if he did not help them.

Unfortunately, Bellah argues, the town father is largely obsolete.
In an era of national and multinational corporations, he cannot protect his community's economic well-being. What is more, his moral
vision lacks coherence in an era when those who suffer do so through
no fault of their own. The town father insists on an ethic of personal
responsibility. He believes that each of us must earn his daily bread, if
he is able, and that we must earn public praise by providing concrete
services to the community.[11]

According to Bellah the Great Society has rendered calls for personal effort and responsibility unjust. Corporate powers control too
much of our economic lives for us to be responsible for our liveli-
hoods. What is more, public service is an ideal we have all but lost.
Our ties to the community have been broken by the constant need to
move for the sake of our career. We now act as members of interest
groups rather than communities, serving our own purposes rather
than the common good. It is difficult even to find a common good because our lives have become splintered and isolated.

The demands of our commercial society—long work hours, com-
muting, frequent moves—along with the impersonal nature of our
public and economic life have split our lives

into a number of separate functional sectors. . . . Particularly
powerful in molding our contemporary sense of things has been
the division between the various "tracks" to achievement laid out

in schools, corporations, government, and the professions, on the one hand, and the balancing life-sectors of home, personal ties, and "leisure," on the other. . . . Domesticity, love, and intimacy increasingly became "havens" against the competitive culture of work.[12]

We now speak and think of our own interests rather than those of the community. Even our families have become disposable consumer goods because family life is no longer part of a larger, communal way of living. We no longer speak of communities but of individuals who join one another only sporadically and to further their own goals.

The public language of the town father cannot defeat the public language of individualism. In fact, the town father paved the way for the individualist. Capitalism grew out of liberal self-interest and has undermined the communities that once reflected and reinforced small town values.

Individualism is *the* cancer infecting our body politic. Bellah finds Tocqueville useful because he called individualism selfish and argued that it undermines communal affection. But Tocqueville cannot point the way out of our current dilemma because he himself was infected with a kind of individualism. Tocqueville praised self-interest so long as it was properly understood. His was the moral language of the town father. He promoted selfishness because it accepted self-interest as a useful tool in fostering local virtue.

We must look beyond Tocqueville to our republican and biblical "second languages" to find how we may replace self-interest with a renewed sense of public duty and commitment.[13] Beleaguered as they are by our dominant individualist language, our republican and biblical languages speak of public duty and so make citizenship possible. Only the struggle for social justice that our second languages demand can produce public virtue.

Bellah defines social justice as economic democracy, which is local community control over the production and distribution of goods, services, and opportunities—all of which are component parts of our true interest: human dignity. Only when local citizens vote on economic issues such as whether a plant should remain open or who should work there is community possible. After all, work itself "should be seen as 'a calling, contributing to the common good and responding to the needs of others as these needs become understood.'"[14]

Our individualist language has sapped local institutions of their ability to give us the proper character—to make us want to establish "an appropriate sharing of economic resources." Good families, churches and local associations still tell us that we should pursue social justice, but our preoccupation with private life has undermined their ability to teach us the habits we need to participate in a just public life.[15]

We now see our families and other local associations as mere objects of leisurely pleasure. Thus we do not take them or their moral lessons seriously. If we are to relearn the virtues necessary for a just public life we must promote and join democratic groups that will guard against private, self-interested activity.[16]

We must become local activists fighting for social justice. We also must become local activists fighting against the centralizing tendencies of our national economy and national government. Both economic and political centralization take decision-making power away from localities, rendering their citizens powerless. Powerlessness saps public virtue by teaching citizens that their actions do not matter, that they might as well not bother trying to affect public institutions because only corporations and the national government can make a difference. Like Taylor Bellah believes we must see ourselves as active, effective participants in political life or we will no longer view the community as the product of our own will. And once we see the community as something other than our own creation we no longer will value or seek the common good.

Like other communitarians Bellah eschews the traditional route of subsidiarity as an answer to centralization. He also rejects Tocqueville's view that local citizens can learn virtue by acting together without calling on the state. Tocqueville insisted that citizens learn to trust and value one another by engaging in public acts, such as removing an object blocking a public road, without calling on any strictly political authority.[17] Bellah insists that it is only through participation in an openly political process that we learn the proper values.

As I noted in Chapter 2, Bellah recommends to us the view that "people's political development—their capacity to organize their common life—is both an end and a means. It fundamentally conditions their ability to participate in other development, including economic development." We learn proper habits through the face-to-face contact of local political activity. Social interactions are not enough. The friendship of merchant and consumer, for example, is meaningless because it is a friendship of utility—each "friend" is looking to his own self-interest.[18] We form proper character only by organizing our lives together, by deciding who shall contribute and receive what from the community as a whole.

Politics is central to Bellah's vision of community. He cites with approval a community activist's condemnation of the "antipolitical system." The antipolitical system is "the network of large corporations that controls most of the wealth of the country, that employs a large percentage of our people, but disparages politics and tries to insulate itself against governmental control." Corporate America thrives on interest group politics. Communities that split themselves into competing factions inevitably lose their sense of purpose and fall under the self-interested rule of the corporations. Proper politics, meanwhile, "begin not from a desire for power, but from 'concerns for security, for justice and for fellowship.'"[19]

We must learn to care for one another but on an organized basis, through public institutions and not through private charity and self-interested attachments. Thus political organizing is "more than a utilitarian means to the end of power. It is also a context in which to nurture a form of moral development on which democratic self-government depends: the practice of citizenship."[20]

Taylor also emphasizes the necessity of politics in the formation of public values and private character. Political parties are a prime example, for Taylor, of "nested public spheres" in which the people come to define their lives together. He goes on to argue that "successful common action can bring a sense of empowerment and also strengthen identification with the political community." We need social movements because our centralized, bureaucratic states make us feel powerless. We must, then, promote a multitude of political "advocacy groups" to involve citizens in a public life of pressuring government to obey their will.[21]

Bellah again uses Tocqueville's name in arguing for a distinctly political vision of local community life:

Tocqueville argues that a variety of active civic organizations are the key to American democracy. Through active involvement in com-

mon concerns, the citizen can overcome the sense of relative isolation and powerlessness that results from the insecurity of life in an
increasingly commercial society. Associations, along with decentralized, local administration, mediate between the individual and the
centralized state, providing forums in which opinion can be publicly
and intelligently shaped and the subtle habits of public initiative and
responsibility learned and passed on. Associational life, in Tocqueville's thinking, is the best bulwark against the condition he
feared most: the mass society of mutually antagonistic individuals,
easy prey to despotism. These intermediate structures check, pressure, and restrain the tendencies of centralized government to assume more and more administrative control.[22]

According to Bellah associations are by nature political. Their
purpose is to provide forums in which the general populace shapes
its own "public opinion." But this opinion must be enlightened. It
must provide the means by which we may subject "the modern economy and the administrative state, to genuine democratic control."[23]

Virtue grows only from local political action that is aimed at producing economic equality. Neither commerce nor centralized political
action teaches true virtue. Neither is centered in local political life,
neither teaches that economic inequality is unjust or demands that
public service is based on a sense of duty to the community. Not even
the family can teach virtue on its own. If not carried out in further-
ance of social justice, familial duties will only produce attachments to
family and neighbor tinged by self-interest. Only social democratic
values, put into action on a local level, can make us love one another
for the right reason: because we all are equal human beings with a
right to public support in our quest for self-fulfillment.

Universal Sentiments and Individual Commitment

His new goal—devotion to marriage and children—seems as arbi-
trary and unexamined as his earlier pursuit of material success.
Both are justified as idiosyncratic preference rather than as representing a larger sense of the purpose of life.[24]

According to Bellah a man's attachment to institutions as intimate and fundamental as the family are senseless if he values these

institutions, and his wife or children, out of an individual, idiosyncratic preference. Even if he values his family for itself he is failing
morally because he does not see its place in a broad vision of life. This
is not to say that local institutions are not important. Clearly they are.
But local affections can be productive only if they are shaped by commitment to the proper vision of what is good and true.

We must reconstruct our localities and even our own moral
actions to bring them in line with the demands of universal benevolence. Bellah does not call for a return to earlier visions of man's place
in the universe. We should not love our children and neighbors
merely to please God or fulfill what our religion tells us is God's plan
for us. Nor should we accept responsibility for our families and communities out of love for our customary institutions and ways of life.
Instead we must serve others on the grounds that all men are equally
valuable and moral creatures. The way we come to recognize this central theological truth of human equality is irrelevant (although it is
self-evident to truly philosophic men). What matters is that we accept
and act on our belief in equality by loving all men equally.

First and foremost we must love mankind. We must love our
community secondarily and only to the extent that it pursues social
justice. Our love of more local institutions, including the families,
churches, and associations that in large part make up the community,
must be conditioned by our broader attachment to universal principles. Principles of universal benevolence and love of equality must always be in the front of our minds and determine for us whether and
in what way we will serve those around us.

Local institutions, in Bellah's view, are not self-justifying. A town
is not good merely because it exists nor are the morals it teaches
proper unless they foster universal benevolence and love of equality.
Local institutions, properly speaking, are the means by which the
people receive their values. Local institutions teach values and moral
habits, so we had best see to it that they inculcate values and habits
that will motivate men to pursue social justice.

We must think globally and act locally. We must put our universal principles into action in our local communities. But to succeed we
must tailor our arguments and even at times our actions so that we
will not offend local customs so much that the citizens reject our program outright.

Like Wills Bellah thinks that leaders must use skillful rhetoric to bring their followers to the proper beliefs and actions. Bellah notes how "the Campaign for Economic Democracy has attempted to combine local organizing on the specific issue of rent control with a larger vision of citizen participation in the control of the economy." A good leader will begin organizing on the basis of an issue close to home, such as rent control. He then will seek to show his followers how their feelings of oppression from high rents point to the illegitimacy of the capitalist system and to the need for economic democracy.

But Bellah saves his greatest praise for the Institute for the Study of Civic Values, a group that "has based its efforts at local organizing and political education on an explicit sense of the biblical and republican traditions of American citizenship. Its program speaks of a notion of justice that is not just procedural but has substantive content. Significantly, it draws leadership and support from churches and labor unions as well as other established community groups."[25]

According to Bellah good leaders compromise with their followers. They understand that they cannot change hearts and minds overnight and so attempt to bring established groups into their larger program bit by bit. Rather than trying to establish economic democracy immediately, the Institute for the Study of Civic Values works locally, reformulating specific issues into the terminology of second languages. It speaks of economic issues in biblical and republican terms and so transforms them into questions of morality. It also makes a point of consulting and including leaders of existing groups in its activities. Showing leaders respect, it increases its chances of winning them over to its point of view.

Bellah does not simply dismiss local attachments or local citizens' claims that men must respect their distinctive culture. Rather, he seeks what he calls "global localism." We must foster ethnic variety and "openness" on a world scale. But we can achieve a proper, just variety only by enforcing democratic principles. "Institutional change comes only as a result of the political process."[26] We must institute a truly democratic political process so that we may use it to eliminate individualism and the capitalism and traditional morality that support it.

In particular, Bellah attacks the traditional small town ideal of self-reliance. The notion that each of us is first and foremost responsible for his own actions presents "a fairly grim view of the individual's place in the social world."[27] It isolates us, forcing us to fall back on our

own economic and psychic resources rather than combining with our
fellows in joint action and communal responsibility.

Self-reliance is bad because it is individualistic. But Bellah does
not wish to replace individualism solely with the pursuit of egalitarian materialism. True to his liberal/communitarian beliefs, he seeks to
promote human flourishing by supporting an ethic of authenticity.
According to Bellah the proper alternative to individualism is "commitment." We develop our character by committing ourselves to great
projects of reform. But we should not be limited to any one specific
moral vision.

In *The Closing of the American Mind*, Allan Bloom criticizes the
moral commitment of today's college students. Students no longer
wish to delve into the roots of our moral habits and ideals. Instead
they engage in shallow moralizing, insisting that the only value
worth defending is acceptance of moral relativism. Bloom also points
out that the students' attitude leads to the self-flattering notion that
"the values I create are just as good as yours." And the conviction
that all values are equal leads only to the construction of superficial,
transitory and individualistic "lifestyles" in which we construct and
constantly change our lives through expensive toys, hobbies, and
fleeting relationship.[28]

Bellah also criticizes Americans' pursuit of happiness through
"lifestyle" changes. He even agrees with much of Bloom's critique of
today's students. But he goes on to chide Bloom for overlooking the
"moral seriousness" of the students Bloom criticizes most—radical
movement organizers from the 1960s. Radicals in the 1960s had
"commitment." They were committed to social, religious, and political experimentation and to an open-ended search for individual and
group fulfillment. Commitment to this form of self-gratification is authentic because it rests on rejection of all authority outside the individual or group will. It produces a variety of moral visions and institutions, many of which contradict one another or themselves. But
commitment itself develops our characters, even when its concrete
results are incoherent.[29]

In *The Good Society* Bellah states that "there is no pattern of a
good society that we or anyone else can simply discern and then expect people to conform to. It is central to our very notion of a good society that it is an open quest, actively involving all its members." Bellah's good man engages in political organizing and debate in order to

bring his ideas to reality. He is doomed to failure because his ideals are too great, because he dreams of a perfection man cannot attain. But this makes all the more heroic his refusal to give up striving for his vision of the good life.

Bellah's good man is not selfish. He attempts to achieve the good life for his entire community. Neither is he a would-be tyrant seeking to impose his will on others by whatever means necessary. He recognizes that tolerance and democratic politics are universal goods. He accepts the equality of all moral visions. Without surrendering his judgment he also accepts the provisional authority of the democratic majority. As Bellah puts it, "The great virtue of the law is that it creates an arena of public debate where current problems can be addressed in light of a body of established principles." Set laws provide a starting point for political conversation and action.[30]

Bellah's good man engages in political conversation, persistently working to have his moral vision adopted, even after losses at the polls. But he also *changes* his moral vision through rational discussion within the political process. He lives, as Taylor would put it, "dialogically." This is a major reason why Bellah's good man is not simply a moral relativist: he believes that the open exchange of ideas produces a better, more fulfilling life for all men. Public discussion, shaped and controlled by democratic procedures and majority rule, allows us to refine our moral vision and learn to respect ourselves and others as equal partners in the creation of moral values.

Thus Bellah's good man makes political democracy the prime arbiter of moral values. Each of us must, to fulfill himself, formulate his own vision of the good life. It is up to the political system to subject these visions to some kind of ordered discussion and vote of the community.

The political system also must provide material and moral equality. Only then can individual and group authenticity flourish. The political community must provide the means necessary for individuals to pursue their own ends. It also must provide each of us with *equal* means so that we will have the same chance, the same feeling that our moral choices are good (and therefore we ourselves are good) and the same material "power" to affect public life. Only when we begin with the notion that all choices of lifestyle are equally valid can we all participate as equals in the political process.

We must see to it that all of our fundamental institutions further the cause of authenticity and personal fulfillment. Only when institutions foster individual flourishing will men commit themselves to them. And only rational, voluntary commitment to institutions can foster community. As Bellah puts it: "We can see among us examples of institutions that are functioning well, that give the individuals within them a purpose and an identity, not through molding them into conformity but through challenging them to become active, innovative, responsible, and thus happy persons because they understand what they are doing and why it is important." We are fundamentally rational creatures. We are fulfilled only when we understand the higher purpose of our actions, and when we feel that we have chosen our own commitments and actions. And we develop loyalty to our institutions only when they fulfill us.[31]

Writing in the 1970s, Bellah expressed hope that the counterculture would produce authentic innovation and transform our public life.

> In the great welter of urban and rural communes, political and religious collectives, sects, cults, and churches that have sprung up in recent years, there are many interesting developments. A new balance of manual and mental labor, work and celebration, male and female traits have been experimented with. Harmony with nature and one's own body, a more "feminine" and less dominating attitude toward one's self and others, an ability to accept feelings and emotions—including feelings of weakness and despair—a willingness to accept personal variety, have all been valued and tried in practice.[32]

Experimentation and a cultivation of varied moral practices should be our goals. The 1960s counterculture provided both these things. Its new-age religions, its communes, its open rejection of traditional sex roles and theological understandings made room for authentic self and group fulfillment. Bellah does not discuss the problems of that era but asks us to look back to it for guidance.

Of course such a moral vision rules out some choices of morality, no matter how voluntarily chosen. Bellah rejects small town values precisely because they stand in the way of moral innovation. Small towns hold on too stubbornly to traditional notions of morality and prevent us from achieving moral as well as physical equality. As important, they stifle authenticity.

Bellah accepts neither traditional values nor moral relativism. Instead he demands that we recognize innovations such as homosexual marriage and the elimination of sex-roles so that truly egalitarian principles may rule local life. We must not merely allow deviations from traditional practice on the grounds that marriage and sex-roles are private matters about which no morally objective truth can be established. That would show a lack of commitment to equality and moral innovation. We must make clear that we as a community morally approve of homosexual marriage and the elimination of sex-roles. These innovations are particularly important because they recognize and reinforce the inherent equality of all human beings and of all authentic moral choices.[33]

Not all existing institutions should be rejected. For example, Bellah does not want to wholly dispense with the traditional family. Indeed, he finds it useful in many ways. But this does not mean that we should accept the nuclear family of husband, wife, and children as the sole legitimate forum for sex and child-rearing, let alone as the proper basis of social life. Rather, we should look to the family as a necessary tool in training good citizens; a tool we must redesign to fit our current needs.

Bellah observes, "We do not argue that the modern nuclear family, which combines the emotional intimacy and sexuality of the parents with the nurture of children, is the only possible or morally respectable form of the family; but because of its importance in bringing children into the world and raising them, it has a kind of centrality and value that we cannot afford to ignore."[34]

According to Bellah we must reconsider the way our capitalist economy and centralized state treat families. Corporations undermine the family because they do not provide enough leave time for parents. The state helps corporations exploit families by not passing laws to establish higher paying part-time work, flex time, job sharing, and other programs that would give parents the chance to spend more time with their children.

But we must not tie ourselves to the traditional family as if it were inherently good. We must engage in a "national discussion of what we expect from the family and how we might better achieve those expectations." Bellah rejects any return to the traditional family because he believes it was part of a social and political system that denied the equality of women and therefore oppressed them. We must seek to "understand what the family as a vital institution today would really be like." We must decide as a national community what we want our fundamental institutions to look like—who should marry whom, how, and for how long. We then should support our moral conclusions with democratically adopted laws designed to reward those who follow our vision and penalize those who do not.

The Authentic Community

Perhaps the greatest problem facing communitarians is that of reconciling authenticity with community. Seeking to convince us to serve liberal democracy, communitarians must show both how this service will help the community and how it will further our own, self-chosen goals. Commitment, then, must serve both as a means to preserve the community and as a means to fulfill ourselves. Ironically, it apparently can achieve both only if we choose to be committed to communitarian ends.

One might argue that the commitment Bellah lauds actually is individualistic. Bloom notes that Americans admire anyone deeply committed to almost any values. We lionize individuals who reject both tradition and personal profit in favor of commitment to "ideals of their own making."[35] Our heroes are authentic value positors, individuals who create their own moral systems and attempt to impress them on the world. Only when these value positors become "intolerant"—only when they deny that all moral beliefs are of equal worth—do we condemn them.

But not just any values will do, for Bellah. We must not posit values that deny human equality. We must pursue economic democracy and democratic rule over institutions as intimate as the family. Only in this way can we be called virtuous.

One might almost argue that Bellah's commitment avoids individualism by "committedly" suppressing individuality. The choices we *must* make render the choices left to our authentic individual wills meaningless. In economics, politics, and even in the realm of social institutions like the family, we can exercise our wills only as part of the collective, general will of the democratic community. Bellah may be seen as a true follower of the eighteenth-century Swiss theorist of communal authenticity Jean Jacques Rousseau. As with Rousseau's general will, Bellah believes we must suppress that part of ourselves which would separate us from the consensus of our fellow citizens.[36]

According to Bellah we create our morality through participation in democratic political life. For example, Bellah views religion as an extension of the political process, and he analyzes the role of religion in American life by looking at conflicts among religious lobbying groups in Washington, D.C.[37] We affect public morals by affecting the political process, which in turn forms and announces the general will.

Rousseau railed against religions (Christianity in particular) that failed to bind "the hearts of citizens to the State," instead "taking them away from all earthly things." He argued that religion's proper goal was to teach citizens "that service done to the State is service done to its tutelary god."[38] Rather than establishing and acting on a personal relationship with God, the citizen, for Bellah and Rousseau, must abandon himself to the religion of the state.

Bellah's virtue is the willingness to subsume our own interests and personalities into the democratic whole; we must pursue the common good. And Bellah, citing another author with approval, argues that "the common good is the pursuit of the good in common." There is no single discernible pattern of a good society. There is, however, the good of communal pursuit of our communal desires and communal control over our lives.[39]

Community requires communal control over social and economic as well as political life. We must decide as a community—that is, vote on who gets paid how much to do what, who shall live where, and what our public associations shall look like. But it is not fair to say that Bellah would leave us with no meaningful choices. After all, the family has always been recognized as the basis of society, so new choices of familial relations—homosexual and group marriage, nonmarital relations in which children are raised, and so on—have meaning.

The effect familial innovation would have on society remains unclear, although our current social breakdown makes it appear inadvisable to say the least. The blurring of the distinction between right and wrong, the rejection of traditional standards of decency, has been accompanied by rampant uncivil conduct. From abandoning one's children to gang-

raping for "fun," conduct once considered scandalous now goes largely
unnoticed because the standards by which to judge such conduct have
lost their authority. One even could argue that this lack of moral judgment renders Bellah's innovations almost meaningless—we cannot apply
any standards of right and wrong to them, cannot even exercise substantive moral judgment when discussing them. Bellah demands that we accept all lifestyles as morally equal. In the end his demand for equal recognition renders moral judgment meaningless if not impossible. If one
choice is as good as another, what reason is there, other than inexplicable
personal bias, for choosing monogamy over polygamy, heterosexuality
over homosexuality, and so on?

But then Bellah's good life does not entail any one particular
choice of lifestyle. It is not a specific innovation but the communal
process of innovation, carried out through democratic politics and in
combination with the pursuit of social justice, that Bellah seeks.

> Communities, in the sense in which we are using the term, have
> a history—in an important sense they are constituted by their
> past. . . . In order not to forget that past, a community is in-
> volved in retelling its story, . . . and in so doing, it offers exam-
> ples of the men and women who have embodied and exempli-
> fied the meaning of the community. . . . The stories that make
> up a tradition contain conceptions of character, of what a good
> person is like, and of the virtues that define such character. But
> the stories are not all exemplary, not all about successes and
> achievements. A genuine community of memory will also tell
> painful stories of shared suffering that sometimes creates deeper
> identities than success, . . . And if the community is completely
> honest, it will remember stories not only of suffering received
> but of suffering inflicted—dangerous memories, for they call the
> community to alter ancient evils. The communities of memory
> that tie us to the past also turn us toward the future as communi-
> ties of hope. They carry a context of meaning that can allow us to
> connect our aspirations for ourselves and those closest to us with
> the aspirations of a larger whole and see our own efforts as be-
> ing, in part, contributions to a common good.[40]

Communities must look backward to historical models of good
behavior and forward to the ever-unattainable fulfillment of the good

lives they envision. Bellah's work is replete with interviews of exemplary individuals. And he clearly intends his examples to show us how we should reform our lives and our society.

Habits of the Heart focuses on a Vietnam war deserter, an environmental activist, and several social democratic political activists. Bellah claims his choices allow him to "describe the most influential forms of middle-class language and moral reasoning about private and public life in America today."[41] One might argue that organizations like the Campaign for Economic Democracy have not been terribly influential on our public life. But for Bellah this is not the point. He seeks to provide examples of how we *ought* to act. Good examples need not be commonplace examples. We must constantly redefine what is properly representative so that we may continue to pursue social justice in changing circumstances.

A community must constantly retell the story of its origins and progress so that it can make its myths and mythical heroes fit its current needs. It must remember the evils it has suffered and perpetrated so that it can maintain its millenarian zeal to pursue social justice. After all, only committed pursuit of social justice makes true community possible.

Bellah assures us that the community he advocates, even with its sense of shared memory or tradition, will not stifle innovation. Traditions, properly understood, do not encourage us to retain the past. Instead a good tradition helps us reshape the past, or at least our memory of it, so that we may use it to further our innovations. According to Bellah a "living tradition is never a program for automatic moral judgments. It is always in a continuous process of reinterpretation and reappropriation. Such a process assumes, however, that tradition has enough authority for the search for its present meaning to be publicly pursued as a common project."[42]

Intellectuals like Bellah have a twofold role in any good community. They must create myths that maintain the people's love and awe of their community. Only in this way can we retain the solidarity necessary for communal self re-creation. But intellectuals also must prevent "self-idolatry" in the community.[43] They must debunk pleasant myths and appropriate or create more critical ones so that the community will remember its need to reform.

Bellah wants us to engage in the common project of finding (or appropriating) a "present meaning" for our traditions. He wants us to use democratic means to reinterpret our past. In practice, intellectuals would reinterpret our past for us. They then would vie with one another in public forums ranging from television to newspapers to scholarly books and the university lecture hall. Etzioni is fond of calling for public "multilogues." In such multilogues citizens would participate in public debate through private conversation, religious sermonizing, radio call-in shows, and television call-in shows like *Larry King Live.* According to Etzioni, multilogues are the proper source of democratic consensus.[44] Although relatively few citizens actually participate in call-in shows and the like, these shows provide a forum in which competing intellectuals can seek to win over the public to their vision of how we can most profitably view our past.

But for most of us reinterpretation is not a strictly intellectual process. According to Bellah we redefine our community's meaning by participating in great projects of communal reform. It is in this light that we can see most clearly the character of Bellah's attachment to local association.

Bellah often agrees with Tocqueville's view that we must encourage individual participation in public life by fostering a variety of vital local associations. It is at this point that he begins discussing the heroic "movement organizer." The movement organizer forged associations to fight "the emerging industrial capitalist order." He "sought to use government at all levels to bring a degree of public responsibility to the new technologies and the wealth they generated."[45]

The movement organizer sought to organize citizens into a group committed to subjecting industrial capitalism to the general will. Good associations seek to chain both private and public power to the will of the majority. Only this subjection makes true democratic politics and any good life possible. Families, religious bodies, and voluntary associations are tools to be used, and when necessary reshaped, to serve the cause of social justice. Egalitarian political action is the essence of citizenship.

It would be inaccurate to say that communitarians seek only service to the general will. Liberals at heart, they continue to see individual flourishing as the proper end of life. They want individuals to form varied political movements seeking to change our nation in very different ways. One might even argue that the communitarian commitment to authenticity in the end undermines community itself. Commitment to democratic reform cannot yield any overarching set of standards that can bind us to one another and to our communities. Politics, then, becomes merely a set of democratic procedural rules that themselves have only limited legitimacy because all existing structures are suspect and subject to change at the whim of the majority. Communitarians provide no set of common goods on which to build social cohesion and stability. Rejecting any full vision of the good life, communitarians cannot provide a coherent prescription for how we can lead a good life in common.

Communitarians attempt to balance the demands of authenticity with the requirements of community. Authenticity remains their goal, but they believe we can only make authentic choices when the political community has seen to our material needs. And communitarians genuinely want to foster solidarity as well as individuality. They believe a solitary individual is a lonely and unfulfilled individual. They believe we can fulfill ourselves only by joining with our fellow citizens to create and accept myths that will teach us to awe our nation and motivate us to pursue social justice.

Communitarians recognize that it is in families and local associations that we develop the habits that allow us to deal with others in a decent manner. They seek to foster local associations so that those groups will continue to teach the habits of cooperation. But they also seek to control local institutions so that those institutions will teach values (primarily toleration, equality, and authenticity) of which communitarians approve.

Communitarians do not trust local citizens to choose social justice and authenticity on their own. They want the national government to guarantee both these values. They leave for local citizens the appearance of community control, but it is a derivative control, one that can be overruled at any time by the true wielder of power and authority: the central government.

This is not to say that communitarians would establish a tyranny in any traditional sense. They would not, for example, consent to heavy censorship of the public airwaves. On the contrary, they seek wide latitude for those questioning traditional standards of morality (what used to be called standards of decency). Community standards must bow down before moral experimentation and free expression.

For example, Etzioni wants the government to force television manufacturers to install mechanisms by which consumers could block reception of certain stations. In this way parents would be able to keep their children from viewing programs of a particularly violent or sexual nature, at least at home. Etzioni sees this as a noncoercive, democratic means to protect families' control over their children's moral education.

But control over the public airwaves would remain with broadcasters in far-off Hollywood or New York City. The community creates and re-creates moral truth through common action. But, according to Etzioni, the *local* community should not uphold its own moral standards. He apparently does not believe that local citizens are the proper judges of what is good for the moral health of their own communities; that the moral character of public entertainment is a public concern properly decided on by local citizens rather than the "Hollywood community."

Communities should not join together to define and apply moral standards to public entertainment. Etzioni is convinced that individual speech and even satiric posters cause real harm to individuals and communities. Indeed, he advocates mass reeducation programs to prevent what he deems harmfully insensitive expressions of opinion on issues such as racism and sexual harassment.[46] But he would keep television, a powerful and pervasive source of persuasive images, free from community control.

Parents could protect their children and themselves from programming they find offensive only by opting out of the public airwaves *as individuals*. They would have to, in effect, turn the television off. This is no difficult task. But it is a quintessentially liberal task. It puts the onus on individuals to flee from an unregulated marketplace of moral visions contained in public entertainment. Indeed, federal laws requiring public access to cable channels have made programs featuring explicit sexual acts and demonstrations of various sexual devices available to children. And even parents who block out channels whose programs they find offensive would have no way to keep their children from viewing offensive programs in neighbors' homes.

Regardless of one's view of the propriety of sexual or violent programming, allowing it on the public airwaves constitutes a moral choice. It says to the public that our nation finds such programming acceptable. It says that those who disagree are squeamish or "puritanical" and may reject such programming only by withdrawing, as individuals, from the public sphere.

Whatever one's view of censorship, Etzioni's proposal clearly would not foster public discussion of moral standards. And it is precisely this moral discussion that communitarians deem necessary if a local community is to have its own vital moral character. If local citizens, acting as members of their communities, cannot keep openly pornographic programs, which intentionally offend traditional moral norms, off their local airwaves, they cannot possibly maintain the moral character of their own communities. Local attempts to establish moral consensus will be impossible. We would be left with only a *national* standard approving all moral visions as equal and positively affirming open violence, nudity, and explicit sexual acts as appropriate fare for public entertainment.

Many argue that any return to communally defined moral standards would politicize art and entertainment. But community standards are arrived at through appeals to tradition and religion as well as more political principles like free expression. Such a process is primarily "political" only if we see political principles as of primary importance; only if we see free expression as more important than tradition, religion, and the community's control of its public standards of morality.

Of course communitarians see families and other local institutions as themselves primarily political. According to communitarians such institutions are proper subjects of experimentation and reform through the political process. Further, Etzioni advocates forcing anyone who expresses the wrong opinions on matters of race and sex to enter reeducation classes. One might, then, wonder why standards of decency are forbidden as "too political" when the family itself is properly subject to political reform. The reason seems to lie in the communitarian distinction between moral visions and concrete, often psychological, needs.

Returning here to Taylor, he argues that we no longer have a coherent set of shared beliefs. Authenticity is our proper goal in part because we no longer share a common conception of the nature of the universe and man's place in it. Overall Taylor is pleased with the destruction of traditional moral horizons because "in principle, people are no longer sacrificed to the demands of supposedly sacred orders that transcend us." Dispensing with the notion that existing institutions reflect God's will we now have more "freedom to be ourselves"—to order our own lives according to our own consciences, however formed.[47]

But we continue to share needs. We need material security, the self-esteem that comes from constant affirmations of our essential equality, and participation in the political process. And we can meet our needs by using democratic politics to eliminate poverty and economic inequality.

According to Taylor there is a kind of moral order, one that demands economic democracy. But outside the economic sphere there are very few rules that apply always and everywhere, save that each of us should follow his own conscience. And such external rules as do exist—for example, Etzioni's favored rules against stealing, drug use, and polluting and in favor of political participation—are largely instrumental. These rules are designed to maintain the social structure, the risk-free freedom, necessary to promote authenticity. There are no set standards by which to judge our choice of, for example, living arrangements, sexual conduct, and forms of artistic expression. Where these choices are concerned, experimentation should rule. Only through democratic politics do we act as a community.

Voting and political organizing, the quintessential political acts, seem rather abstract forms of common action, relying more on rhetoric than on the affections that grow from habitual interaction. But communitarians are left with little else. They have rejected vital local communities for fear such groups will promote "puritanical" values. They are left with local institutions that serve only as means of what Taylor calls "citizen mobilization" to enforce national standards of political and economic justice.[48]

What, then, of the *spirit* of community? Are we bound to our fellow citizens only by our mutual subjection to the general will? If we all must serve the causes of universal benevolence and egalitarian materialism, what is left of local liberty? What of individual authenticity? What of local affections? And what will be the effect on our spirit as a people?

Religious Authenticity

Communitarians continue to worry about our lack of a common moral vision. Taylor recognizes that the loss of belief in transcendent standards has produced individualism. No longer bowing before God, we also no longer bow to any standards of right and wrong—including those created by the community. And this has led to "an abnormal and regrettable self-absorption."[49]

Unfortunately, communitarian attempts to reconcile authenticity with our need for a common moral vision result in the very religious individualism they loathe. Commitment to our own authentic, self-generated religious beliefs breeds a self-worship that eviscerates common standards of conduct and makes it even more difficult for us to join with our fellows in constructing a moral life in common. And the communitarian response to this dilemma—the further politicization of religion—hardly seems capable of providing the common standards on which any cohesive society relies.

Bellah shares Taylor's concern over the loss of communal standards. He laments in particular the fizzling of the communes of the 1960s. No longer joined in communal experimentation, Americans now reject all external codes of conduct. Each of us has come to see himself as the sole source of morality. The result is a plethora of individualist religions, or what Bellah calls "Sheilaism."

In *Habits of the Heart*, Bellah summarizes a series of interviews with a woman named Sheila Larson, who exemplifies the individualism into which Americans have descended. She has divorced herself from others and from any collective standard of faith or conduct. She "named her religion . . . after herself" and she literally made herself her own god.

According to Bellah, Sheilaism is "significantly representative" of American mores. Because Sheilaism is consistent with our prevalent individualism it "suggests the logical possibility of over 220 million American religions, one for each of us." Despite his love of religious experimentation, Bellah finds this particular example of religious diversity to be, in the end, selfish.

Sheila calls her religious beliefs a "faith," indeed one which has "carried me a long way." But her faith entails no particular church religion and has very few tenets: "Just my own little voice." And Sheila's own little voice bears a constant message: "It's just try to love yourself and be gentle with yourself." Only after this self-love is made clear as the basis of her religion does Sheila add, as a derivative afterthought, "You know, I guess, take care of each other."[50]

Sheila refuses to formulate any rules or tenets for her faith other than the call to "take care of each other." She is uncomfortable expressing even this commandment, although she adds the observation, "I think He would want us to take care of each other." "He" appears to be a reference to some sort of god. But He is no traditional God, handing down commandments from on high; He is much closer to Sheila's home. Indeed, Sheila and "He" may be different aspects of the same being—at least for Sheila.

According to Bellah,

> "Sheilaism" is rooted in the effort to transform external authority into internal meaning. The two experiences that define her faith take [such a] form. One occurred just before she was about to undergo major surgery. God spoke to her to reassure her that all would be well, but the voice was her own. The other experience occurred when, as a nurse, she was caring for a dying woman whose husband was not able to handle the situation. Taking over care in the final hours, Sheila had the experience that "if she looked in the mirror" she "would see Jesus Christ."[51]

Sheila acted virtuously. Her unselfish care for a dying woman might even be characterized as Christlike. But Sheila, in her own eyes, did not merely emulate Christ, she became him.

Sheila cannot comprehend any authoritative, church expression of the duties and meaning of life. Thus she interprets her experience in the most personal way imaginable. She becomes the source of the goodness she exhibits.

External codes of conduct—a transcendent God—entail man's surrender of ultimate judgment and his admission that he owes duties to his fellow man. Far better, for the individualist, to create God out of oneself and command oneself to do one's own bidding. One may even care for others if one so chooses, although one had best not ask *why* one cares for others. This might force one to consider why one sees Christ—a commonly recognized religious figure—rather than one's self in the mirror.

Ironically, Sheila closely resembles the ideal communitarian character type. She has vast self-esteem. After all, her faith is based on a self-generated commandment to love herself. Sheila also is truly authentic. She bows to no standard save her own conscience. And her conscience, the voice of God within her, is hers alone. She is the true value positor, the true creator of morality, because she is a self-created, self-worshipping god. Rhetoric has changed her life. She has convinced herself, by naming her religion after herself, that she needs no outside authority to tell her how to lead a good life.

But Sheilaism has a fatal flaw for Bellah: it is individualistic. Sheila's faith is solitary. She looks to no communal standard, feels no solidarity with her political community, and does not create morality in dialogue with her fellow citizens. She is woefully self-sufficient.

Sheilaism, with its 220 million potential varieties, closely resembles another, more general phenomenon of American religious experience discussed in *Habits of the Heart:* pantheism. Bellah criticizes certain religious environmentalists who identify the earth with God and living "in harmony with nature" with a godly life. He argues that values based on a rejection of man's special status "lack a notion of nature from which any clear social norms could be derived. Rather, the tendency in American nature pantheism is to construct the world somehow out of the self."[52]

Pantheists see self-realization as the highest good. They deem holy anything that helps them transcend their particular circumstances and achieve union with a mystical higher self. Using techniques borrowed from Eastern religions like Buddhism, adherents of nature religions often seek personal communion with nature. But the nature worshipper does all this in order to "define my own self." He seeks to act as a god, creating his own being and creating a world out of his own self-generated perceptions and meanings. He acts on his own impulses, communing with only a vague, mystical universe that does not constrain him. He avoids communal religious and political practices.[53]

Nature religions make the earth a god but do not construct any communal code of conduct to go along with this god. Adherents of nature religions share with Sheila and Americans in general a tendency to deify themselves and call holy that which they happen to fancy. Their faith is rooted in self-gratification rather than communal dialogue.

Bellah finds environmentalism morally compelling. Virtuous men can worship the "Earth Mother." Indeed, commitment to the environment, and to a form of pantheism, is a necessary outgrowth of Bellah's commitment to equality. His concern is that we serve the earth through common political action and develop through this action a common vision of proper conduct.

If looked on properly, environmentalism can produce lessons of which Bellah approves. "A rare species of squirrel examining an acorn on the intended site of a power plant, as shown in a television sequence, can remind millions that wonder is a gift not monopolized by humans. In such public reactions we see the capacity to identify our destiny with fellow creatures in the great web of nature."[54]

Television producers can use rhetoric to convince us that wonder is universal. Equality transcends even the limits of humanity because all creatures are parts of a divine nature. All of us are valuable, and at least partially divine, because we are parts of the god that is the universe.

Tocqueville also discussed pantheism. But for him it was an outgrowth of the drive for equality and the individualism this drive breeds.

> As conditions become more equal, each individual becomes more like his fellows, weaker, and smaller, and the habit grows of ceasing to think about the citizens and considering only the people. Individuals are forgotten, and the species alone counts.
>
> At such times the human mind seeks to embrace a multitude of different objects at once, and it constantly strives to link up a variety of consequences with a single cause.
>
> The concept of unity becomes an obsession. Man looks for it everywhere, and when he thinks he has found it, he gladly reposes in that belief. Not content with the discovery that there is nothing in the world but one creation and one Creator, he is still embarrassed by this primary division of things and seeks to expand and simplify his conception by including God and the universe in one great whole. If one finds a philosophical system which teaches that all things material and immaterial, visible and invisible, which the world contains are only to be considered as the several parts of an immense Being who alone remains eternal in the midst of the continual flux and transformation of all that composes Him, one may be sure that such a system, although it destroys human individuality, or rather just because it destroys it, will have secret charms for men living under democracies. All their habits of mind prepare them to conceive it and put them on the way toward adopting it. It naturally attracts their imagination and holds it fixed. It fosters the pride and soothes the laziness of their minds.[55]

According to Tocqueville, the conformity and enormity of democratic society awe the individual. Torn from the vital local attachments
that once gave him responsibility and a feeling of personal connection with his fellows, democratic man sees only his tiny, insignificant
self and the vast mass of the political community. Mankind has become one organism, of which he is an insignificant part indistin-
guishable from any other. His response is to deem the universe and
everything in it holy and godlike. Because he now is part of a "national community" or even a "community of mankind," he no longer
feels intimate ties to his family and neighbors.

Tocqueville argues that democratic man is too lazy to set about
finding a natural ordering to the universe, in which various men and
creatures play distinctive roles. He loathes distinctions because they
smack of inequality and he fears personal responsibility because it
brings with it the possibility of failure. By calling everything outside
himself God he creates a world in which all is self-evident and all is
well; in which we all are equal parts of an inexplicable but self-justifying organism.

But Tocqueville's democratic man also is full of pride. He thinks
he is independent from his fellows because he does not share his life
with them. He thinks he is the equal of other men because he refuses
to acknowledge their differences. By declaring the universe itself a
god he also declares himself to be at least a part of God; a holy creature who serves the universal purpose by doing whatever he happens
to choose because the universe is all knowing and all powerful and
would not allow him to do wrong.

Democratic man comes to think that his powers are puny as an
individual but godlike as a group. He comes to believe that he can
eliminate mistakes, tragedy, and bad luck. He comes to believe that
vast social movements can perfect both himself and the world.[56] According to Tocqueville democratic man is tragically mistaken. He cannot perfect anything because perfection is not to be had in this life.
What is more, his projects of reform undermine the habitual attachments that make community and any decent life possible.

Bellah, of course, seeks to promote the social movements Toc-
queville feared. He seeks to foster the very drive for material equality
Tocqueville saw undermining the well-ordered liberty he admired in
America. But where Tocqueville saw in pantheism an excessive sur-

rendering of human individuality, Bellah sees in it a selfish moralism that rejects communal dialogue.

According to Bellah we must participate in mass political movements that will create new moralities for us as they re-create our existing institutions. Pantheism, unfortunately, allows us to reject any common standard in favor of our own unguided will. We come to see our individual will, which we often confuse with our reason, as the sole judge of what is holy and what is useful. We lose our ability to come together and decide as a group how we ought to relate to one another and to our world.

At this point Bellah asks, "How did we get from the point where Anne Hutchinson, a seventeenth-century precursor of Sheila Larson's, could be run out of the Massachusetts Bay Colony to a situation where Anne Hutchinson is close to the norm?"[57] The answer for Bellah is, of course, individualism. Americans have come to accept only their own individual reason as the arbiter of moral truth because they have come to be concerned only with themselves as beings, moral or otherwise. As in all else, the "anti-political system" has destroyed religious community by taking away its proper role as a political force (or "social movement").

Religion has become only a form of therapy. We create moral rules to satisfy our own largely psychological needs. We do not create a common code of conduct to regulate our lives together. Instead we shape our moral rules to fit and to justify the way of life we as individuals happen to find pleasant.

Bellah's lament over the fate of religion must not be taken too literally, however, for he is no enemy of the therapeutic imperative—rightly understood. Bellah is quite willing to rely on the psychiatric authority of Sigmund Freud in discussing the need to remember so that "unhealthy" suppressed memories will not continue to haunt us.[58] What is more, his exemplary model of a "basic Christian community" consists of an adult education group wherein "you begin to go around the group, naming one's oppression," be it alcoholism, cultural alienation, divorce, or unequal treatment by one's family.

A Christian community achieves its goal, for Bellah, as one "puts oneself in a broader context and comes to see how one is caught in a web that binds us all." Having come to this realization, group members further realize that they must work to eliminate "institutional" as well as personal sin through group consciousness-raising and political action.[59] Therapy is actually good to the extent that it is shared and produces egalitarian political action.

Bellah judges religions good or bad according to their political affects. He places "conservative or fundamentalist religion" and Sheilaism at opposite ends of an antipolitical spectrum. According to Bellah both those religions that concentrate on the need to live a good life in one's private endeavors (and within a particular religious community) and the religious individualism or self-deification represented by Sheilaism share a destructive opposition to political life. "One seeks a self that is finally identical with the world; the other seeks an external God who will provide order in the world. Both value personal religious experience as the basis of their belief." Both "conservative" religion and Sheilaism are individualistic. They alienate us from one another because they concentrate on promoting individual virtue and, because they are based on faith, are "unreflective."[60]

Bellah's good remains the very liberal one of making men like gods. He wants us to create the meaning and morality that will order our lives. But the creation of morals requires common action. It also requires democratic socialism. Religious action becomes another form of social action, which itself is the political pursuit of equality.

Only within a uniformly egalitarian community can we flourish as individuals. Only when we can "experiment" with morality without fear of material inequality or discomfort can we fully form our own characters. But it is only by committing ourselves to equality and economic democracy that we can develop the institutions and the character necessary to lead full, godlike lives.

The question, then, is how we are to produce the commitment necessary to reform our society. Communitarians cannot merely serve as intellectual critics of current practice. To be true to themselves they must form a new social movement to win over the people to their vision of social justice and authenticity.

Chapter Five

Liberalism as Social Movement: Communitarianism in Practice

According to communitarians good character comes from, as it fosters, good politics. But communitarians maintain the traditional liberal distrust of governmental institutions. Indeed, they see character formation as something that takes place in *opposition* to established, corrupt, political institutions.

Etzioni styles communitarianism a "social movement." He argues that "when social scientists examine the ways in which we may significantly alter a society as complex and as free as ours, they often conclude that the government is too heavy-handed, costly, and inappropriate an agency to confront most moral and many social issues." Social scientists know best, according to Etzioni, and they agree that only social movements such as those committed to environmentalism, feminism, and civil rights have "profoundly shaped and reshaped our values and social lives." Thus, *"what America needs now* is a major social movement dedicated to enhancing social responsibilities, public and private morality, and the public interest. We need you, your friends, your neighbors, and others we can reach to join with one another to forge a Communitarian movement."[1]

Etzioni unabashedly promotes his movement. He implores his readers: "Please do not just read this book. Please try to respond. We in the Communitarian movement are keen to hear from you, and we hope you will tell others about the Communitarian framework . . . lead the way by organizing Communitarian groups." Etzioni's book facilitates such "leadership" by providing addresses and telephone numbers so that supporters can contact communitarian headquarters. To bolster morale and convince possible followers that they are joining a group with clout, he includes on the book's red, white, and

150

blue dust jacket a picture of himself with Vice President Al Gore at a communitarian function. To reassure potential followers that leaders like himself will allow them to participate in a meaningful way, he informs them that he is "quite sure that success has not gone to our heads."[1]

Etzioni presents himself as a savvy version of Bellah's heroic movement organizer, in fact as the leader of a cadre of savvy organizers. He argues that "social movements are much more effective than mere waves of public opinion because they have a steady core of leaders. . . . They draw on strong shared values and molding symbols. They command cadres that mobilize the rank and file to whatever social action is called for." Social movements are effective because intellectuals like Etzioni use civil religion to form their followers into a cohesive group; a group that will fight for social justice by boycotting, demonstrating, and otherwise pressuring government to obey their will.[2]

Communitarians recognize that their social movement and its organizers break down the traditional liberal separation of politics from the private sphere. But they do not believe that this separation is appropriate. Taylor argues that "in a modern democratic polity, the boundary between political system and public sphere has to be maximally porous."[3] Liberalism now demands that politics be freed from the constraints put on it by liberalism's former, now outdated view that we can lead good lives in our own isolated, private worlds.

The community's highest goal is to create and re-create its moral identity through democratic means. The individual's highest goal is to participate in this process. Given such goals, preexisting structures are dangerous at best. Governmental structures are particularly dangerous and morally suspect because they are public institutions that individuals now living did not create and to which they therefore cannot fully consent. The very fact that political institutions were created in the past means that they interfere with the people's moral autonomy and authenticity. The only way to make such structures good is constantly to reform them—to make them ever more responsive to the will of the democratic majority.

According to communitarians we must encourage political discussion and action so that citizens will see their nation as the product of their own will. The action must be local because only in this way will citizens recognize the effects of their own efforts and feel empowered. But the cause all must serve is universal: democracy. All political activity, if it is to be legitimate, must aim at tying the government more closely to the will of the people.

Democracy fulfills us, and we need not fear that the democratic majority will come to oppress us because all our voices will be heard. Each of us will participate in an advocacy group that will influence public policy and ensure that liberal tolerance retains sway. What is more, because everything is subject to constant democratic revision, our choices always have the potential of becoming the people's choices. We have no right to complain, then, if the majority happens to distribute income or honors disadvantageously to us or take other actions we do not like. The point is to maximize democratic power and participation.

One of the movements to which Etzioni points for inspiration is early twentieth-century Progressivism. Progressives sought to remove local and private interests from government activity; they wanted "clean" government. They also sought to increase public participation in political life. The progressive reform Etzioni singles out for highest praise is establishment of the direct election of senators. A Senate appointed by various state legislatures is too undemocratic. Senators were tied closely to their localities under the old system. But this, for Etzioni, was bad. Local allegiances made Senators all the worse, in his view, because it made them serve local interests rather than building a more equal and democratic nation. That states and the localities, represented by state legislators, might achieve and maintain greater local coherence and autonomy by choosing their common representative in Washington apparently either does not occur or is not important to Etzioni.[4]

The political goals of equality and democratic control are paramount. Communitarians will mobilize local citizens and cadres to fight for the universal political standards they value. The difficulty lies in winning over local citizens to the view that they must serve the national community by making it more equal and democratic. If citizens are committed to their own varied political ends (or "things that matter") and individual lifestyles, it will be no easy task to conceptualize, let alone gain adherence to, a common vision of the common good. Communitarian civil religion intends to solve this problem by teaching individuals that it is holy to struggle for "the American way" defined as democratic politics.

Because democratic politics allows for variety and individual flourishing, it is good. Because our civil religion asserts that to be an American is to be committed to making ever more progress toward a democratic polity, we all should join the struggle. Because the struggle, and the survival of liberal democracy itself, depends on certain instrumental virtues like honesty, hard work, attention to children, and a modicum of personal responsibility, we should practice all these for the sake of our nation-as-family.

The communitarian "social movement" specifically aims at *political* reform. And it is through reengineered social programs that communitarians hope to reengineer American citizens, making them more virtuous and thus more effective proponents of liberal democracy. We will use government to teach the people the habits necessary for them to lead authentic individual lives while maintaining the society that makes such lives possible.

But how is this civil religion to be promulgated? How are communitarians to convert the unconverted and so build individual virtue and communitarian democracy? Clearly the answer lies in education. Why else would communitarians spend so much time and effort reconstructing our past? But education for communitarians must be carried out at several levels: educating groups and classes in proper habits through reformed government social programs; teaching children the proper values in schools; and learning by everyone of liberal virtues in democratically reconstructed businesses and civil associations.

New Democratic Reforms

Most observers identify contemporary liberalism with the Democratic party. Communitarians identify themselves with that party as well but seek to redefine public perceptions of democratic liberalism. They are "new democrats." As new democrats they promise to oversee a new liberalism, one tougher, more disciplined, and more insistent on private and public virtue.

Like communitarians in general, candidate Bill Clinton at first presented himself as a new kind of democrat. In the 1992 presidential election he argued that his administration would transcend partisan politics to fight crime, poverty, and hopelessness. He would forge a new democratic community in which the government would protect us from want but also insist that we act with virtue. We would serve the public as it served us, doing our best not to burden, let alone victimize, our neighbors. Clinton would reform crime and welfare policy and even "reinvent" government to give us back our streets and our sense of responsibility to ourselves and our communities.

One of the more sensational legislative battles of Clinton's early years as president was that over his crime bill. Having passed the Senate, it unexpectedly was held up in the House of Representatives by conservative Democrats and Republicans upset at its inclusion of several billion dollars for neighborhood "crime prevention." Opponents argued that the bill's crime prevention programs—including after school sports, community activities and training to build self-esteem—constituted 1960s-style social spending. The bill's supporters charged that opponents actually were attempting to kill its provision banning sales of certain weapons. But the bill passed with this ban intact after several billion dollars were cut from crime prevention programs. The battle then was replayed unexpectedly in the Senate when the revised bill came up for a vote—with the same results.

What is interesting for our purposes is that Clinton's crime prevention programs were self-consciously communitarian. They aimed to fight crime by having the federal government rebuild local communities. Clinton's bill also promised to fund 100,000 new police officers nationwide, another attempt to rebuild communities.

Additional police officers would engage in "community policing." They would get out of their squad cars and walk beats. Policemen would know the neighborhood better because they would walk through it on a regular basis. Local residents would come to know their policemen because they would be in contact with them on a daily basis. Residents and policemen would come to trust each other and work together to catch the few criminals ruining life in their community. And this experience, along with common participation in federally funded activities, would have spillover effects, teaching residents that they can and should work together on other projects to make their neighborhood a better place in which to live.

But the federal program actually would fund fewer than fifty thousand new policemen nationwide—and very few for each neighborhood. What is more, federal funding soon would end. Communities then would be left with only a federal mandate, and would be required by law to find money on their own to keep and hire more policemen.

In essence, the federal government would tell local communities how many policemen they must hire. But this would be no departure from current practice. The federal government persistently tells local communities and businessmen whom to hire. Affirmative action quotas and disabilities acts (instituted under Republican as well as Democratic administrations) put the burden on employers to prove they had good reason not to hire applicants in certain protected categories. And these are only the most visible federal hiring mandates. A plethora of federal programs aim to force employers to act virtuously, to hire the "right" applicants so that we will have a more equal society. They further the liberal goal of risk minimization by "insuring" that no applicant will be denied a job for any reason the government deems irrelevant. But such programs clearly restrict the freedom of local communities to set their own standards and run their own lives.

In creating a mandate the federal government tells states (and localities and individuals) that it wants something done without having to do it itself. Welfare, crime control, and other Clinton proposals to "reinvent" government are not intended to free states and local communities from federal control. They (and a number of Republican proposals also attempting to enforce moral standards from Washington) do little to free local citizens and communities to experiment with new programs or otherwise take greater control of their own lives.

Clinton's proposed "enterprise zones," for example, were called market and community oriented during the 1992 campaign. They would entail tax breaks and a loosening of some regulations for businesses operating in economically distressed areas. But Clinton's enterprize zones would involve significant government oversight. Only businesses agreeing to employ a high quota of local residents deemed disadvantaged by the government and to prove reinvestment in the area would be eligible for special dispensations. Government agents would have to approve detailed business and local government plans before any consideration would be forthcoming.

Clinton also promised to give local communities and individuals greater freedom by reinventing government. Streamlined, efficient, and decentralized administration would provide more services more cheaply while allowing communities and individuals more choices concerning how they might meet their obligations to the federal government. But the thinking behind these proposals renders unsurprising the real effect of such reform: further extension of the liberal regulatory state.

Often called the "Bible" of the Clinton administration, David Osborne and Ted Gaebler's *Reinventing Government* seems distinctly new and unliberal. In it Osborne and Gaebler gather together and systematize arguments they made both before and during the 1992 campaign. These men favored privatizing a number of government activities, rearranging bureaucratic duties and attitudes to emphasize "client" service, and providing more discretion to administrative managers. Such reforms, according to their proponents, would make government cheaper, more responsive, and thus more efficient.

But Osborne and Gaebler's reforms would not aim to reduce the *role* of government in our lives; they explicitly aimed to make government *better* at reordering our lives. As the authors put it, "Government is the mechanism we use to make communal decisions." The authors "believe deeply in government," in its role in educating us, solving our "collective problems," and establishing "equity."[5]

Reinvented government aims to achieve traditional liberal goals, only more efficiently. As the old model had, so reinvented government would attempt to provide the forum and means with which to solve our national, collective problems. One of Osborne and Gaebler's favorite notions was "anticipatory democracy," that is, government that tries to prevent problems (minimizing risks) rather than deal with problems when they occur. Thus they endorsed preventive regulations, such as bans on nonrecyclable packages, and favored government "futures commissions" and strategic planning. Such programs would reorient government, in their view, allowing it to transcend outmoded New Deal and Progressive Era administrative structures in which the government attempted to do all the work itself. Now, they said, government would steer the ship but leave others to do the rowing.

Such reforms clearly would entail change. But they hardly constitute a rejection of liberalism. Even the privatization Osborne and Gaebler recommended was far less than revolutionary. The sanitation and other basic services Osborne and Gaebler would privatize would not become the subjects of free competition but of competition "managed" by the government—with wages, working conditions, and even specific employees mandated by that government. The state would give up direct control but would continue to mandate who would do what, when, where, and how.

The goal apparently is to give individuals the impression that they are participating actively in the government programs that affect so much of their lives, making them believe that these programs are in some way their own. But any such impression would be illusory. Individuals would remain under the effective control of unelected bureaucratic elites, albeit ones careful to act with the appearance of democratic concern.

Federal mandates, whether of welfare payments, numbers of policemen or hiring quotas, all seem to leave local citizens freer than direct laws. Instead of telling us exactly what to do, mandates tell only what results we must achieve. They leave us free to figure out the details on our own. But when one combines mandates for, say, a certain number of police officers in a certain area with race- and sex-based hiring quotas and throws in federally mandated work and antiharassment rules and Environmental Protection Agency mandates restricting where and how to construct facilities like police stations, there no longer is a great deal of room left for "creativity"—or for anything resembling local self-government.

Osborne and Gaebler (and Clinton) sought "entrepreneurial government." What this meant, in effect, was that reinvented government actually would exacerbate the problem Lowi sees in liberalism. Bureaucrats would be further divorced from the consequences of their actions because they would have more power and less accountability. They would find it easier to regulate because regulation, now involving only mandates rather than detailed regulatory schemes, would seem more benign, fair, and easy. No longer saddled with the task of determining precisely how goals such as workplace safety and decreased pollution could be accomplished, bureaucrats would find it easier to dictate that communities, companies, and individuals do so. The liberal impulse to regulate everything now would rule unquestioned.

Only one thing would change: the increased emphasis on mandates would put the onus on states, localities, companies, and individuals to change their behavior more radically and with more initiative than would actual laws. Where specific laws require only acquiescence to government dictates, mandates require initiative on the part of "mandatees." Mandatees must determine exactly how they might obey the will of the state without going bankrupt.

Reinvented communitarian government would require citizens with cooperative, active, and inventive characters. This requirement is ironic because communitarian government would stifle the very communities that foster public spirit and initiative. Of course these communities already had fallen into disarray, and this was another problem Clinton sought to correct through federal programs.

Communitarian Welfare

Welfare reform was a Clinton solution to the breakdown of families and inner cities—one based, ironically, on a new and universal "right." All Americans would be entitled to universal health care and pensions. But this new right would be linked to the responsibility to work. As before under welfare liberalism, everyone would be given the right to government education and training so that they could liberate themselves from their dependency. Now they also would be guaranteed against the compound tragedy of suffering some form of illness and having to seek treatment from a charity hospital or the charitable auspices of a private hospital or physician.

Individuals now would have every opportunity to seek employment and would no longer need to avoid it in order to keep their government-supplied health benefits. But individuals also would have the responsibility, enforced by government sanctions, to take advantage of these incentives, to get jobs and get off of welfare whenever possible. Once welfare-dependent individuals were working, Clinton reasoned, they would get married, teach their children the value of work, bring money into their communities, and fight harder against criminal elements.

Government would instill habits of hard work and personal responsibility by demanding real effort on the part of aid recipients. Some called such proposals punitive or even "racist" because they would affect the poor (among whom minorities were disproportionately represented) rather than all Americans. But Clinton was not to be so criticized. He and his aides quickly pointed out that sanctions would apply only to those who "could" work, and that this category would be defined narrowly, leaving out the vast bulk of welfare recipients.

The proposal that emerged emphasized the same elements of training, public jobs programs, and subsidized day care that characterized Jimmy Carter's Comprehensive Employment and Training Act. The plan would be aimed largely at unmarried mothers in their late teens or early twenties. It would exempt recipients born before 1972—who make up the bulk of the welfare caseload. It would not place recipients into private sector jobs but rather into training and public works programs from which for practical purposes they could not be fired.

The administration continued to mandate welfare payments as before, leaving little room for state reforms. Still, a few states attempted to change the federal welfare payment structure, eliminating increased payments to mothers who had additional children while already on welfare. Such changes produced outrage from many quarters. Some criticized the argument that government programs increase illegitimacy and unemployment and foster welfare dependency.[6] Critics deemed this impossible because the real, after-inflation value of welfare benefits has decreased since 1970 while illegitimacy and welfare dependency have increased.

But few of us consider only money when we decide how we should act. Some poor people even today refuse both charity and public assistance out of pride. Some well-off teenagers steal and burgle for "kicks." Motivations to human action are varied. But one very powerful motivation is habit. Individuals who have become accustomed to relying on the government for support and are unaccustomed to self- and family reliance will not suddenly get married and look for work because their welfare check does not go as far as it once did. Instead they will become angry that their "entitlement" has decreased in value. Political activism, along with increased crime among those who have been taught that their society is oppressive, are the natural outgrowths of marginal decreases in welfare benefits.

The Clinton administration avoided such issues by emphasizing work and training programs, along with rhetoric aimed at making aid recipients feel guilty if they remained on welfare for too long. Curiously, the administration also instituted an experimental "freedom card" for welfare recipients. Using this card, anyone on welfare may purchase goods with government funds as if using a credit card. In this way they could avoid the "stigma" attached to users of food stamps and other government payments.

But communitarianism rests on social pressure. Eschewing open coercion, communitarians would use public shame to make individuals conform to community standards. One would think, then, that a community standard saying that it is a bad, even a shameful, thing to be dependent on government payments would be in keeping with communitarian values. Such a standard would use nonlegal means to teach those dependent on the community that they must attempt to become independent as soon as possible.

The Clinton administration seems more concerned to redistribute wealth than to resuscitate the traditional work ethic. Social justice defined as equal wealth must trump, in their view, the small town value of personal responsibility. In effect, Clinton's reforms reduce even further the stigma of welfare dependency and increase the role of the federal government in local life. But then the communitarians' goal is not to preserve our communities. It is to transform them.

Freeing Minds

Communitarians often praise what they call communities of memory. A shared past helps a people form and maintain moral coherence. Common experiences of joy and sadness give the people a certain commonality of character. Each member reacts to shared memories in much the same way. Consensus about their past helps citizens maintain consensus about the moral standards they want to apply in meeting present and future circumstances.

Etzioni claims Americans have a consensus concerning certain key democratic values, principally nonviolence and nondiscrimination. But the values communitarians see, or wish to insert, in our collective memory demand great reforms to eradicate perceived injustice and inequality. Thus Etzioni disparages the "Leave it to Beaver" morality he believes predominated 1950s America. He also condemns what he asserts were the characteristic racism, sexism, and homophobia of that era, along with its tolerance of inequalities of wealth and political power.[7]

We must rewrite our past, using it to teach ourselves and especially our young to strive for a more tolerant and egalitarian future.

Communitarian social scientists seek to extend the logic of liberalism by "freeing" our minds from unwanted prejudices. As earlier liberal revolutions freed peoples from oppressive government, as welfare liberalism seeks to free us from poverty and the consequences of the actions of others and ourselves, so communitarian liberalism seeks to free us from certain unthinking beliefs.

All liberalisms seek to free us from constraints on our individual, authentic wills. But where earlier liberalisms saw these constraints as coming from outside forces (military police or poverty, for example), communitarian liberals see obstacles to our true authenticity coming from inside ourselves. Communitarians believe existing and historical institutions, beliefs, and practices have given us ideas and habits that prevent us from seeking the truly authentic lifestyles we otherwise would pursue.

Communitarians combine the rationalism of American pragmatism with a romantic commitment to individual sensibility in their quest for the truly authentic self. Their goal is to unchain our wills and desires from unexamined beliefs they deem harmful and restrictive. They would use pragmatic, "value neutral" social science to free what they believe are our essentially benign natural drives and sentiments.

Of course communitarians cannot free us from all prejudice because a prejudice is merely an unexamined belief, and no society can exist without a myriad of such beliefs. If each of us stopped to examine such fundamental prejudices as those concerning the laws of aerodynamics, for example, airplane flight would come to a halt. And the same goes for cultural beliefs. If each of us individually must be convinced of the "truth" of the prejudice that it is wrong to commit murder or to abandon our families, society will crumble.

Communitarians do not want to eliminate all forms of prejudice. Instead they want to replace certain forms of prejudice—primarily the racism, sexism, and homophobia they find inherent in America's small town values—with prejudices more in keeping with their own goals and values. Communitarians wish us to believe without question that all individuals are equal, save those bad ones who presume to judge the personal conduct of others or who oppose pursuit of social justice through government redistribution of wealth. Equality, democracy, and social justice are to become the new prejudices of the age. We are to learn them from birth as a holy creed, much as communitarians assert our existing institutions have indoctrinated us into racism, sexism, and homophobia. Public schools and government subsidized and regulated day-care centers will teach our children the democratic faith—democratically, benignly, and without undue coercion.

This creed can lead to somewhat embarrassing rhetorical excesses. Nonetheless, communitarians should not protest too loudly when the words of a former university chancellor, cabinet member, and often quoted spokesman on educational issues are used to show their influence on Clinton administration policy. The words are from a speech given by Clinton's Health and Human Services Secretary Donna Shalala at the University of Chicago in November 1991. In this speech Shalala drew a picture of what a typical little girl (named "Renata") would be learning and thinking about in the year 2004: "Renata doesn't know any moms who don't work, but she knows lots of moms who are single. She knows some children who only live with their dads, and children who have two dads, or live with their mothers and their grandmothers. In her school books, there are lots of different kinds of friends and families."

After Renata leaves kindergarten, she goes to a small day-care center outfitted by the city. "Sometimes she and her best friend, Josh, play trucks; sometimes they play mommy and daddy, and Josh always puts the baby to bed and changes the diapers, just like his own dad does at home."

Even holiday celebrations have been transformed: "At Thanksgiving time, Renata's teacher will tell a story about how people from Europe came to the United States, where the Indians lived. She will say 'It was just the same as if someone had come into your yard and taken all your toys and told you they weren't yours anymore.'"

But Shalala does not want us to complacently await this paradise in which traditional sex-roles and shared pride in an immigrant heritage have been destroyed. All of this will not just happen; to believe that it will is to resuscitate the old liberal fallacy of spontaneous progress. Utopian tolerance will come because "we made it our top priority in our communities and in our Congress."[8]

The Clinton administration made Shalala's project a top priority. Soon after Clinton took office his Education Department proposed legislation establishing federal oversight to make certain states and localities adopted "gender equitable and multicultural materials."

The federal government would mandate that localities rewrite their texts and their history to see to it that children reject their racist, sexist, and homophobic past in favor of sexual and cultural egalitarianism.

The federal "Goals 2000" Act would provide national standards for teaching history that would emphasize egalitarian character transformation. The new standards do not mention our Constitution but highlight the early feminist gathering at Seneca Falls, New York, and the founding of the Sierra Club. They discuss Harriet Tubman, a black rescuer of escaped slaves, six times and ask students to discuss the grandeur of Mansa Musa's court in the West African nation of Mali while mentioning Alexander Graham Bell, Thomas Edison, Albert Einstein, Jonas Salk, the Wright brothers, Daniel Webster, and Robert E. Lee not at all.

Clinton's standards emphasize the achievements of other cultures and the failings of our own. Their goal is to teach children the equality of all cultures and individuals, and to have them ruminate on the sins of our past so that they might more determinedly seek communitarian social justice. The standards rewrite history in order to promote communitarian virtue.

We must create a meaningful community by re-creating our children. We must change "the system." We must learn a new kind of virtue for a new kind of community; a virtue created by social scientists, educators, and bureaucrats, members of professions in which communitarianism is most influential.

Teaching Democratic Virtue

Etzioni is particularly anxious to use the state to teach virtue. He criticizes currently popular "values education" for failing to teach students the proper values. In values education teachers only lead children to explore for themselves how they might examine moral dilemmas. Teachers present ethical problems to their classes and guide them in thinking through the issues analytically, but do not "impose" any particular solution. Etzioni dislikes this approach because in his view it is the state's responsibility to see to it that all children learn the *proper* values.

What values should children learn? Etzioni claims there is no real issue here. "Nobody considers it moral to abuse children, rape, steal (not to mention commit murder), be disrespectful of others, discriminate, and so on." We all can agree on the basic values necessary for civilization to exist (honesty and forbearance from violence) and on the need for equality (nondiscrimination). As to other more difficult issues such as abortion, we must multilogue to create consensus.[9]

Etzioni does not state the basis on which we should determine what a proper value is. He refers to neither rational principles nor any natural ability such as conscience as a source of knowledge concerning values. But the values he chooses to emphasize are truly communitarian—they emphasize the inherent equality of all individuals and groups. What is more, they rest for their legitimacy on the democratic principles of consensus and open discussion. The problem arises when majorities choose unliberal, small town values. These majorities, communitarians argue, must be freed from their prejudices so that they will join the proper, communitarian consensus.

But even obvious values often are difficult to teach. For example, crimes of violence have become all too common over the last few decades. Etzioni has little to say about how to enforce the "obvious" moral rule against crimes such as murder. Instead he spends much time explaining how schools should teach nondiscrimination. He praises Emory University for requiring students, faculty, and staff accused of making sexist remarks to attend "workshops" orchestrated by administrators to teach them about the dangers and pervasiveness of "sexual harassment." Apparently due process rights (such as the presumption of innocence) for those accused of "intolerant" remarks would interfere with the communitarian goal of inculcating the proper sensitivity on issues of sex.

In regard to both sex and race, inegalitarian values must be stomped out through public seminars, news conferences, personal confrontation, and especially professionally orchestrated consciousness-raising sessions. Etzioni endorses a plethora of mandatory workshops, "cultural awareness" programs in which students are exposed to the ideology of multiculturalism, mandatory sensitivity training sessions for all students, and arbitration seminars in which those accused of insensitive remarks are exposed to large numbers of students, faculty, and administrators telling them that their views are offensive, harmful, and un-American. Using such means, Etzioni argues, educational authorities can teach individuals the proper values without "coercing" them. Such means are noncoercive apparently because so long as they agree to sit through these sessions and do not object or criticize them, involuntary participants will not be fired or expelled.[10]

Critics have observed the authoritarian possibilities of communitarian consciousness-raising. Leon Wieseltier notes in a *New Republic* article titled "Total Quality Meaning" that communitarians owe much of their vision of community to W. Edwards Deming. Deming revolutionized economics, particularly in Japan, through a vision that treats all organizations alike and puts them all in single-minded pursuit of one goal: quality.

Quality, like authenticity, means achieving whatever the organization's goals happen to be but very well. "Quality," wrote one Deming disciple, "must become the new religion." All members of the group must sacrifice for the common good of quality output. They will be formed together in this purpose by the great leader. Deming writes that "transformation in any organization will take place under a leader. It will not be spontaneous . . . the job of a leader is to accomplish transformation for his organization. . . . He possesses knowledge, personality, and persuasive power." Monopolies are best, for Deming, because they leave the leader most free to mold his organization to achieve quality.[11]

It may be unjust to accuse Deming's followers of having a totalitarian mindset. Their goal is, after all, competitiveness. One seeks total quality management because one wants to defeat the competition in the marketplace. But Wieseltier notes that the Clinton administration (whose gurus Osborne and Gaebler openly use Deming's ideas) has followed Deming in conflating moralism and managerialism—of confusing better means for a system of ends.

Labor Secretary Robert Reich, for example, promises to construct "a new America" by forcing companies to pay all employees more nearly the same wage and allow more independence for employee work groups. According to Reich workers would be more satisfied and productive if allowed "to experiment in rearranging the data to provide new insights into what is being produced and how it can be refined." Justice demands that workers be given equal material rewards and greater opportunity to act authentically.

Wieseltier worries that communitarians' love of managerial authenticity has led them to devalue private life and make it a slave to their political vision. Certainly communitarians' desire to raise our consciousness on cultural and economic issues does nothing to dispel these worries. But communitarians are convinced that they would free us by enrolling us into these various totally managed organizations. These organizations would "free our minds." They would dissolve our improper prejudices and replace them with liberating prejudices like instinctive belief in equality and authenticity. And according to communitarians the organizations themselves would not be coercive. They would not force individuals to join but only force them to act in certain ways, or at least participate in certain orchestrated discussions.

Communitarians' attachment to democracy goes hand in hand with their opposition to open coercion. They want each of us to feel that he is an integral part of the community. Feelings of inclusion and empowerment promote individual self-esteem and group solidarity, both of which communitarians feel are necessary for the pursuit of authenticity.

Only when we feel that we are an important part of a community we helped create will we have the self-confidence to fully participate in its public life. Taylor recommends extension of the welfare state largely because it will make the beneficiaries feel more a part of the political community. On cultural issues too groups must feel that they are recognized, valued, and heeded by the community. Equal acknowledgment, equal material wealth, and equal access to public forums must be maintained, or real injury will be done to those "excluded" and to the community that will lose some of its solidarity. Individuals no longer will be empowered because they will not feel that they contribute to the public discussion on how best to achieve social justice. They no longer will feel good about themselves, and feeling good about oneself is both the basis and the goal of authenticity.[12] It is because they are committed to self-esteem that communitarians seek to construct communities within which each of us may pursue his own ends secure in the knowledge that he always will be accepted and supported by the community.

The Community of Self-Love

Clarke E. Cochran has argued that communitarians have only a "thin theory of community." According to Cochran communitarians are unwilling to look with depth and care into essential elements of community, particularly authority, loyalty, and commitment. They have no means by which to understand the varieties of tradition that make communities—from the French in Canada to the various ethnic groups fighting in the former Yugoslavia—differ as radically as they obviously do.[13]

But communitarians do not want communities to differ in fundamental respects. Their community must be thin (that is, based only on abstract democratic values) lest differing moral judgments destroy moral and economic equality. What is more, moral judgments may harm individuals' self-esteem.

Close-knit communities are slow to accept outsiders and may even shun those who have customs, lifestyles, or appearances different from their own. Racial bigotry and even violence are examples of the dangers of community identity (although racism itself is a pseudoscientific theory that warps and magnifies cultural prejudices).

What concerns communitarians most, however, is not racial violence, which they clearly abhor, but discrimination in all its esteem-damaging forms. According to communitarians most traditional religious and moral views, if held and expressed strongly, are dangerous, because they constitute negative judgments concerning others' beliefs and practices. And negative judgments lead to statements of moral disapproval that are dangerous to the hearer's self-esteem.

Communitarians find traditional religion and moral values too confining in and of themselves. They are "illiberal" except to the extent they help preserve liberalism itself, which cannot exist without the moral absolutes it by nature abhors. How, then, is liberalism, even with its communitarian face, to survive? Through group therapy.

Taylor decries the "triumph of the therapeutic." So do other communitarians. Indeed, Taylor cites Bellah when he criticizes therapeutic shallowness. Our contemporary tendency to see psychological therapy as a cure-all keeps us from asking ourselves important moral questions. Failing to posit any standards beyond self-fulfillment, we seek only to become "well-adjusted" through group therapy, and this "encourages a kind of shallowness." When we refuse to look to standards outside our own wants and desires,

> the very language of morals and politics tends to sink to the relatively colourless subjectivist talk of "values." To find the mean-

ing to us of "our job, social class, family and social roles," we are
invited to ask questions like this: "In what ways are our values,
goals, and aspirations being invigorated or violated by our
present life system? How many parts of our personality can we
live out, and what parts are we suppressing?"[14]

According to Taylor such self-involvement is self-defeating. "A total
and fully consistent subjectivism would tend towards emptiness:
nothing would count as a fulfillment in a world in which literally
nothing was important but self-fulfillment." Only if we commit ourselves to causes greater than ourselves, only if we authentically pursue social justice, can we fulfill ourselves.

    This does not mean that psychological therapy, with its emphasis
on mutual toleration and support for all individuals as they construct
the lifestyles they believe will help them flourish, is bad. On the contrary, Taylor, Bellah, and other communitarians consistently advocate
group therapy as the proper means to achieve self-understanding
and morality in public life. So long as it is not coercive and so long as
it aims to achieve social justice (so long as it promotes the communitarian civil religion), group therapy is communitarian.

    Etzioni seeks to eliminate all forms of discrimination through
workshops that use therapeutic techniques (rather than overt coercion) to inculcate sensitivity. Clinton administration reforms, from
"crime prevention" to welfare reform to economic policy, all aim to
give individuals a sense of effectiveness and self-esteem. Communitarians want us to feel good about ourselves. Indeed, self-esteem in
many ways appears to be the true goal of communitarianism. Discrimination is bad, even "wounds" us because for communitarians it
harms our love of ourselves. Democracy is good because it makes us
feel good—like effective, important participants in public life. Economic inequality is bad because individuals may take their possession of fewer than average goods as a sign of failure and so love themselves less. The prejudices of human equality and the equality of all
lifestyles are good because they allow each of us to pursue his own vision of the good life without fear of being judged morally inferior,
without risking his reputation and self-love.

    One might ask at this point why I am singling out communitari-
ans' commitment to self-esteem. After all, the pursuit of self-esteem
is a veritable mania in America today. Everything from unemploy-

ment to violent crime to low corporate profits has been blamed on low self-esteem. Educators in particular have become enamored of the notion that it is only by building children's love of themselves that we may produce well adjusted, educated individuals. Elementary schools and day-care centers across the country have something akin to Minnesota's "Very Important Kid" program or the Halsey school's system of holding awards ceremonies every six weeks to boost students' love of themselves.[15]

Self-esteem programs in many schools rely on tools such as talking stuffed animals to teach children to love themselves. One program uses "a loveable young dragon puppet who helps children overcome 'negative self-talk' and learn 'positive thinking skills.'" Children are being taught the skills necessary not to achieve any particular goal or goals but to love themselves no matter what.[16]

Emphasis on self-esteem is a popular liberal communitarian development. It rests on the assumption that individuals will flourish—find what they are good at and practice it while harming no one and even serving the common good—if only "freed" from self-doubt, from the improper prejudice that their abilities are limited merely because their achievements have been limited. What we do is less important than how we feel about it. The only caveat is ironic: one cannot have self-esteem if one is behaving criminally or dysfunctionally because, the assumption is, one who loves himself will perform well and treat others well.

Thus California's state-appointed Task Force to Promote Self-Esteem concluded that "the lack of self-esteem is central to most personal and social ills plaguing our state and nation." Other states, the national government, and the National Education Association all have followed California's lead in promoting self-esteem as a safeguard against vice. Self-esteem programs have been built into the primary school curriculum throughout the United States. Self-esteem also is taught at higher grade levels in the form of drug awareness and sex education programs based on the assumption that self-satisfied children will not use drugs or have sex.[17]

We know our children have self-esteem because they invariably answer the plethora of "self-esteem tests" correctly, showing that they love themselves and feel that they are intelligent and capable. But somehow our children still manage to score lower than children from other advanced countries in math and science, still manage to tries, and still manage to have a much higher crime rate, particularly among youths, than that in other advanced countries. As to drug and sex education programs, those seeking to instill self-esteem as a guard against undesirable behavior actually *increase* the incidence of drug use and teenage sexual activity.[18]

Self-esteem is not an effective tool of public policy. It does not protect us against the lures of vice but encourages us to experiment with vices we find enticing. Dr. William Coulson, a former leader in the self-esteem movement, observes, "If I'm really quite wonderful . . . then whatever I decide to do must be wonderful, too."[19] Self-esteem programs break down traditional barriers to undesirable conduct—respect for the authority of one's parents, laws, and social norms—in favor of reliance on individual judgment. They encourage students to question authority and the very basis of morality so that they may come to their own conclusions concerning proper moral conduct. The result is moral experimentation.

But self-esteem programs further the communitarian agenda. They bring together groups of individuals, led by professionals "expert" at making us feel good. They encourage us to tolerate and support one another, punishing only cynics and doomsayers with public disapproval. They seem to impose no rules but in fact seek, through the pressures of group opinion and the authority of scientific expertise, to shape our conduct and character along communitarian lines.

Etzioni and others have questioned the propriety of teaching children to question democratic values, but they share the self-esteem movement's goal (self-love and authentic individual conduct) and its primary assumption—that properly educated individuals will choose to act in a socially beneficial manner almost all the time and under almost all circumstances. They assume that we will choose to do the right thing spontaneously and even in the face of great temptations and/or peer pressure to steal, take drugs, or otherwise practice vice.

Like communitarianism, self-esteem is an attempt to save liberal culture from itself. Liberalism has freed mothers from the home and the duties of child-rearing. It has produced a society in which it is typical for both parents of even small children to work outside the home, and child-rearing increasingly has become the job of professionals. Unfortunately, this new freedom, or rather prejudice in favor of universal work outside the home, has brought problems.

Day-care centers cannot provide constant loving care. Their employees are just that, employees. No matter how caring they are they often must leave for various reasons and in any event have too many children to tend to give individuals extensive personal attention. School programs to build self-esteem attempt to fill the void of loving care by having groups of children recite flattering cheers for themselves. One Illinois school, for example, put up a banner proclaiming "We applaud ourselves."[20]

One aspect of self-esteem is the need for what psychiatrist Stanley Greenspan terms "a constant and loving caregiver . . . a fundamental sense of safety and security." It is difficult for children growing up in warehoused day-care centers or elementary schools, who come home only to the television, to gain these feelings of safety and security; they have no constant caregiver, only passing moments with parents who are consumed—often out of economic necessity—with their separate lives.[21]

And parents, and communitarians in particular, have been led to believe that children actually will be made into better adults if we let educational experts train them. Social scientists have promised at least since philosopher John Dewey began his educational experiments a hundred years ago that children would become more accomplished, flourishing adults if put into democratically structured environments from an early age. Dewey, founder of "Progressive" education, argued that educators should bring out the natural goodness and capabilities present in all children by teaching them "democratically." Teachers would shape students' natural inclinations rather than impose what Dewey saw as outdated beliefs and habits.

According to Dewey we flourish only when we learn to integrate our individual capacities into a coherent mode of life (form our own character and lifestyle) and lead this life in solidarity with our fellows. "We can," Dewey argued, "distinguish between the false and unsatisfactory happiness found in the expression of a more or less isolated and superficial tendency of the self, and the true or genuine good found in the adequate fulfillment of a fundamental and fully related capacity." True happiness could be achieved only when individual capacities and desires were harmonized with one another and with society as a whole.[22]

Thus Robert Westbrook argues sympathetically that for Dewey "the development of a character that aimed at the social good was not only necessary but sufficient for true happiness." We can only find happiness in the pursuit of social justice. But this pursuit must itself be authentic and spontaneous. It was, for Dewey, the social scientist's task to form happy, integrated selves concerned with social justice out of the individual material at hand. The social scientist should fuse "the sympathetic tendencies with all the other impulsive and habitual traits of the self."

The social scientist should not impose a character on the individual, according to Dewey. Instead he should help the individual in his task of moral self-creation. The social scientist should form "out of the body of original instinctive impulses which compose the natural self . . . a voluntary self in which socialized desires and affections are dominant, and in which the last and controlling principle of deliberation is the love of the objects which will make this transformation possible."[23]

According to Dewey the social scientist's task was to bring out and shape into liberal form the individual's spontaneous desires and drives.[24] Only if their natural drives were shaped properly could individuals achieve true, effective freedom or "positive control of the resources necessary to carry purposes into effect, possession of the means to satisfy desires; and mental equipment with the trained powers of initiative and reflection required for free preference and for circumspect and far-seeing desires." Like the communitarians, Dewey believes that the good man is the tolerant value positor who pursues his own vision of the good life, as played out in the democratic community. Also as for communitarians, for Dewey the state must play a prominent role in helping us flourish. It must free us from poverty, prejudice, and ignorance so that we may develop and exercise our capacities to the full.[25]

None of this meant, for Dewey, that happiness required moral training in the traditional sense. Quite the contrary. Dewey strenuously argued against using either punishments or incentives to prod students in their schoolwork. Rather, educators must design curricula in which "the child has a question of his own, and is actively engaged in seeking and selecting relevant material with which to answer it." In this way teachers would "permit the intrinsic wonder and value which attach to all the realities which lie behind the school curriculum to come home to the child, and to take him up and carry him on in their own onward sweep."[26]

Teachers should not teach their students ethics or mathematics but rather the techniques of how to think. However, unlike some educators today, Dewey recognized that he was not seeking to impart an empty set of tools the child could use however he desired. Rather, he was indoctrinating the child into a particular way of thinking, that of "science." Of course, Dewey would build on spontaneous desires: "The native and unspoiled attitude of childhood, marked by ardent curiosity, fertile imagination, and love of experimental inquiry, is near, very near, to the attitude of the scientific mind." But scientific thinking requires specific virtues—-free inquiry, toleration, and free communication—along with the conviction that intelligence is the product of group interaction. Dewey's science is, as Taylor would put it, "dialogical." And only individuals who respect, out of prejudice, the universal reliability and applicability of the scientific method, in Dewey's view, could participate and flourish in democratic society.[27]

Science would noncoercively shape our character. By teaching us to think according to scientific criteria social scientists would, in Dewey's view, teach us good citizenship. The choice of subject matter to be taught ("scientifically") also would influence character development. As for contemporary communitarians, for Dewey history was a particularly important subject and tool in teaching children how to act and should be taught as an "indirect sociology" in which students would learn to appreciate "the forces which favor men's effective cooperation with one another, to understand the sorts of character that help and that hold back." History should be a tool for teaching virtues much like those advocated by communitarians today.[28]

According to Dewey democratic values should determine both the ends and the means of education. Students should be shaped into good, tolerant, scientifically minded democratic citizens. But character shaping must not involve "a line of action contrary to natural inclinations." Rather, the educator must reengineer these natural inclinations, shaping them into a more democratic whole.

Dewey rejected both the notion that children must be overtly taught their moral duties and the knowledge and customs of their civilization and the "romantic" notion that the inclinations and actions of the child are self-justifying. Instead Dewey argued that what he saw as the child's natural impulses, to communicate with others, construct, inquire, and improve or express in finer form objects and statements he comes across, must be used and developed. The teacher's task was to form the child into a good democratic adult by making him see the relevance of accumulated knowledge and the scientific method to his concrete experience, and to make learning natural by designing problems in which children would use and develop their natural impulses.[29]

Of course Dewey's theories, like those of communitarianism, assume that children's natural impulses are fundamentally constructive—that we, even when very young, seek to construct and improve rather than deconstruct, destroy, or merely control what is in our power. Dewey sought to bring out both the sociability and the critical reasoning he was convinced already existed in the child. But Dewey also recognized the revolutionary nature of his project. He urged his methods on the nation as a means of ending capitalism's division of labor (which he considered undemocratic) and inequalities of income and power. Such an education would produce "individuals not complacent about what already exists, and equipped with desires and abilities to assist in transforming it."[30]

Indeed, Dewey saw educational reform as the source of liberty, equality, and fraternity. Educational reforms demanded and would produce, in his view, social justice. They required an egalitarian society, with children "freed" from political oppression and material want. The reforms themselves would free students from the constraints of preexisting social structures and facilitate individual and collective flourishing.[31]

Students in Dewey's own schools were led through practical projects, such as constructing a replica of a colonial room, intended to teach them the concrete nature and utility of history. In addition, such projects were intended to integrate practical skills, such as carpentry and reading, with analytical and cooperative skills that Dewey deemed more important. The goal remained the formation of democratic character. And this goal was reinforced continually in Dewey's laboratory schools. As friendly observers noted,

> At the beginning of the period, the children were given time for the exchange of amenities of the day usual to a group of persons meeting after an absence. The general conversation was soon directed by the teacher to the business of the day. the results of the previous work were reviewed in a group process, and plans for

further development were discussed. Each child was encouraged to contribute, either out of his past experience or his imagination, ways and means of meeting the problem of needs that might arise under new circumstances. These suggestions were discussed by the group, and with the aid of the teacher, the plans for the work of the day were decided upon and delegated."[32]

Teachers would lead students in developing the habits of governing by committee. They would teach students democratic habits and virtues from the earliest age on the assumption that children feel fulfilled when they deliberate in groups. Ironically, Dewey's experimental school died as the result of bureaucratic infighting.[33]

But Dewey's theories influenced generations of philosophers and educators. And Dewey's prescription for the great society—democratic education coupled with reform and social action to create a more egalitarian character and community—meshes perfectly with communitarian ideology, itself most popular among social scientists and other professionals concerned with character and its formation. For Dewey as for communitarians, professionals must lead us to a more equal and accepting society in which democratic participation adds to feelings of empowerment and self-esteem, thus bringing out the individual's innate abilities and sociability.

Communitarians believe that if we just love ourselves we will find ways to be more effective. Soon after taking office President Clinton took his advisers with him to Camp David for a group counseling session. As reported in *Newsweek*, "specially trained group leaders spent several hours teaching America's most powerful to open up and trust each other. The president started the ball rolling; he told a story about being teased as a fat child."[34]

Public policy itself now must find its moorings in the culture of consciousness-raising. As Clinton had learned to love himself despite being discriminated against on account of his girth, so his administration would deal with the intransigent Washington establishment by exuding self-love and self-confidence. Decrying the "authoritarianism" of traditional community but recognizing that community could not be dispensed with, communitarians sought to construct a "thin" community based on shared feelings of pain and inadequacy and instilled through the ministrations of professional facilitators.

Ironically, the cult of self-esteem smacks of the Sheilaism Bellah so abhors. We must love ourselves no matter what and all will be well. Bad and even criminal behavior is a sign, not of bad character but of a lack of self-love. Refusing to insist on universal standards of right and wrong, communitarians and Americans in general are left with only one common, shared value: love of oneself and one's own beliefs. We are afraid to insist on standards that owe their authority to tradition and religion. These would be "puritanical" and intolerant. Instead we seek solidarity on the basis of beliefs that happen to be widely held. Thus we are left with beliefs that also are self-serving, that feed our pride and undermine our attachment to the community.

Answering to no one but ourselves, convinced that our inner voice tells us what is right, we come to believe that our desires are self-justifying, that if we want something we have a right to have it. We lose even our belief in tolerance and equality because, after all, these are just others' beliefs, ones we ourselves did not create; they are mere prejudices to be discarded when they become inconvenient. And so ends community.

The 1992 elections brought the victory not just of mass communications but of mass "community." The ties that bind us were stretched thin as candidates sought to appear morally sincere while offending no one. The result, not surprisingly, was a thin morality based only on a very thin sense of common affection and purpose. But then the goal itself was morally thin—to make Americans more moderate in their selfishness and so allow the continuation of a "liberal democracy" devoted to the pursuit of physical and psychological comfort.

Chapter Six

Covenant, Contract, and the Power of Interpreters

> Democracy and the one, the ultimate, ethical ideal of human-
> ity are to my mind synonyms. The idea of democracy, the
> ideas of liberty, equality, and fraternity, represent a society in
> which the distinction between the spiritual and the secular has
> ceased.
>
> —*John Dewey*

Bill Clinton did not promise a "new deal" for America as had Franklin Roosevelt. He proposed instead a "new covenant." And the difference is significant. A deal is much like a contract, a voluntary exchange of goods or services. What Roosevelt promised was a government that would deliver the goods better than had previous administrations. The deal was "vote for me and I will use government to put you back to work and improve your living conditions" or "hire me as President and I will solve the Great Depression."

A covenant is not a mere "deal" between individuals and their government. It is a pact sworn before God. When we enter into a covenant we join together as a people, agreeing to aid one another as we follow divine rules. Thus one of Bellah's books, *The Broken Covenant*, is an indictment of the American people who according to Bellah have failed to carry out God's will. Our forefathers swore an oath before God to lead godly lives as a people. And we have failed to live up to this promise.

But what exactly was the oath our forefathers swore? What was the godly life they, and we, were to lead? It was, in the communitarian view, a sanctified egalitarianism. God demanded and the people promised a tolerant society, ruled by democratic means, in which all were treated equally and ensured equal material well-being. Such a society cannot be achieved with perfection. There always will be inequalities, failures of will, and lapses in judgment. But according to communitarians the democratic process by which we pursue egalitarian materialism is itself holy. It wipes out the distinction between the spiritual and the secular. If the people's intentions are divine, then the people themselves partake of the divine.

In effect communitarians applaud the *process* of millenarianism. They want us to join in the impossible project of bringing God's heavenly reign to earth, as that God and His reign are defined by the democratic process. They want citizens to band together to pursue an unattainable level of equality and social justice. Although the final goal cannot and perhaps should not be attained, striving after a perfect egalitarianism is holy and sanctifying, so long as the effort entails democratic rhetoric and procedures.

What matters is not that we construct a paradise of equality and authenticity, but that we constantly strive to do so. Indeed, paradise in a significant sense consists, for communitarians, of the collective pursuit of paradise. It is only in striving that we can assert ourselves and find within ourselves the capacities and talents that make us unique and allow us to flourish as individuals and parts of the group.

Just as achieving a concrete goal is less important than striving after an ideal, so for communitarians the covenant is less important than and subordinate to the idea of covenantal relations. Where the Puritans looked to specific passages in scripture by which to guide their conduct, Bellah sees the Bible and God Himself as explanatory devices by which we come to understand our own lives. Thus the covenant is not really entered into or sworn to before God. For communitarians the covenant is entered into by a people with and for itself.

This is not to say that no communitarians are religious believers. But for communitarians the point of the covenant is to set in motion a series of social movements aimed at producing ever more democracy and equality while leaving ever more room for the expression of individual authenticity. The goal is to serve mankind by advancing the cause of equality. If one believes that God demands this goal so much the better—this belief will motivate one to work even harder for equality. Private religion is not ruled out, but communitarians see it as relevant only to the extent that it helps or hinders the pursuit of social justice.[1]

A Question of Will

God's dictates to His people, in the communitarian view, may be summed up in the phrase, "obey thy will." This is shown most forcefully by the communitarian attitude toward both contractual and covenantal documents. Most communitarians deem the Constitution a mere contract among self-interested parties. As such they find it morally suspect and have no qualms about seeking to change it fundamentally through constant reinterpretation. But communitarians see even the Declaration of Independence, for them a covenantal document setting forth the ideals and way of life of the American people, as essentially nonbinding. Communitarians feel that succeeding generations need not obey the letter or even the original spirit of either the Constitution or the Declaration. Instead they argue that we must treat our Founding and even "sacred" political texts as material to be reshaped through the democratic process, redefined as we progress toward ever more equality and social justice.

But if the people are the source as well as the followers of divine will, how are we to have constant, lasting, and authoritative principles to guide our actions? If morality is based on consensus, and consensus constantly does and should change, then why should we obey the rules that happen to be in effect at any given time? Why not steal? Why not get several teenaged girls pregnant and then abandon them? Why not sell drugs? Why not, all in the name of living by your own code, of flourishing as an authentic thief, "stud," or pusher?

Here the communitarian movement organizer enters the picture. Communitarianism attracts a large number of social scientists, educators, and other professional facilitators; individuals who see it as their calling to structure public policies, educational programs, and living and working environments to bring out the best in their clients—the most productivity, the most virtue, the most happiness. With the help of media elites communitarian facilitators will free our minds and characters from old, selfish ways and make us *choose* to follow the will of the democratic majority. We all will achieve our authentic lifestyles and selves by participating in communal reform projects. And this paradoxical relationship between individualist ends and collective means will work, communitarians argue, because our communal projects all will aim at equality; they will promote a tolerant environment within which intellectual and moral experimentation can be pursued without significant risk to one's person, property, or self-esteem.

But this brings us back to our original question: how is a society devoted to individual self-satisfaction to call forth the virtue communitarians know it needs in order to survive? A covenant is holy only to those who accept the existence and authority of a higher being, a God whose will must be followed. If we are to dedicate ourselves as a covenanted people, religious faith would seem a necessary ingredient.

One also could attempt to teach the people virtue by arguing that we achieve our nature, fulfill our human potential, or otherwise flourish best by serving others. Taylor in particular comes close to making this argument. But even Taylor refuses to argue for any common standard we all must follow, like it or not, if we are to lead virtuous lives. According to Taylor we must posit or at any rate choose our own standards, our own things that matter. Otherwise we surrender our will and authenticity. And according to Taylor one who surrenders his authenticity surrenders his essence, becoming less than fully human.

Communitarians want us to promote a universal, egalitarian form of society but in the name of an individual authenticity that undermines and delegitimizes all inherited institutions, including liberal democracy. Communitarians can save liberalism from itself only if they can convince the people that they must practice the necessary if somewhat shallow virtues democratic liberalism requires in its citizens. As liberals in the eighteenth century sought to convince the people to give up some of their natural rights to society so that they might more securely enjoy the rest, so communitarians today seek to convince the people to sacrifice some of their own authenticity so that the society that makes possible their own authentic self-fulfillment may survive.

Heaven and Utopia

The communitarian tool for teaching liberal virtue is civil religion; with it they hope to convince the people that it is holy to serve the liberal state. The word holy should not be taken in a literally religious let alone specifically Christian sense, however. The ultimate reward for communitarian service is not eternal bliss in the next life but fame in this life and the blissful utopian pursuit of a perfect society here on earth.

Utopia means "nowhere." We can neither find nor construct it. But its pursuit for communitarians constitutes sufficient reward for true believers. Machiavelli thought himself virtuous because he loved Florence more than his own soul. The reward he sought was fame and a position of sufficient power to reform his city, strengthening its spirit and institutions so that it might attain some of the lost, mythical glory and virtue of the old Roman republic.

But communitarians do not merely bring the ends of religion down to earth. They see religion itself as essentially material and earthly in character. Religion for them is a means by which we come to understand ourselves, including our values, or that which is for us sacred and holy. For earthly purposes at least, there no longer is for them a God above whose will we must obey. There is instead a voice inside each of us that tells us which values to posit and how best to put them into action.

Our authentic inner voice now *is* God. Thus to follow it and to construct a society that enables everyone to follow their own inner voice without obstacle or risk is to serve both oneself and a higher purpose, the highest purpose possible in a secular liberal society. Of course it is not truly holy to serve a secular state devoted to individual authenticity. But communitarians use religious language and symbols to convince us that the path to personal fulfillment or holiness is found through democratic public service.

As the sacred and the secular fuse in democracy so do the public-spirited and the self-serving. We fulfill ourselves by serving the one true cause: democratic liberalism. Because this service gives our lives meaning, it also must be the will of God, that voice within us that bids us to fulfill ourselves.

Communitarians are not alone in identifying the democratic process with the will of God. Woodrow Wilson sought to "make the world safe for democracy" more than seventy-five years ago. Even many who claim for themselves the label "conservative" exude utopian enthusiasm for democratic forms, seeking to spread the majoritarian political process throughout the world.

Often called a conservative, George F. Will praises the congressionally funded National Endowment for Democracy for preparing "the stony ground of authoritarian societies for the seeds of democratic skills—organization, mass persuasion." Our government apparently has a duty to export the infrastructure of the democratic process and transform indigenous societies in the process. Local institutions, beliefs, and practices—traditions with which the people have lived for centuries—must give way or be destroyed in the name of democracy.

Democratic transformation can take place through many means. Neoconservative journalist Ben Wattenberg praises the spread of American democratic "culture." We are winning the world for democracy, he argues, through overseas sales of videocassette recorders (on which natives watch "mostly American movies and music"), American newspapers, and viewership of the Cable News Network.

What these democracy boosters share with communitarians is the belief that a political process can embody the will of God; that we can achieve the Great Society if only we construct the proper political machinery. Even some who speak openly of their religious beliefs see God's will as something that unfolds and comes to fruition within history, in this world and not in the next. Political philosopher Eric Voegelin referred to such beliefs as a Gnostic fallacy in which men and peoples seek to "immanentize the Christian eschaton." By this Voegelin meant that these men seek to achieve in this life that perfection Christianity promises only in the next.

Gnosticism has proven powerful throughout the history of Western civilization. It promises heavenly rewards in this world and has spawned numerous millenarian movements and rebellions. Men gladly have given their lives in pursuit of a definite, earthly salvation. If only the Holy Land were retaken from the Muslims; if only the pope were defeated; if only the people followed the ways of a given religious leader, men believed, God's reign on earth would begin. The very thing most liberals abhor about religion, its tendency to promote intolerance and violence, is the result not of religious faith but of millenarian heresy. The great historical movements of religious millenarianism all have sought to change *this* world in order to usher in a time of godly rule and many have died in the name of such causes.

Communitarians seek to avoid the pitfalls of religious millenarianism by reducing religion to its political components. They seek to tame the religious impulse by chaining it to overtly political principles and goals. Civil religion, they believe, will be "civilized." It can be used to teach tolerance and to teach us to seek, not heaven in the next life, but a utopian earthly existence in which we continually pursue our own authentic goals. But civil religion has been around much longer than Bellah or the Founders or even Machiavelli. And until recently thinkers have recognized that civil religion's costs are quite high while its benefits are woefully short-lived.

Perhaps the first self-conscious civil religion was Plato's myth of the metals. Plato thought the only way to assure harmony in his perfect regime and ensure that each class of citizens would be satisfied with their lot in life was through a "noble" lie—a lie that would promote good ends. Plato would convince citizens that their city's land was their mother. Born of the earth, they were raised in her bowels, where their souls were mixed with different metals giving them different natures. The rulers or guardians had gold mixed into their souls, the military men or auxiliaries silver, and the workers bronze or iron. Believing this myth, Plato argued, citizens would see one another as brothers, spawned by a common mother and destined by her to fulfill a particular function in the city. Each individual then would do his duty and protect the city against foreign and domestic threats.

But Plato recognized that this lie could not stand on its own. The people would believe it only after the force of tradition had taken hold, only after they had heard it told many times without contradiction.[2] And not even tradition could make adults truly believe the tale. Thus, for this and other reasons, Plato thought it would be necessary to banish adults and young adults from his city so that the young might be brought up hearing only his salutary lies. And even then the perfect city would not last. It would degenerate over time as the temptations of luxury and licentiousness overcame the call to virtue.

Machiavelli sought measures at least as draconian as Plato in building his good republic. Blood sacrifice and public executions were necessary, he argued, if the people were to value the city more than their souls. Only if the fear of earthly punishment were real and terrifying would the people obey their rulers and serve the public good. What is more, the people inevitably would become corrupt. Then the only hope for the city would be brutal retribution against important transgressors to terrify the people once again into virtuous service to the state.

Pursuit of an earthly paradise neither ended nor reached its brutal zenith with Machiavelli. The horrors of the Soviet gulags, the Chinese cultural revolution and the Cambodian killing fields all were instituted to liberate men from capitalist or Western corruption and free the new socialist man trapped in their bosoms. Thus freed, this new man would lead a utopian existence, pursuing his own various callings and desires without fear of tyranny, deprivation, or the psychological traps of consumerism and careerism. Hitler promised his chosen people a thousand-year reign if only they would exterminate the Jews and subjugate other supposedly inferior races.

Few today would go as far as Machiavelli or Plato, let alone Stalin or Hitler, in seeking to instill their civil religion in the people. Communist mass murders need only be mentioned to elicit cries of "foul" and "that is not at all what we intend." And communitarians seem to have a deep aversion to overt coercion. But communitarians like all millenarians, be they Christian or communist, urge us to bring heaven down to earth. Also like other millenarians, communitarians recognize that they must transform our very character if we are to become capable of pursuing utopia.

An Egalitarian Elite

Communitarians present themselves as defenders of equality, but this claim seems untenable in light of their desire to reeducate all of society. Reeducation is by nature inegalitarian. In any program of reeducation a self-selected group of intellectuals asserts that it has the authority to decide what kind of character and beliefs everyone should have. Even Etzioni's "multilogue" is only a means by which intellectual and media elites decide on a course of action and convince the citizenry to follow it.

Communitarians seek to use curricular reforms and federal, local, and school regulations concerning racial, sexual, or other forms of harassment to teach sensitivity and tolerance. Whatever one thinks of such innovations, few of them have been instituted through democratic means. Most of these measures have been put into effect by unelected judges and government or university bureaucrats subject to only the most cursory oversight from legislators or university boards of trustees, with little or no input from the general public. Communitarian reeducation is being instituted through means that bypass the very political process communitarians claim to value.

School administrators are not elected. And they maintain many of the self-esteem programs communitarians advocate through parental ignorance and, when faced with parental objections, deception.[3] Perhaps most dangerously, the "multilogue" format of public discussion led by intellectual and media elites has helped undermine our already weakened commitment to the formal political process. Despite the politicization of our public life in recent decades, relatively few Americans bother to vote. Americans see little reason to cast ballots because the communitarian view that laws are indeterminate has taken hold and concentrated power in the hands of unelected judges and bureaucrats. Nowhere is this more true and more damaging than in regard to our "indeterminate" Constitution.

It is in some ways convenient for communitarians to view the Constitution and laws in general as provisional rules to be reinterpreted and changed at will. In this light new rules and constitutional interpretations cannot be seen as oppressive or inegalitarian because they too may be replaced or re-interpreted. It also is convenient for communitarians to portray facilitators as necessary but neutral technicians who merely free us from prejudices and other constraints keeping us from leading our own authentic lives. In this light those who refashion our schools, our government bureaucracies, and even our most local social institutions are not coercing us but rather freeing us from improper constraints.

Galston argues that judges themselves are communitarian facilitators. Even though judges are not elected, according to Galston, we must look to them to redefine and improve the character of our Constitution and people. Judges are experts on our "civic consciousness" whose will we should obey even if it contradicts the majority's will. Although the people may not want to change the way they organize their lives, they eventually will see the wisdom of the judges' decision and confirm it.[4]

Etzioni splits interpreters of the Constitution into two camps, those who openly admit that the courts, especially the United States Supreme Court, treat the Constitution as a living document that may be modified to respond to the changing times and changes in our moral values. [And others who] argue that the Constitution is to be treated as a sacred text that is unalterable. The latter group of legal scholars does its adjusting of the Constitution by interpreting what they see as the Founding Fathers' intent. In either case, we are not irrevocably bound by what was written two hundred years ago.[5]

Because the Constitution, like all of history, has no definite meaning, we may choose only between those who openly change it to fit their reading of what the people need and those who surreptitiously do the same thing. According to Etzioni, we cannot be bound by the Constitution because it has no intrinsic meaning. Thus we must allow our judges to rearrange our government and society and should trust only those who do so openly, in the name of social justice.

Of course, even the Founders felt that we should not be *irrevocably* bound by the Constitution. They set up a system in which we could unbind ourselves from any or all of its provisions. But the Founders would have us unbind ourselves through open political means, by amending the Constitution rather than by allowing judges to reinterpret it.

The rules of the American political process are laid out largely in its Constitution. According to constitutional theory, the people should decide on their basic framework of government—for example, by what means it should select its representatives—and set it down in written form. Laws passed thereafter should take effect only if they are in keeping with the framework of government set forth in this constitution. Ex post facto laws, for example, would not take effect because our Constitution forbids them on the assumption that it is unfair to punish as illegal a deed that was not forbidden at the time it was committed.

Because mistakes may be made and circumstances may change, the Constitution should be liable to amendment. But because the Constitution is the basic document of government, because it outlines the people's expectations concerning the process by which they are to be governed (though not the specific laws by which they must abide), it should be changed with caution. More than a majority is required to amend our Constitution because our Founders believed that a free people should change its basic rules only if it was reasonably clear that the rules needed changing. Otherwise instability would engender disrespect for the government and its laws, and the result would be anarchy and a loss of liberty.

Publius argues in *Federalist* 41

> that useful alterations will be suggested by experience could not but be foreseen. It was requisite, therefore, that a mode for introducing them should be provided. The mode preferred by the convention . . . guards equally against that extreme facility, which would render the Constitution too mutable; and that extreme difficulty, which might perpetuate its discovered faults.[6]

Even if the Constitution is "racist, sexist, and homophobic" one cannot advocate amending it through judicial or bureaucratic "re-interpretation" while claiming to be in favor of popular rule. Injustices may exist in the system, but respect for law and in the end for the will of the people requires adherence to constitutional forms. Even if one is improving a woefully imperfect document, one must either abide by its rules or openly repudiate it and seek to replace it *through democratic means* if one is to be a true democrat.

Communitarian Law

If the people are to rule themselves they must do so through settled laws. Locke himself argued that laws must be settled and generally known. It would be unjust to expect anyone to follow a law not knowing what it commanded or forbade.[7] The communitarian reading of our Founding documents results in the very legal indeterminacy against which Locke warned. It keeps the meaning of laws and even the Constitution "open" to constant reinterpretation by unelected officials, individuals whose values and opinions change significantly over time. What is more, this indeterminacy puts government out of the people's reach. By subjecting our documents to reinterpretations of their own, by calling our rules indeterminate, communitarians deny to the people the ability to judge for themselves by what rules they should act. This may be necessary, in communitarian eyes, so that we may liberate the people from their inherited prejudices, but it hardly seems in keeping with their oft-stated love of democracy.[8]

One who uses judges and bureaucrats to change the Constitution denies by his actions the importance of democracy. He shows that his true goal is to have his own view of what is true and good—for example, that children who do not believe in God should not be forced to listen to any public prayer in school—win the day and come to rule his society. By claiming that the Constitution has no set or at least no legitimate set meaning, communitarians might justify leaving important decisions to the people or their legislators. But they cannot justify leaving these decisions to unelected officials not amenable to the majority's will and still claim to support democracy. Unfortunately, in the name of democracy and authenticity, this is precisely what has happened.

The current system is undemocratic. It also provides no set rules by which the people may judge their own conduct. Its pronouncements make no inherent sense and do not rest on long-held beliefs and customs that could make them come to be natural to the people. Neither philosophical argument nor history makes the current system legitimate. Not knowing what their fundamental documents say, the people must obey the will of their documents' interpreters. Facilitators, those most skilled at manipulating language and the media, become the new elite, interpreting for the people the documents through which they understand their own past and purpose.

One communitarian, Mary Ann Glendon, argues that Americans today expect too much clarity and literalness in their legal and social relations with one another. We speak to one another in "rights talk," demanding that everyone respect our absolute, unattainable rights. And this leads to friction and constant disappointment. As Glendon points out, "When we assert our rights to life, liberty, and property, we are expressing the reasonable hope that such things can be made more secure by law and politics. When we assert these rights in an absolute form, however, we are expressing infinite and impossible desires—to be completely free, to possess things totally, to be captains of our fate, and masters of our souls."[9]

Glendon argues that rights are inherently limited by social duties as well as the rights of others. Laws, in her view, must be reformed so that they will encourage virtue and discourage our rampant individualistic selfishness. She recommends, for example, laws that would require passersby to come to the aid of the injured and endangered.[10]

As important, in Glendon's view, we must cease conceptualizing and adjudicating rights as if they were clear and absolute. To demand that laws and legal decisions mark out and guarantee absolute and well-defined rights is to invite disappointment and bad feelings. It also is to undermine our *social* relations with family and neighbors because it leads us to see everyone around us as potential enemies or infringers of our rights.[11]

One answer to this dilemma is limited government, which leaves most decisions to communities or individuals. In this way the state allows its citizens to solve their own problems together through mutual cooperation and accommodation. The people develop friendships, traditions, and customary prerogatives and duties. These in turn give rise to general rules the people can follow in their daily lives without resorting to the coercive ministrations of the state. Not dependent on the state for their comfort and well-being, individuals learn to cooperate with one another for their mutual benefit.

But this is not Glendon's answer. A communitarian, she argues that our Constitution promises individuals too little support from their government. Glendon would have us borrow from European constitutions, which explicitly recognize economic rights and the government's duty to provide for its people. Unlike the haphazard, rights-based American system, European countries emphasize the individual's duties to the public as well as the state's duty to insure everyone against material privations.

As Glendon argues,

> The principal virtue of the European constitutional formulations . . . does not lie in what is most obvious—their relatively greater attentiveness to the economic and social responsibilities of the state. . . . It is, rather, that they keep responsibilities—of citizens and the state alike—prominently in view, along with rights.[12]

The law must apprise us of our duties because its primary purpose is pedagogical. Lawmakers and judges teach citizens their duties through laws, constitutions, and legal decisions. Thus they must craft their proclamations carefully so that they may teach citizens the proper virtues, the virtues necessary if liberal democracy is to survive. Perhaps most prominently, they must teach citizens their duty to pay taxes to support social welfare programs.

Laws and their concrete interpretations set the boundaries of what is and is not appropriate conduct. They tell us what we should and should not do and accustom us to acting in the prescribed manner by setting up standards that we may be punished for transgressing. Thus, in Glendon's view, drafters of laws and legal opinions should be careful to send the proper messages; to encourage tolerance and other liberal virtues while discouraging selfishness, judgmentalism, and other vices along with clearly recognizable crimes such as murder.

According to Glendon the law did not always play its current, central role in our moral lives. But now, quite properly in her view, we demand more from our lawmakers and law interpreters; so now our legal leaders and rhetoricians must be careful about the messages they send. Government must pass laws to support families through subsidized day-care and other programs, and these programs must be set up and justified in ways that teach responsibility toward one's family and society.

Glendon occasionally laments the Supreme Court's habit of usurping the legislature's policy-making function. But for her the Court's job is not to defer to the intent of the legislature or the Founders. The Court's function is rather to concentrate on establishing broad outlines of appropriate conduct and legislation that will foster liberal virtues while leaving practical details to elected bodies.[13] Perhaps most important, judges must write decisions that consider the feelings of those involved in controversies that come before them; they must send messages of tolerance, inclusion, and social duty.

Glendon decries the Supreme Court's decision in *Bowers v. Hardwick* not for its result but for the callousness of its reasoning. The *Bowers* court upheld a law banning homosexual sodomy. Unfortunately, in Glendon's view, neither the majority upholding the law nor the minority who wanted to strike it down confronted "the tragic dimension of the case: the fact that a decision either way was bound to be felt as a real affront to the deeply held beliefs of many people." Like all too many recent decisions, according to Glendon, *Bowers* gave members of an unpopular or powerless group the impression that they were "outside the community for which we Americans have a common concern."[14]

Once again, for communitarians what matters is that the government protect everyone's self-esteem. In Glendon's view a legal decision is a form of rhetoric. The decision may only affect a few of us directly, but it affects all of society through the messages it sends concerning who is inside and who is outside the community. For communitarians, law, like history, leads us though its language to believe, to feel, and to be a certain way. Thus those who interpret the laws must manipulate their language to see to it that they promote liberal virtues and self-esteem.

But in our system judges are not supposed to control the law. Rather, the law is supposed to determine what the judges do and decide. Jefferson, no enemy to liberal democracy, insisted that a free people must bind all its public officials "with the chains of the Constitution."[15] The Founders allowed for judicial review of federal laws— the ability to strike down laws because they violate the Constitution— because they wanted to ensure that legislators and executive officers would not overstep the powers granted to them by the Constitution and thereby tyrannize the people.

Publius argued that judges would protect rather than destroy state and individual liberties because their job would be merely to interpret law. And judicial review merely meant interpreting the Constitution. A judge might hold an act of the legislature or executive unenforceable because a previous and higher law, the Constitution, forbade it. This meant, however, that the Constitution itself must be treated as a written law, with terms that have definite, identifiable, and applicable meanings:

A constitution is, in fact, and must be regarded by the judges as, a fundamental law. It therefore belongs to them to ascertain its meaning as well as the meaning of any particular act proceeding from the legislative body. If there should happen to be an irreconcilable variance between the two, that which has the superior obligation and validity ought, of course, to be preferred; or, in other words, the Constitution ought to be preferred to the statute, the intention of the people to the intention of their agents.[16]

The Massachusetts Constitution of 1780, adopted seven years before the federal Constitution, made clear that Americans saw constitutions as means to protect the people from the very creative and expansive judicial interpretations Glendon advocates. In a section paralleled in a number of other state constitutions, the Massachusetts document notes that "a frequent recurrence to the fundamental principles of the constitution . . . [is] absolutely necessary to preserve the advantages of liberty and to maintain a free government. . . . The people . . . have a right to require of their law givers and magistrates an exact and constant observance of them."[17]

Raoul Berger notes "that judges are not required by Article VI, s. 3, [of the Constitution] to take an oath to do justice but rather 'to support this Constitution.'"[18] The reason for this oath seems clear: the Constitution was meant to ensure that the people would be ruled by laws and not by the will of either legislators (their agents) or judges (those entrusted with the power to apply the law to concrete situations). Loose reinterpretations of fundamental law confuse the populace and reduce respect for law. But more important, for Publius, "every breach of the fundamental laws, though dictated by necessity, impairs the sacred reverence which ought to be maintained in the breasts of the rulers towards the constitution."[19]

The people adopted the Constitution. It was their will and thus should be followed by the public officials who are, after all, mere agents or employees of the people. The Constitution was a limited grant of power; it gave only certain powers to federal officials, reserving the rest to the states and to the people. If the people wished to grant it more power they had only to amend their Constitution. But to allow public officials to add to their own powers by "re-interpreting" the document to mean something the people did not intend is to give them the power of tyrants. Judges who take on this role are, in the words of Justice Story, "usurping the functions of a legislator."[20]

Jefferson also believed that the Constitution's words must rule public officials' conduct: "Our peculiar security is the possession of a written Constitution. Let us not make it a blank paper by construction."[21] Thus when he became president Jefferson pledged to administer the Constitution "according to the safe and honest meaning contemplated by the plain understanding of the people at the time of its adoption."[22] For the same reasons Justice Oliver Wendell Holmes argued that not only the Constitution but also any amendments to it should be read in a "sense most obvious to the common understanding at the time of its adoption."[23] To reshape the Constitution, or any law, to make it better serve the needs of the moment is to take on the role of a legislator. To "educate" the people by making the words of constitutions and laws mean or imply things the drafters did not mean or intend to imply is to usurp the power that belongs to the people.

Of course many contemporary observers object to the notion that we should interpret laws to mean what their drafters intended to say. Leonard Levy, for example, believes judges should dismiss the intent of those who drafted the Fourteenth Amendment, which guarantees due process and equal protection to all Americans. Judges should read that amendment as they choose because "there is no reason to believe that [the drafters] possessed the best insights or ultimate wisdom as to the meaning of their words for subsequent generations."[24] In essence Levy argues that we have progressed in our moral understanding beyond the level attained by the men who drafted the Fourteenth Amendment. What is more, in Levy's view words by nature have no definite fixed meaning, and so must be reinterpreted by every new generation of judges and legal academics.

The judicial rhetoricism Glendon praises has its roots in the view that written laws mean what judges say they mean—that "the constitution is what the Supreme Court says it is" or, as Felix Frankfurter wrote to President Franklin Roosevelt, it is the justices "who speak and not the Constitution."[25] Attempts to discern the meaning of the Constitution have been criticized as "absolute artifacts of verbal archeology," "strictly, a matter of concern only to rhetoricians," concern for "the idiosyncratic purposes of the Framers," and based on a "filiopietistic notion."[26]

Still, judges of all stripes claim to be applying rather than rewriting the Constitution. Even Justice William O. Douglas, in his decision in *Griswold v. Connecticut*, felt it necessary to base his creation of a "right to privacy" on the constitutional text. Douglas argued that while there is no explicit right to privacy in the Constitution, "specific guarantees of the Bill of Rights have penumbras, formed by emanations from those guarantees, that give them life and substance."[27] Douglas was overturning long-standing precedents and traditional practices. But he felt it necessary to look not to a theory of the indeterminacy of language but to the text of the Bill of Rights as his primary justification. Only with this touchstone in place did he then proceed to "reinterpret" the document to grant federal judges the power to overturn laws in the several states concerning issues like the free availability of contraceptive devices.[28] For Douglas the Constitution has meaning, but one that judges can stretch and manipulate to serve their own vision of what is just.

In allowing themselves latitude to "reinterpret" the Constitution in ways not intended by the Founders, judges rely on two arguments: that the original meaning of the document is too shrouded in mystery to be discerned and that the original meaning has become irrelevant because circumstances have changed.[29] H. Jefferson Powell combines these two justifications into a single formulation, arguing that the very nature and purpose of the Constitution has changed so radically that its original meaning and intent is indecipherable and irrelevant.

According to Powell, the Constitution's original intent "was determined . . . by consideration of what rights and powers sovereign polities could delegate to a common agent without destroying their own essential autonomy." Because the Constitution set up a federal government with only limited powers, it left the states with the bulk of their power and authority intact. The Founders assumed and desired that states would remain the primary focus of political and social life. In this view the Constitution listed specific powers that the states delegated to the federal government. The government that the Constitution created would use these powers to achieve specific ends such as a stable, uniform currency, a stronger and more unified foreign policy, and the elimination of domestic trade barriers. The Constitution, then, should be interpreted in such a way as to allow the federal government to carry out its functions without endangering state sovereignty.[30]

So much seems beyond question. But to reason from this premise, as does Powell, that it is useless to engage in "historical inquiry into the expectations of the individuals involved in framing and ratifying the Constitution" simply makes no sense. Powell's argument assumes that because the character of our nation has changed (one might argue largely by means of judicial reinterpretation), the Constitution must be rewritten constantly by judges to make it "relevant."

But constitutional government is based on the assumption that only the people should change the meaning of their basic charter. If times change, if the people believe the purposes of their national government should change, they have the power to amend the Constitution. If the people do not so choose, it is the judge's duty, if he is the servant and not the master of the people, to apply the law as written, as its authors intended. And the very examples Powell uses to show that determining the Constitution's meaning is impossible and in any event not in keeping with the Founders' desire in fact prove quite the opposite.

Powell argues that two conflicting theories of interpretation were pursued actively during the Founding era: "Protestant anti-interpretivism," or strict reliance on the document's language, and the common law tradition. Powell argues that the Protestant tradition rejects the role of judges as interpreters because it looks to individual conscience as the proper guide to one's actions. As Protestants rejected the Catholic hierarchy's authority in interpreting scripture, Powell reasons, Americans must have rejected any role for judges in interpreting the meaning of the Constitution. Precisely. The Protestant emphasis on the literal meaning of the Bible easily translates into the early American emphasis on the plain meaning of the Constitution. Thus intricate theories of judicial interpretation such as Justice Douglas's are particularly illegitimate in the American context.

What is more, Protestant literalism calls into question the Supreme Court's long-standing practice of justifying its decisions on the basis of its own prior rulings. The words of the text, not the interpretation of that text given by a previous set of judges, should rule in any given controversy. Only in this way is the literal meaning of the text protected from the accretion of a succession of bad, potentially tyrannous interpretations. Precedent, the authority of previous court decisions, cannot override the text's clear meaning. It only can help show how the text applies in action to a particular set of circumstances.

Powell next somewhat oddly argues that the other interpretive tradition active in the Founding era, common law reasoning, was inconsistent with Protestant literalism.[31] But common law reasoning is merely the attempt to discern what words mean to a people. The "rules of law" and "common understandings" that Powell's exemplary judges sought were not, in this light, a form of authoritarian interpretivism but rather a form of research into the meaning of words. Even today lawyers often use Latin phrases to capture rules of law that have existed for centuries. The goal is not to obscure but rather to maintain the commonly understood meaning of important phrases around which people have developed expectations.[32] Powell notes the framers' concern to eliminate vagueness in the Constitution so that its express language would be clear to succeeding generations and continue to bind their rulers. And clear language is only helpful if interpreters stick to it, construing it strictly and applying it as it was intended to be applied.[33]

It may be true that our nation has changed. It may even be true that our public philosophy and the very character of our society have changed. But it seems doubtful that lawyers and judges have the training or foresight to construct a new Constitution or new public philosophy. And even if this class of reinterpreters had such expertise, it hardly is in keeping with communitarian egalitarianism to cede them, or any of the other professional classes, this kind of power. In the face of such concerns, attempts to regain our understanding of what words like "due process" meant to those who put them into our Constitution seem nothing more than prudent attempts to recapture an understanding of the rules Americans as a people chose to govern themselves. Having recaptured our understanding of the Constitution we might choose to change it. But at least we would know what we were choosing to change and be capable of deciding for ourselves what rules we *wanted* to change and how.

Reinterpreting Culture

The communitarian view that our Constitution is an indeterminate or "living" document amounts to a rejection of written rules in favor of the shifting opinions of intellectual elites; elites who have taken it upon themselves to reinterpret the will of God and man. But this view is merely one element of the communitarian commitment to reinterpretation. Communitarians seek to reinterpret not merely our laws but also our customs and even our forms of spirituality.

We must change the very beliefs that give our lives meaning to make them serve the communitarian cause. We must transcend small town values. We must leave behind supposedly sacred systems that once ordered our lives. We must tame religion to make it serve the needs of democratic socialism.

Indeed, the most convenient aspect of the communitarian theory of linguistic indeterminacy is its tendency to give intellectual elites, our interpreters, great power to transform social values and our very culture. What does the Constitution mean? Look not to the text but to the "experts"—judges and legal academics. What or who is God? Look not to scripture or religious tradition but to academic theologians and sociologists. What does a particular piece of art "mean" or "signify?" Look not to the object but to the "expert" artists and critics. Thus cultural elites are born.

The Constitution once defended moral consensus. We could not change it unless a large majority of us believed it needed to be changed. Now judges feel it is their right and duty to change the Constitution as needed to fulfill their own visions of what is just and good. Some, such as Justice William Brennan, even presume that "when Justices interpret the Constitution, they speak for their community." Brennan means not merely that justices speak on behalf of the community that did not elect them. He means that justices lead their community in a manner of which Wills would approve. The judge must craft his decision so that it will be "received as legitimate" by the people while fulfilling our "faith in progress" and equality.[34]

Subjectivism and indeterminacy inevitably lead to rule by experts. They just as inevitably make experts of those who hold positions of practical power and influence—those who hand down judicial decisions, criticize artistic work (and so either attract the public to it or repel them from it), and all those in a position to "interpret" for the masses. Rule by a new class of intellectuals and policy experts is undemocratic. Many in this new class claim that we have no choice but to follow them in our age of mass democracy and bureaucratization. A large, complex nation on this view can only be run by experts. We can sustain democracy only if our experts build social structures to elicit the proper opinions from the people and help them attain their full potentials. This, after all, was Dewey's point and his hope for social democratic reform. But the view that interpreter/experts are inevitable wielders of power is the product of the same ideology that produced the new class in the first place.

Scholars such as Louis Dupré have argued that modernity itself began with the vision of man as a creature whose character could be molded through schemes of social engineering. During the Renaissance, thinkers and statesmen began rejecting the classical and Christian view that man is by nature a social animal who achieves his potential only in society. As Dupré puts it, increasingly "the idea of fostering and developing an existing potential started giving way to man's need to assert himself independently of nature's arrangement. He began to regard the entire socialization process as a construction of his own free will and insight. Only by surpassing his given humanity would he grow fully 'human.'"[35]

Because thinkers from Machiavelli to Dewey believed man has no fixed nature, they devised methods by which to "improve" man and society. Culture and nature are distinctly different in this view. Whether a blank slate or clay ready to be molded, we come into this world ready to be shaped into radically different forms depending on the social institutions with which we come in contact.

Because the shape of our institutions can create radically different human beings, those who have the power to shape these institutions are society's true rulers. The intellectual classes who control the school curriculum, who can rewrite legislation to transform basic institutions like the family (or replace it with socialized child-rearing), constitute the vanguard of culture; they create our future and can help us progress toward utopia or at least toward more self-fulfilling lives. Indeed, only such intellectuals can lead full lives because only they can posit values *and put them into action for the community.* Only the vanguard can shape character.

We generally call this vision "modern," although "technocratic" might better capture its fascination with mechanisms of social and behavioral control. It is a liberal vision, indeed it constitutes the foundation of liberalism. Liberalism claims we can free ourselves from the bonds of the past because we can reconstruct our fundamental institutions, beliefs, and practices through force of reason, ignoring or even overcoming tradition and cultural consensus. This view is entirely opposed to the more truly cultural view it has supplanted in large part in our courts and universities. The older view saw each of us as intrinsically social. More important, it saw culture as something natural and deep-rooted.

The Latin word *colere* refers to cultivation in the sense of agriculture. From this term we derive both culture and cult, a root word for religion. The intimate links between these words show the sense in which for Western man religion, culture, and ritual were seen until recently as part of the same essence—the essence of man. Each of us developed his inherent tendencies—to come closer to the divine presence that gives our lives meaning, to follow and uphold common conceptions of what is good and right, and to bond with our fellows by acting in common with them. Social institutions do not create human nature in this view; instead they cultivate or bring out a God-given nature that already exists in each of us.

Because we have an inherent, limited nature, social institutions are both less and more powerful than liberals assume. They are less powerful because there are real limits to how much they can change us. The sin of pride in particular always is with us and causes us to overreach, to attempt what we cannot accomplish and bring tragedy to ourselves and those around us. Pride is an unchanging part of our nature, ironically one that produces recurrent bouts of millenarianism. Pride produces the drive to reengineer our characters but cannot itself be stamped out through social engineering because it is natural to us.

Social institutions are more powerful than liberals assume in that they are part of us. We develop our characters only by interacting with our families and neighbors. And these interactions are shaped by customs dating back generations, customs to which the people give tacit, unthinking consent because they build their lives on the expectation that their neighbors will abide by them. To change these institutions radically is to endanger civilization itself by leaving the people with no habituated and universally accepted rules by which to organize their lives.

The new liberal vision never completely supplanted the older cultural vision. Not only so-called "organic" conservatives like Edmund Burke but also more popular and seemingly liberal thinkers like Tocqueville were convinced that cultural institutions and religion in particular are not subject to our rational will. We attempt to change these institutions at our peril because they are expressions of our social nature, in a real sense *part* of our nature, rather than mere artifacts we may change as we desire.[36]

The cultural vision's emphasis on the limits of reform dates back at least as far as the ancient Greeks, who "did not consider themselves called to control nature or its processes but, rather, to keep all instrumental activity strictly within the fixed boundaries set by nature. . . . the work of the craftsman does not intend to change or even to humanize nature. To create, then, is primarily to adjust oneself to nature."[37]

The Greeks did not see nature as something opposed to culture, as do even modern environmentalists. Rather they believed that culture (our shared, customary rituals and practices) and the civilization that is its flower are bound by nature. They believed we can lead good lives only by recognizing human limits and cultivating the substantive and universal human virtues, such as bravery and magnanimity, that make social life possible.

This vision is inherently theological. It rests on the conviction that each of us, singly and in our several groupings according to profession, ethnic group, and so on, has a purpose and an inherently meaningful place in the universe. The Greeks, including Aristotle, wrote of the influence of heavenly bodies on human fate.[38] The Jewish emphasis on God's plans for his chosen people is well-known. Christian thinkers saw man as a microcosm of the divine universe. On this view, Dupré notes, "The entire universe is conceived as a gift endowed with a meaning that is man's task to discover and express. In fulfilling this task man finds at the same time his own meaning, the content of which is given in the two books of nature and revelation."[39]

Man looks to nature and to God's revelation to find out about himself. He must accept what he finds as true and good because it is the gift of an all-powerful being on whom he relies and who gave him everything, including his own being. The life that is given man, in this view, is not to be transcended, let alone created, out of his own, self-posited values. It is to be accepted with thanks.

The modern vision, on the other hand, aims at "a conquest of nature on man's own terms." Nature has no intrinsic meaning but rather is material to be reworked by man. But in the process, Dupré argues, technology itself

> has ceased to be a means. The world we inhabit has been built by technique and for technique. Even though technology renders unprecedented services, it is anything but man's handmaid; for the services, in a classical reversal of the master-and-servant role, have made their dominion irreversible. The skills acquired by modern science and technology are not of the kind one can choose to use or not to use. For not to use them would destroy the very nature of the enterprise. Nor can theory once again be detached from technical practice, since theory itself has become a function of practices—and *vice versa*. In the instrumentalist universe of modern science, all is *function*; nothing refers *beyond* the closed circuit of its own connections.[40]

Communitarians seek to humanize this technological world without fundamentally changing it. All has become function precisely because liberalism demands that state and society not dictate to individuals what their lives should be aimed at or what they should mean. The liberal state seeks merely to "enable" us to fulfill our own selves and life plans. In the process it has put technology and expert practitioners in the position of defining for us how we can go about our lives.

The communitarian view of human nature does not free us from the grip of technological elites because it remains based on the claim that we create our own lives and meanings. According to Taylor our characters are formed dialogically, in conversation with those around us. Communitarians believe that we create our own dialogue—create, control, and give meaning to the words that make us and, in their view, make the world. But this does not make each individual the creator of his own meaning or his own universe. Instead it places immense power in the hands of reinterpretive elites. On this view we need facilitative experts to define and reinterpret words to make them, at least provisionally, mean the same thing to all of us. Only in this way will we be able to communicate at all, let alone form a coherent community.

As Dupré notes, both Hannah Arendt and Martin Heidegger—patron saints of communitarianism—saw the irony of our current predicament:

> In the age when man became most worldly (that is, most exclusively interested in subjugating the world), the world itself has lost all intrinsic meaning. It has become reduced to a mental abstraction. What started by being a pure object ends up being devoid of any substance, a mere projection of the subject. Everywhere man encounters only himself and his own fabrications in this closed, autistic universe. Yet, Heidegger adds, nowhere does man encounter himself *in truth*, that is, in his own essence.[41]

The universe has become a reflection of our own will. But we ourselves have become empty, devoid of any intrinsic meaning. This is a necessary aspect of the modern vision because it alone allows for the control over human nature that liberals demand.

Dupré points out that man's view that he would control nature was possible only after God was cast out of the natural world: "A crucial step in this process was the transition from motion *externally imposed* to *self-motion*." Only after man came to see nature as self-ruling, and not the product of divine will, could he see it as something he could manipulate. In the early modern era even the most daring philosophers admitted the existence of a divine being. Mechanistic deists merely argued that God was a machine maker who built the natural world and set it in motion, then retired to some faraway region to become irrelevant. The modern vision increasingly saw nature as merely a series of *automatic* processes requiring no transcendent presence or source. Evolution and life itself came to be seen as the products of purely mechanical forces of nature. Thus man himself seemed another accidental product of natural processes; processes those expert at such things might manipulate.[42]

Man has become the object of scientific inquiry and also of scientific experimentation in our schools and through government and judicial policies. The interpreters of our culture now seek to reinterpret our very nature to make it fit their theories and their vision of social justice. Politics has become the servant of a cultural elite that uses the people for its own ends, and it was precisely this use of the people that our Founders sought to forestall through constitutionally limited government.

The constitutional system provided protection for the local institutions, beliefs, and practices that foster nonpolitical and nonbureaucratic rules of conduct. Political action was largely local and based on the cultural beliefs and practices of local citizens. Politics was merely one aspect of a larger, richer, and more diverse public life.

Moral rules were the product of custom, reason, and revelation. They were not perfect. They certainly were not egalitarian and did not embody any desire for "social justice" as that term currently is used. But custom and convention allowed for mutual accommodation and compromise in the light of enduring standards. These standards, or virtues, held more content than the liberal virtue of tolerance. They demanded more from the people. They also rested on the assumption that many of the standards that rule our lives lie outside our ability to change overnight, and in many cases even in the long run.

The view that we have a definite nature, reflected in God's creation and bound by His will, does not allow for the value-positing self-fulfillment of liberalism. But, as I will argue in the next chapter, this other vision, still active at our Founding, was a more effective basis for community than the pursuit of self-fulfillment possibly can be. It provided better means by which to maintain decency and allow us to fulfill our duties to family, neighbors, and society while maintaining a decent self-respect and independence.

Chapter Seven

Religion and the Ends of Communal Life

> And Judah and Israel dwelt safely, every man under his vine and under his fig tree.
>
> —*1 Kings 4:25*

The biblical passage from 1 Kings was a favorite among Americans of the Founding generation, both those in favor of the Constitution and those opposed to it.[1] This is fitting because the picture it draws of pastoral contentment in large measure sums up the vision of the good life held by the bulk of that generation. And its derivation from the Bible shows the roots of American liberty in a religious understanding of man and society that transcends even as it affects politics.

In pamphlets, speeches, and sermons, Americans did not merely cite the passage from 1 Kings. They expanded on it to set forth their arguments concerning the goals of life and the proper ends and limits of political action. In opposing the new Constitution, Patrick Henry argued in part that it was unnecessary. Those who thought the United States was in peril of its existence, or even in serious distress, in his words should "go to the poor man, ask him what he does; he will inform you, that he enjoys the fruits of his labour, under his own fig-tree, with his wife and children around him, in peace and security."[2]

Henry, supposedly a classical republican, did not sum up the good life in political terms. Instead he argued that the good life consists in large part of each man's pursuit of his own occupation and his enjoyment of its fruits in the nonpolitical felicity of family life. Yet this idyllic picture is neither antipolitical nor individualistic. It captures the social as well as the private character of American local life. When combined with public worship and other social pursuits, Henry's vision of familial life under the fig tree reflects the integrated nature of the early American community.

Men on both sides of the constitutional debates shared with their American predecessors a commitment to the way of life that had become traditional in their land. This way of life consisted of participation in various local associations, bound together by a commitment to well-ordered liberty and to the system of manners and morals taught through public worship and private habituation. Most important, it was a way of life in which virtue was the goal and was defined as adherence to universal religious standards of piety and morality.[3]

There was in early America, as in most places during most eras, a streak of millenarianism about in the land. Puritans in particular at times felt that they were bringing God's reign down to earth by building a pious and moral community. But the dominant tone in early America was not so revolutionary.

Americans saw politics in particular as a guardian of deeper understandings and practices more central to the leading of godly lives. There was no hesitation to demand universal assent to the moral code set forth most explicitly in the Ten Commandments and to some form of theistic belief. Only the form and extent of the required religious beliefs changed from community to community, and even here the emphasis on Protestant Christianity was strong.

Politics was the guardian of social life and cultural consensus. Political leaders were drawn from the ranks of social and often religious leaders. Their duty was to guard the more fundamental social and religious institutions in which virtue was taught.[4]

A Covenant of God's People

From the start each New England community was bound together by a covenant. Covenants could take a number of forms, many of them nonpolitical. Donald S. Lutz points out that the covenant tradition on which our constitutional system is based has roots going back through early Puritan codes of law, early protoconstitutions like the Mayflower Compact and radical Protestant church covenants of the late sixteenth and early seventeenth centuries, and finally to the Old Testament.[5] One might add that the Puritan experiment in the New World was supported in part through economic arrangements and agreements among dissenting Protestants that took covenantal form.

Whatever their purpose, all covenants bound a group together under a specific set of corporate rules by binding specified people in a limited geographical area and for specific public purposes, be they religious, political, or economic. The purpose of the corporation in turn defined each individual's rights of representation. One was represented only when and where one had genuine interests and duties, much as a stockholder gains representation in a corporation by reason of his stake in the company.[6]

One outgrowth of American covenantal relations was the conviction that majority rule is inherently limited. The majority rightfully could control only those matters relevant to the community's purposes, set forth in the covenant. Acts aimed at controlling other matters or undermining these purposes were improper and could rightfully be resisted. If necessary, dissenting minorities had the right and even the duty to respond to oppression by leaving to form their own government and people.[7]

The covenant tradition was neither limited to New England nor short-lived in America. As Lutz points out, "Wherever dissenting Protestantism went, so too went their church covenants." Thus "this basic form was repeated throughout New England, part of the central colonies (including the Dutch colonies), and later in the piedmont regions of the South."[8]

The covenant is the basis of American constitutionalism. When Americans organized for common action they habitually turned to the covenantal form. Early Americans sought eagerly to establish themselves in the new land as a people devoted together to walking in the way of their Lord. Lutz quotes one early church covenant and notes its connections with later constitutional forms:

> We can note several foundation elements contained within this document. First, God is called in as a witness to the agreement. . . . Second, it explains why the agreement is necessary: to create a church in the wilderness to support their living together in a manner "as becometh all those whom He hath Re-

deemed. . . ." Third, it creates a people: "We whose names are hereunder written. . . ." Fourth, it creates a church. Fifth, it defines the kind of people they wish to become—a people who walk in the ways of the Gospels, God's ordinances, and in mutual love.[9]

Early colonial codes of law were followed by state constitutions, many of which were merely reenacted colonial charters and codes of law. All of these combined Lutz's "foundation elements" to form political communities. Later documents called on the people rather than God as witness to the pact, but the goal remained that of forming a godly people. The people's duty to enforce the covenant on their rulers and themselves now was explicit. But the goal remained a godly life lived in common, and rules of proper, godly conduct still were to be found in scripture as the ultimate evidence of God's will.

Codes of law from the colonial period well into this century enforced overtly religious rules. All states with the possible exception of Virginia required that public officials swear to their belief in God before taking public office; in five states such religious test oaths survived until the turn of the century. At the beginning of the Revolution nine states also required allegiance to a particular form of established religion and even burdened minority religions through unfavorable taxes and other laws.[10] Formally established religions were common, if varied, in the states well into the nineteenth century. Witnesses could not testify in many state courts without affirming their faith in God. Political struggles raged throughout the colonies and early states on the issue of religious establishment. The conflict was purely political, as churches were established or disestablished according to their political strength in the community.[11]

In daily morality as well, political institutions upheld religious rules. Courts routinely enforced laws against blasphemy and deviant sexual practices and upheld the marriage tie against most attempts to divorce or abandon one's spouse. At least as important, churches played a vital role in the community's public life. In addition to religious and social events, churches were entrusted with the community's charitable work. Religious organizations tended the sick, supported the poor and attempted to rehabilitate those who had fallen into bad or sinful ways.[12]

Religion was an integral part of daily life, and the people, whatever their failings, sought to uphold and live by its rules in their social, political, and private relations. As Harold Berman points out, even to speak of church and state, let alone the separation of the two, in early America is to mischaracterize the nature of public life in that era. The First Amendment speaks of "religion" and "Congress." Madison used the terms "religion" and "government" throughout his work on religious freedom. Jefferson's use of the phrase "a wall of separation between church and state," decades after the Founding, is highly atypical.

There was neither church nor state in early America as those terms currently are used. Even colonies and states with established churches granted minority religions a highly unusual degree of toleration for the times. They protected minorities' right to gather and worship when almost all nations made such minority practices illegal. There was no single established church in America but rather a variety of religious organizations and establishments. Further, America had no single "state." Instead it had a variety of governments at the city, county, state (or colonial), and later federal level. As John Noonan points out, "religious and governmental bodies not only coexist but overlap." And this was particularly true in early America. The individuals who made up the political as well as the social and religious community acted as both believers and wielders of power.[13]

Many.today profess horror at the restrictions on personal liberty entailed in early American religious practices. But such criticism ignores the roots of liberal philosophy. Liberalism builds on the traditional Christian understanding of the equality of all men in the sight of God. Locke derived man's inalienable rights to life, liberty, and property from his status as God's creation. Because each of us owes his life to God, Locke argued, only God can decide when we should die. Thus anyone who seeks to kill us or put us in his power such that he could kill us if he wished unjustly usurps God's role. He also breaks God's law if he takes what we have made our own through our labor—our use of our God-given capacities. Our individual efforts give us the right to particular pieces of property, but our capacities and even our selves are gifts from God to be protected out of deference to Him.[14]

The Judeo-Christian tradition teaches that each of us must answer to God for his own deeds, regardless of his riches or inherited station in life. The ideas of personal responsibility and God's ultimate enforcement of that responsibility are deeply ingrained in our culture. We inherit from our ancestors an attachment not merely to a particular liberal ideology but to a way of life and code of conduct that rest ultimately on religious belief and practice. The duty to care for one's own, to love one's neighbor, to refrain from theft, and so on have their roots, for Americans, in the Judeo-Christian tradition. The Bible historically has been the source of moral teaching for Americans and, as Galston notes, it is doubtful whether most Americans would glean the same lessons from philosophical treatises.

Even Bellah admits that all societies rest on "a common set of religious understandings that provide a picture of the universe in terms of which the [common set of] moral understandings make sense." Bellah also states that this set of understandings is the basis of our notions of good and bad, right and wrong.[15] No community can survive if its members do not share a basic vision of the order of the universe (for example, the belief that sins in this life will be punished in the next and common notions of what constitutes a sin).

Communitarians believe we can retain our social cohesion without its moral and religious basis, provided that intellectuals rear the masses in the proper *civil* religion. This assertion seems untenable. It rests on a highly exaggerated view of the power of words taken by themselves and on the belief that intellectuals can create new myths in the space of at most a few years or generations. But myths are not mere stories "got up" to convince the people to serve their masters. Myths grow and change over time precisely because they are a people's way of trying to understand truths that are beyond human knowledge.

Myths, particularly of the afterlife, have been with us longer than civilization itself. Men from all over the globe have sought to understand their place in the universe and in eternity since the childhood of the race. They continue to do so today, as the explosion of "near death experience" stories attests. Myths from Virgil's *Aeneid* to Dante's *Divine Comedy* help us understand our permanence. They explore the unchanging character of our souls and the circumstances we will encounter when we leave behind the shells of our bodies.[16]

It is popular among intellectuals to disdain these myths and to seek to construct better ones more suited to a life lived solely on this earth. But their success at building more humane societies on the basis of more strictly human myths has been nugatory. Man's search for meaning cannot be satisfied by peace and prosperity. And too much emphasis on these limited, if in no way improper, goals can lead to millenarian reaction (an undisciplined rush toward an unknown meaning) or to debilitating cynicism.

We can never sate our appetites for material pleasure. Thus to define justice as a "fair" distribution of material goods is to invite mass dissatisfaction and selfishness. It is to invite envy against those who have *any* more than we do without spawning the feelings of common affection that dampen such unsocial vices.

A political religion cannot hold a society together for long. But societies require public religious affirmation if they are to survive. Social cohesion and moral conduct both require that public institutions, including government, affirm religion. Public prayers, days of thanksgiving, and other once common religious observances solidified, sanctioned, and supported private belief. They also supported the private and social undertakings (charity chief among them) that bind a society together while teaching individuals the habits and customs of duty and decent, neighborly conduct.

The customs and ceremonies that bind a people together into one culture grow from the cult, from the beliefs and practices we share in our search for meaning in an ordered universe. If there is no order to the universe, if we as individuals must create our own meanings or accept those given to us by great leaders, then there is no intrinsic reason why we should pursue the good of anyone save ourselves. Only brute force is left to control men's appetites, and ordered liberty becomes impossible.[17]

Taylor is correct to point out that our moral lives changed as we changed the way we perceived the nature and role of conscience. Increasingly for intellectuals since the eighteenth century and more and more for everyone, conscience no longer is a faculty that allows us to determine what is right—how we must act to fulfill God's will as set down in permanent, natural laws like the Golden Rule. Conscience today is seen as an internal instinct or voice in each of us that naturally (that is, automatically) tells us what is right. This view necessarily leads to moral relativism because each of us *desires* to do many different things. And our desires and appetites, themselves "voices" speaking to us from within, obscure our view of natural law.

A hungry man will have more trouble following the commandment not to steal if theft is his only quick means to food. A man convinced that his appetites are by nature just may not even pause before stealing. His aversion to stealing is merely one passion among many, and one that often brings unpleasantness. We each have a conscience. But unless it points us outside ourselves, to a moral law that binds us in spite of our desires, conscience will lose its coherence and its commanding role in our lives, becoming just one impulse among many.

Liberalism at one time was explicitly religious. And Locke himself pointedly refused to argue for toleration of atheists. In his view atheists could not be trusted because they could not even properly take an oath. Not believing in God they had no entity before which to swear to tell the truth and no fear of heavenly reprisal for lying.

And Locke's view of atheists resonated during America's Founding era.[18] Jacob Rush argued in 1796 that the obligation of an oath depends on belief in a deity who abhors falsehood and will punish perjury. Further, oaths are necessary for the maintenance of peace and justice among men. Therefore "it clearly follows that a belief in the existence of God is necessary for the support of civil society. . . . Whatever therefore relaxes the religious sentiment upon which an oath is founded, is injurious to society; because it lessens the restraint which the belief of that salutary principle imposes upon the human mind."[19]

Also during the Founding era, Gad Hitchcock, for example, preached a sermon on the subject of Proverbs 29:2—"When the righteous are in authority, the people rejoice: but when the wicked beareth rule, the people mourn." Hitchcock encapsulated his view of the public official in a quotation from Saint Paul: "He is the minister of God to thee for good."

Atheists were by definition not righteous and so could not promote the public good. They even made it more difficult for the people to be righteous because they set bad examples and interfered with the propagation of God's word. Invectives against atheists were relatively rare because the closest thing to an atheist most commentators considered at all was the Deist, a man who believed in a divine creator but not in the divinity of Christ. It was the philosophical deist, overrepresented among America's Founders, who was the object of solicitous defense from some prominent Americans of the time and the charge of atheism from others.[20] But the Deist was defended on the grounds that he was no threat to the people's piety and virtue and thus their happiness.

Virtue, Happiness, and Good Government

Communitarians note that liberal democracy requires a certain set of virtues. The Founding generation was convinced that well-ordered liberty requires something more. True liberty in their view requires belief in transcendent standards of right and wrong; it requires religious faith. It requires that local associations constantly teach and reinforce God's universal laws. Only with these aids can the people lead good lives, following their God (itself the ultimate goal) and enjoying—as a kind of side benefit—earthly peace, independence, and contentment.

Americans believed that they needed virtuous rulers to keep them on the godly path. The Founding generation listened to and gave literally hundreds of election sermons aimed at reminding the people of how important the task of electing rulers was. Not only was voting an important right but its exercise was a great trust because a bad choice of rulers could ruin society.

A people that chose a ruler without virtue faced disaster. Daniel Shute argued that "vice is detrimental to society in some degree in *any* of its members, but is more so in *those* who manage the public affairs of it. It disqualifies for public service at the same rate, as it debases the mind, weakens the generous movements of the soul, and centres its views in the contracted circle of self-interest."[21] Hitchcock put it more succinctly: "The measures which rulers pursue, are generally good or bad, promotive of the public happiness, or the contrary, as are their moral characters."[22]

In order to serve the common good one must have a proper moral character, the virtuous habits that cause one to put the needs of one's fellows above one's own wants and desires. And a ruler would seek to serve the public only if he sought to serve God. As Samuel West put it, "If a man is not faithful to God and his own soul, how can we expect that he will be faithful to the public?" West continued:

> It certainly implies a very gross absurdity to suppose that those who are ordained of God for the public good should have no re-

gard to the laws of God, or that the ministers of God should be despisers of the divine commands. David, the man after God's own heart, makes piety a necessary qualification in a ruler: "He that ruleth over men (says he) must be just, ruling in the fear of God.". . . A people that have a right of choosing their magistrates are criminally guilty in the sight of Heaven when they are governed by caprice and humor, or are influenced by bribery to choose magistrates that are irreligious men, who are devoid of sentiment, and of bad morals and base lives.[23]

For early Americans the link between justice and fear of God was clear. Political and religious leaders who did not fear God would despise, corrupt, and oppress their followers. A people that chose such rulers deserved its fate.

Shute argued that each people's religious health by nature affects its social state. If the religious "state" is in ill health, the disease will be transmitted to the social state, causing vice and dissension.[24] The good governor recognizes that the social and religious states are linked. He seeks to promote the public welfare by saving the weak, seeing to it that all citizens follow and work at their vocations, seeing to it that proper, virtuous education is promoted, and of course supporting religion.[25]

Man learned how to act in large part through religious instruction. Worship also bound him to society. There was, then, a necessary and intimate connection between religious and human law. Human law was to be obeyed because this was God's will.[26] But precisely because religion was so central to the moral life of the community, only proper laws could be followed by righteous men. The purpose of law as of government itself was to support virtue and punish vice; laws that did the opposite must not be obeyed.[27] Good laws in some way promoted religion, religious education, and various forms of "social worship."[28]

Religious doctrine was not the sole means by which the people were taught virtue. Government promoted virtue through its laws against conspicuous consumption and by maintaining the well-ordered schools needed to form well-ordered character.[29] Early Americans learned virtue in a variety of local institutions. George Mason argued that republican government was based on an affection "for altars and firesides."[30]

Family as well as religious life, Mason's firesides as well as his al-tars, and the habits learned in both led men to recognize their du-ties.[31] Political, social, and religious life were interdependent. One must, on this view, defend liberty for the sake of one's family and fel-low citizens. One must recognize that without liberty, virtue and reli-gion would be lost.[32]

Early Americans valued liberty as an important element in a good and godly life. Men must *choose* to do what is right if they are to be truly virtuous; this was, after all, the reason they had been given free will. Of course, liberty did not mean license. Only men of decent habits would know how to choose as they ought. Men must be taught virtue within a system of well-ordered liberty. Government must support religion, but not take over its tutelary role.

Only if law protected and cooperated with religion could the so-cial state necessary for liberty and virtue be maintained. With this co-operation a good life for the people—a life that was happy because virtuous—could be attained. As Joseph Lathrop argued,

> Let rulers, influenced by the fear of God, and by love to mankind use all their power and authority to encourage righteousness, protect innocence, redress wrongs and banish iniquity; let laws be made with a single design to advance the general interest, and be executed with diligence and fidelity; let people, in all ranks, conscientiously discharge the duties of their respective stations; let justice and integrity take place in all private intercourse; let benevolence operate in all exigencies to excite mutual aid and succour, so that no man shall be miserable, while it is in his neighbour's power to relieve him; . . . let every man, in his pri-vate capacity, maintain sobriety, purity, temperance, industry and self-government, and attend more to the culture of his mind, the improvement of his virtue, and the regulation of the manners of his domesticks, than to the indulgence of pleasure or the accu-mulation of wealth; let this be the general spirit and conduct of mankind, and what will be wanting to make them as happy as the condition of mortals will permit, or as beings in a state of probation can reasonably desire?[33]

This is not just a call to treat one another well, although it clearly is that. It is also an exposition of the requirements for local virtue.

Lathrop sums up his argument as a call for "a general reform of manners."[34] Manners—the habits of social interaction—are formed in local associations and "stations"—economic and social positions. Men will form the necessary associations on their own, but because men are sinful these associations and the manners they teach may be corrupted, The state must help reform manners by upholding justice and maintaining the social order within which virtue is learned.

The Roots of Subsidiarity

Early Americans felt they owed duties to God, country, and particular groups. To fulfill these duties, in their view, one must be trained in various local associations—families, churches, and local communities. Only with such local training could one recognize one's duties to the country and ultimately even to God. Thus John Adams informed his wife that

> My Opinion of the duties of Religion and Morality comprehends a very extensive connection with society at large, and the great Interest of the public. Does not natural Morality, and much more Christian Benevolence, make it our indispensable Duty to lay ourselves out, to serve our fellow Creatures to the utmost of our Power, in promoting and supporting those great Political systems, and general Regulations upon which the Happiness of Multitudes depends. The Benevolence, Charity, Capacity and Industry which exerted in private Life, would make a family, a Parish or a Town Happy, employed upon a larger Scale, in Support of the great Principles of Virtue and Freedom of political Regulations might secure whole Nations and Generations from Misery, Want and Contempt.[35]

The practical virtues of benevolence, charity, capacity, and industry may be practiced in the most local of associations—families, parishes, and townships. But unlike the communitarians, Adams argued that individuals will not naturally exert their virtues on behalf of more distant and artificial political communities like the nation. Nations can elicit virtue from their citizens only by appealing to the great principles of virtue and liberty. And one learns to recognize and apply these principles only in one's natural, local associations.

This is not to say that early Americans saw politics as unnecessary or unnatural. As "The Preceptor" put it in 1772, man's God-
given nature was such that it "cannot be confined within the circuit of
a family, of friends or a neighborhood; it spreads into wider systems,
and draws man into larger confederacies, communities and common-
wealths. It is in these only, that the higher powers of our nature attain
the highest improvement of which they are capable."[36] What is more,
as Daniel Shute argued, without government man's natural tendency
toward sin would remain unchecked and create constant war.[37]

One pamphleteer, "Americanus," argued that social compacts
must deal with men per se and also men as their characters are
molded by their stations in life. Society and the legislature in particular must respect the individual's rights in regard to both his abstract
nature and his "second," socially formed nature.[38]

To say that men should be treated differently, according to their
station in society is not to deny that each of us is equal in the sight of
God. But such diversity of treatment denies that the communitarian
call for equality of condition is just.

All abstract rights may call into question the classical/Judeo-
Christian view that nature and society are one and the same. But for
early Americans, while all just governments protect men's lives, liberties, and property, men naturally are social and differ widely in their
capacities. Society shapes them into different beings with different
specific rights and duties. Samuel Williams, for example, argued that
equality demands that we respect only "natural" distinctions. But for
him such natural distinctions are many and produce distinct classes;
classes with their own rights and responsibilities.[39]

Abraham Williams observed that

> As in the natural Body, the several Members have their distinct
> Offices, for which they are adapted, and when in their proper
> Order, they perform their natural Functions, the body is in its
> most perfect State; so in the politic Body, when its several Orders
> attend to their respective Duties, proper to their Rank; the Wel-
> fare of the whole Community, and of every Individual, is secured
> and promoted.[40]

The Founding generation did not wish to create a homogeneous,
fundamentally political community. Early Americans believed that

human differences and eternal standards of right and wrong demand differences in social status. One's status should vary according to one's performance in a number of areas of life. For example, a rich man who neglected his duty to care for his poor relatives would be thought ungodly.

Americans had a variety of attachments and obligations. Indeed, they formed a variety of peoples. The colonists held that they had the capacity and even the duty to form separate peoples when dictated by circumstances such as isolation or oppression. Depending on the circumstances, the "people" might be a group much smaller than all Americans. One early American author, going by the name "Monitor," argued that New England had its own constitution and its own people.[41] A number of revolutionary writers defined "people" as the inhabitants of a given colony, with whom George III either had broken faith or over whom he had never had legitimate dominion.[42]

The fundamental unit of society was the "people." But the people was a rather amorphous unit, combining or separating depending on the context and circumstances. Inhabitants of a town, county, state, colony, or nation might be called a people to emphasize their distinct society and manners. In the same way, Americans often referred to their county, colony, or state as their "country," thereby highlighting the inherent ambiguity of that geographical term but also highlighting the unique characteristics of their locale. Americans joined together in a variety of places and communities, from church to local community to colony to nation. All of these communities had their own customs and shaped their members into various peoples.[43]

Because each had its own distinct ways of doing things, peoples could overlap in various ways but also could come into conflicts, some of which might require explicit separation. As the people of America found it necessary to separate from the people of Great Britain, so the people of one state or even one county might find it necessary to separate from another. This was just, provided it was done in the proper manner.[44] All associations, whether of individuals (for example, partners in a business) or of peoples (for example, the British empire) had specific purposes. If the association was no longer serving its purpose or if its leaders were acting incorrigibly outside their scope of proper authority, the association should be dissolved.

Further, as men become less attached to one another because they are less intimately involved with one another's day-to-day activities, legitimate power becomes more narrow in scope. Samuel West noted that given the diversity of manners, it was miraculous that the colonies joined to fight for independence. And local diversity showed, for West, that the national community formed by the Revolution had very limited purposes.[45]

Men naturally engage most constantly and fully in the activities of their most local associations. We are most attached to our families, then associations like our church or local club. Our ties to larger organizations and the nation in particular stem from our more local attachments. Early Americans loved their nation because it protected every man under his own vine and fig tree, leading his life of local involvement and felicity.

True Localism and the Interests of Politics

"The Impartial Examiner" argued in 1788 that each of the states constituted its own separate society, with its own unique interests, needs, and circumstances. To rule or even tax all the states in the same way would constitute oppression. Local laws, on this view, must vary to fit local circumstances. And local circumstances vary greatly, not least because over time they produce a variety of local customs and habits.[46]

British policy had encouraged localism in America from the start. As Lutz observes,

> The typical colonial charter, beginning with the first, . . . left the design for local government to the settlers, so long as local law was not contrary to the laws of England. . . . the grant of local control, the impossibility of running any colony from London given the distance involved, and the preoccupation in England with the English Civil War gave the settlers considerable latitude in running their own affairs. The legal situation, geography, and the perilous circumstances led each colony to move quickly to secure the cooperation of everyone in the community, and this was naturally accomplished in small communities by meeting together regularly to plan and make collective decisions. Town or colony meetings were often a regular event before any foundation document was written and approved.[47]

From the beginning Americans relied on fellow members of their local communities for their very survival. Working together they came to trust and feel loyalty toward one another and to their community as a whole. Local control was necessary at the start and soon became habitual. And this habit was deep and long-lived. The Constitution itself mentions the states either directly or indirectly over fifty times. As Lutz notes: "The United States constitution, as a complete foundational document, includes the state constitutions as well. We operate under a constitutional *system*, in the sense of an interlocking set of constitutions."[48]

The Founders recognized that the people were most loyal to their own communities and states rather than to what James Wilson called the newly created "system of republicks." Adams and Jefferson echoed Wilson's view and his concern to protect what Jefferson called America's "little republics."[49] Men on both sides of the ratification debates sought to construct a system that would make the best of man's natural, local attachments and bring America's republics together into a more perfect association without consolidating them into one all-powerful central government.

Herbert J. Storing perhaps captured best the Founding's central issue: Did the new structure strengthen federal authority so much that it destroyed the federal principle?[50] Both sides argued for a federal form of government, one in which the states would delegate certain powers to a national government.[51] The debate concerned whether the Constitution gave the central government so much power that the states would no longer be able to defend themselves against the encroachments of federal politicians intent on extending their power beyond its proper bounds.[52]

Federal thinking was deeply ingrained among Americans before the break with Britain. Shute, for example, defined Britain's empire as a federation. Particular states would form their own societies and laws, bowing to the central authority only as far as was consistent with their inherited rights.[53]

The township was the center of life and font of virtue; the federal government would be merely a mechanism for protecting townships from outside forces and certain internal ills. Because its powers and functions were to be limited to issues of foreign policy, interstate transactions, coinage, and the like, the federal government would not be the source of human virtue. Further, because it was so distant from the everyday activities and attachments of the people, it was not designed to be entirely dependent on human virtue. The Founders set up a system of "mechanical" checks and balances because they recognized that the central power they were creating was derivative and artificial.[54]

The federal Constitution was constructed to deal with a fundamental dilemma of political and social life: each of us has conflicting loyalties—to ourselves, our local groups, and the natural law that tells us to pursue the common good. Publius argued that the Constitution's extensive republic would make it more likely that public-minded men, those with "fit characters," would be elected to office. The Constitution's system of representation would "refine and enlarge the public views by passing them through the medium of a chosen body of citizens, whose wisdom may best discern the true interest of their country and whose patriotism and love of justice will be least likely to sacrifice it to temporary or partial considerations."[55]

The constitutional system would bring together those most likely to pursue the public interest. It also would provide mechanical checks and balanced avenues of self-interest to block would-be tyrants. The "double security" provided by the partition of the legislature into two branches—each watching over the other as the executive watched over both—would protect the rights of each branch, and of any minority that might be the object of schemes of oppression.[56]

More important, the inherent variety of differing local customs, interests, and loyalties would prevent any legislative majority from forming around any scheme of oppression. According to Publius, "In the extended republic of the United States, and among the great variety of interests, parties, and sects which it embraces, a coalition of a majority of the whole society could seldom take place on any other principles than those of justice and the general good."[57] This is not a mere statement of political mechanics. It is an assertion that something happens within the various interests and "sects" in America that renders their representatives capable of pursuing justice and the general good. It is an assertion that virtue is possible precisely because each of us belongs to associations more local and more primary than the federal government. Where communitarians insist virtue is possible only among those committed to universal social justice, for early Americans virtue was the product of local attachments and the habits formed in local communities.

The constitutional system balanced men's various interests and associations against one another, but also respected their rights and encouraged them to cooperate for the common good. Its drafters recognized that each of us holds a variety of interests and loyalties that cannot be destroyed without destroying liberty itself.[58] They sought to make our baser natures, our ambitions, counteract one another so that our higher nature, led by our moral sense and formed into the habits of virtue, could lead us to the common good.

American Virtue in Action

Many critics dismiss the early American vision of the good life because Americans of that era mistreated particular individuals and groups. They point to slavery and the lack of modern women's rights as particularly heinous crimes, irreversibly damning our Founding as they damn Western (though for some reason no other) civilization. Early in this work I pointed out my own misgiving that the Founders placed too much faith in man's natural sociability. I might have added that Americans quickly came to assume, wrongly in my view, that religion can carry on its role of teaching manners and duties to the people with little or no aid from government or society.

But in most circumstances the Founders' system allowed for the ultimate protection of liberty—freedom to leave uncomfortable social and political surroundings to form a new people. It also allowed for the extension of rights to minority groups, provided there was social consensus for such changes. Today by contrast we seem incapable of constructing a consensus on anything save perhaps the desirability of virtually contentless virtues like tolerance. Today we face massive social breakdown and the crumbling of our way of life in the face of illegitimacy, crime, and a general loss of moral bearings.

One source of our troubles is the fact that we define tolerance so broadly that it requires a public square emptied of "intolerant" religious and moral forces. The result is intolerance toward those who would harness religion for the social good or, more properly, serve their God in part by aiding those in need. In *The Tragedy of American Compassion*, Marvin Olasky shows the vital role once played by America's churches and religious folk in tending the needs of the poor and helping those on assistance develop the habits of industry and self-reliance required for economic success. He also details the means by which churches, local organizations, and their former partners in government came to rely solely on bureaucratized and largely political schemes of poor relief, to everyone's impoverishment. The mistaken notion that religious belief is the source of intolerance combined around the turn of the century with a millenarian zeal to use government to "solve" poverty. Government redistribution of money replaced face-to-face charity. The poor were abandoned to the care of faceless bureaucracies, and local virtue decayed.

Poverty is not new in America, nor are illegitimacy and other social problems that often accompany it. But America had no separate "underclass" in the eighteenth, nineteenth, and much of the twentieth century because the poor were treated as members of local communities. We did not have illegitimacy rates of 80 percent in our inner cities as we do today.[59] We did not suffer from these extreme conditions in large measure because we did not have the kinds of inner cities we have today—rigidly separated by income, cut off from other neighborhoods, and inhabited by thugs, with atomized individuals and single mothers serving as their virtual hostages.[60] We had poor neighborhoods, often separated by ethnic rivalry. But we did not abandon our poor to the debilitating ministrations of bureaucratic organizations more concerned to protect their own status and prerogatives than to help families and individuals out of destitution.

Americans of earlier eras did not leave it to their government to support the poor by redistributing money. Instead they voluntarily supported and/or participated in an extensive network of neighborhood organizations that provided assistance through face-to-face contacts and moral education. They saw it as their religious duty to be their brother's keeper. They did not merely give him money and tolerate (that is, ignore) his choice of lifestyle. Instead they sought to reform his habits and spirit where necessary to make him independent of charity in the future. They recognized that economic dependence breeds irresponsible conduct and also that escape from dependence requires adherence to certain objective standards of behavior, like hard work and honesty. Perhaps most important, they recognized that we will habitually live up to these standards only if we think it is morally as well as economically necessary to do so.

Led by their ministers, Americans of moderate to comfortable means founded private charity banks and insurance companies to loan money and pool resources for the working poor. Often receiving local and state government funding, these organizations generally were based in the local neighborhood. Whether providing insurance, work, or homes for orphans, charity workers relied on coalitions of prominent citizens and politicians to organize and carry out their work.[61]

Politicians by and large sought to protect this system from state interference. In 1854 President Franklin Pierce vetoed a bill that would have provided for federal construction and maintenance of mental hospitals. He did so because he feared the precedent would encourage construction of a full-scale federal welfare system. Such a system, in his view, would harm the needy by discouraging local charity. "Should this bill become a law, that Congress is to make provision for such objects, the foundations of charity will be dried up at home."[62]

This is not to say that government did not take part in providing charity, but the emphasis was on bonding those in need of aid to their families, religions, and ethnic groups. Those applying for aid typically were asked if they had relatives on whom to call for help. If they did, the local charity organization would, if necessary, contact the relative to apprise him of the situation, and that relative was expected to provide the needed support. As late as 1937, two-thirds of the states required that relatives with sufficient resources support those in need of charity or face prosecution.[63] Thus government worked to support community values including family solidarity. Religious and ethnic groups also aided those in need, and charitable organizations actively encouraged this reliance on "one's own" by putting aid applicants in touch with the appropriate ethnic or religious organization.[64]

Instead of giving aid directly to those in need of assistance, government bodies reimbursed volunteers and organizations who took on the actual charity work. Traditions of hospitality and charity have roots in America going back to the Puritans, who honored local townspeople for taking in orphans and others in need. But the expenses of such care would likely as not be taken care of through reimbursements from the town council, the county, or even the colonial and later state government.[65]

Some Americans worried that caregivers would become insensitive to their wards and come to value them only for the extra income tending to them would bring in. But the rewards were slight and the work hard. Further, by dealing frequently and intimately with their wards, caregivers developed affection and a sense of mutual interests with them. One charity leader argued that taking in and *suffering with* a child from the slums should not be economically draining since it was already emotionally draining: "Habits are patiently corrected, faults without number are born with, time and money are expended [out of] a noble self-sacrifice for an unfortunate fellow-creature."[66]

Volunteers were honored more for their time and effort than for their financial sacrifices. And aid recipients also were expected to work hard, as well as show gratitude for aid received. Benjamin Franklin opposed cash payments to the poor because he observed that such a system in Britain made them "idle, dissolute, drunken and insolent." Famous abolitionist journalist Horace Greeley campaigned in the mid-nineteenth century for more openhanded charity and came to regret it. The soup kitchens and other forms of mass-delivered charity his reforms brought to New York City produced, in his view, "chronic beggars" and "thriftless vagabonds." Greeley's experience showed him that "the poor often suffer from poverty, I know; but oftener from lack of capacity, skill, management, efficiency, than lack of money."[67]

Somewhat late Greeley came to accept the basic assumptions of American charity relief: first, the aid giver must be careful to instill proper character in his charges, and second, this is done most effectively through a combination of religious dogma and practical training in an intimate atmosphere. As one charity organization put it, "Until the feelings, opinions, and practices of the great mass are governed by sound principles, and Christianity pervades and renovates the habits of social and civil life, there is no reliable foundation for prosperity." Jewish groups also were a part of the nexus of charitable organizations, and the common message was clear: religious belief is necessary for moral practices, which in turn are necessary for economic independence.

Early American charity rested on the conviction that "the best politics and the most complete form of government are nothing if the individual morality be not there." And individual morality was seen as having a theological base.[68] Both caregivers and aid recipients would have to work hard to live up to these theological standards and put their morality into action. As one minister told his congregation:

To cast a contribution into the box brought to the hand, or to attend committees and anniversaries, are very trifling exercises of Christian self-denial and devotion, compared with what is demanded in the weary perambulations through the street, the contact with filth, and often with rude and repulsive people, the facing of disease, and distress, and all manner of heart-rending and heart-frightening scenes, and all the trials of faith, patience, and hope, which are incident to the duty we urge.[69]

Aid recipients, for their part, had to work if they were able or be sent away. They were subjected to persistent sermons, lectures, and manual labor. But all this was provided by caregivers they came to know on a personal basis, who frequently visited them in their homes and who quite intentionally bonded with them as individuals and families.

Churchmen in particular insisted on personal care-giving. Even the earliest forms of bureaucratic relief (massive soup kitchens and the like) produced "a dependent feeling, a dry rot, which leads the recipient of city bounty to look upon it as something due as a reward for destitution." Charity workers sought to prevent this dependence by relying on face-to-face contacts and a work ethic they found grounded in scripture. As Olasky puts it, in the late nineteenth century

Christians observed that Jesus neither abandoned the needy nor fed them immediately—instead, He taught them. (In Matthew 15, Jesus feeds thousands after they have listened to Him for three days. In Mark 6, Jesus first teaches—"He had compassion on them, because they were like sheep without a shepherd"— and only late in the day multiplies five loaves and two fish, so all eat and are satisfied.)[70]

Religion motivated charity work and gave it its early character. Charity workers sought to emulate Christ (or follow the dictates of the Torah) by serving others and teaching them proper faith and morals. They sought to reform individuals, teaching them to follow an objective standard of conduct to which all must conform if they are to lead good lives. Charity workers, their wards and in the end America's neighborhoods and towns drew strength from a religious vision that provided constant standards of conduct and showed the way to a meaningful life as individuals and as productive members of communities.

Virtue's Decline

The first serious challenge to the American charitable vision was developed by utilitarian economists and sociologists now generally called "social Darwinists." In fact this label is misleading because even Herbert Spencer, perhaps the most biologically minded of these thinkers, did not use Darwinian catchphrases like "natural selection" or "survival of the fittest." So-called social Darwinists in fact were rather old-fashioned liberals who were particularly enamored of scientific arguments. They argued that the automatic processes of the free market alone could produce progress and prosperity. Thus charity, and especially mass charity, was counterproductive and even cruel because it encouraged the biologically inferior and economically doomed (the poor) to procreate, thereby burdening us all.

The social Darwinists argued against charity on the grounds that it produced more paupers than it elevated to the working or middle classes. But their answer to this dilemma—elimination of all forms of charity—produced a fierce counterreaction, the effects of which we still feel today. Social Darwinists appealed to market forces and other impersonal powers and structures as the final judges of right and wrong conduct. They defended irreligious, even vicious behavior so long as it produced increases in overall material well-being. They were confident that economic forces would reward and punish efficiently enough to produce material well-being, and that wealth in turn would produce moral progress. Praising faceless economic processes and ignoring virtue, social Darwinists undermined the religious vision of man and society on which the Judeo-Christian vision of charity in America relied.[71]

Many charity workers continued their struggle to reform the poor. They called for a return to neighborhood charity, workhouses, and other forms of face-to-face care-giving. But many others seized on social Darwinism as the means to put forward a different vision of reform and charity work. Building on the scientific theories of social Darwinism, member of the new "Social Gospel" movement in the late nineteenth century argued that it was, indeed, true that the poor could not be reformed through face-to-face charity work. But the answer, for them, was not the elimination of all forms of charity. Instead the answer lay in a radical restructuring of American economics and society.

Social Gospelers reinterpreted Christian teaching, dropping its demand for spiritual education and calling for a millenarian quest to eliminate poverty and all forms of social injustice. These activists demanded "philanthropy of governments" or rather "coercive philanthropy" to "establish among us true cities of God." Poverty would be eliminated not by reforming the character of the poor but by using government to reform the structures of society. As Olasky puts it, "Their faith was clear: the only reason some people did not work was that they were kept from working, and the only reason some lied about their needs was that they were forced to lie."[72]

Social Gospelers called unjust older mechanisms like the "work test" whereby only those willing to do manual labor, if able, were given aid. Aid workers began to ask, "Who are we to judge" the morality of aid recipients? More and more the religious element of charity became an embarrassment to those who gave the care.

And caregivers increasingly came to be professionals, trained by Social Gospelers to provide nonjudgmental aid to the poor while working though the political system to eliminate capitalism and all other forces they believed created poverty.[73] Neighborhoods no longer were the centers of charitable activity or loyalty. And the nation came to take on the churches' roles as caregivers and the sources of religious awe. As one prominent Social Gospeler observed, "When we think of [the nation] as becoming, as it must do more and more, the object of mental regard, of admiration, of love, even of worship (for in it preeminently God dwells) we shall recognize to the fullest extent its religious character and functions."[74]

The nation, on this view, was the source of material progress. Because men are naturally good and act badly only because of material deprivation, material progress would produce moral progress. This made government the ultimate source of moral improvement. Thus compassion came to consist of tolerating bad behavior until social and economic conditions could be put right and man's nature thereby improved.[75]

"Human improveableness," in the words of Social Gospeler

Owen Lovejoy, became the new creed around the turn of the century. And the phrase grew in power and influence. Social engineers came to dominate among social workers and replaced those who once gave voluntarily of their time and effort in the name of God. God Himself was reduced to a social force for the new caregivers. Lovejoy appealed to an "invisible church" that he defined as that "bond of union among congenial spirits which under whatever name is bound to work itself out in those cooperative activities of the human race." He referred to the "apostolic succession"—the followers of Christ—as all those who are "keen in the service of humanity."[76]

The Social Gospel movement was millenarian. Its members sought to bring God's reign down to earth by reconstructing society to make it more "fair." They thought they could improve man's very nature by increasing his material well-being through the engine of government. In the process Social Gospelers reduced God to a servant of the social engineer. Small wonder, then, that when faced with the extreme crises of the Great Depression, private charity already was too weak to do much good, and the bureaucratic structure set up to deal with the emergency quickly became an accepted part of the political and social landscape.

Once policymakers saw "the system" as the root cause of poverty, moral education became obsolete. Charity work then became the organized giving of money and goods to the poor. Government promised to distribute this aid more efficiently and effectively than the already bureaucratized but haphazard charity system that had developed by the 1930s. We already had given up on the values that made bureaucratized charity seem detrimental. It was only a matter of time until the Great Society would do away with the last vestiges of work requirements and other merit-based rules intended to improve the characters of aid recipients.

Institutions of Faith and Community

Olasky points to a series of factors that helped charity workers in the nineteenth century see some success in their efforts. Poverty was not and could not be eliminated because those saved from poverty would be replaced by new arrivals, youths with bad habits or those who had fallen or refallen into bad habits. But charity workers continued to work and to see success every time they turned an aid recipient into an independent, working member of society. How was this done? Through a combination of tactics intended to foster personal and community bonding, habits of hard work and independence and an unabashed emphasis on religious faith.

In particular, the emphasis on faith steeled caregivers to their clients, encouraging them to follow biblical examples and live with and care for their wards—but only after they had turned away from sin. Those who showed a desire to live by alms rather than work their way out of poverty were shunned. Those who persisted in bad habits like drunkenness, gambling, and so on also were shunned. Only those willing to work with their caregiver to aid themselves would continue to receive help. Economic incentives combined with the threat of the humiliation of being cast out even from the almshouse motivated the poor to pull themselves out of their predicaments.[77]

Until recently the public dole, and even private charity, was considered shameful. Today we hear of the "humiliation" of low-paying, low-skilled labor and the need to "preserve the dignity" of those on public assistance. This reversal of shame has theological as well as philosophical roots. Where once men believed they served God by caring for their families, neighbors, and communities, today we seek to fulfill ourselves by controlling our own lives.

The "humiliation" of a low-paying job arises from its involuntariness. No one, we believe, would actually choose to shine shoes. The work is too unpleasant, the lifestyle it affords too confined. Thus to shine shoes is demeaning. By the same token, demanding government entitlements to support one's authentic lifestyle is said to show moral courage.

But if lifestyle and authenticity are not the proper goals of life, if decency and duty better capture the means to a good life, then we should honor the shoe-shiner more than the youth who depends on public money to finance his lifestyle. Unfortunately this choice will mean little to the man who shines shoes if he believes all he can look forward to is poverty, social disdain, and an early death followed by nothing. Civil religion builds on one central truth of the human condition: we require the holy in our lives if they are to have meaning. We can accept the inevitable pain, suffering, and defeat that is life only if we commit ourselves to something beyond it. Philosophers may find that something in their own words and theories, but most of us need something more concrete, something that promises to give our life meaning. And those who believe that man has a definite nature would argue that man's need for the holy is one important proof that the holy is real, is transcendent, and is the ultimate goal of life.

Religion may be "the opiate of the masses" in the sense that it helps them deal with the inevitable tragedies of life. But one might say the same of most philosophies—they are attempts to make sense of our lives and of the world in which we live. If it is coherent, a philosophy is ultimately theological; it attempts to explain the universe and our place in it. What religion adds to this is the recognition that universal order is divine; that there are rules we all must follow lest we endanger our society and impoverish our souls.

Natural Law, Natural Attachments, and Community

In early America social life was based not on mere calculating reason but on man's natural moral sense; a sense leading men to seek the good of their neighbors and their community. Not only Jefferson but many writers in America accepted the view of Francis Hutcheson and other Scottish enlightenment thinkers that there is a natural law meant to guide human actions which is ascertainable not by mere reason but by an instinctive "moral sense."[78] James Wilson argued that we need precisely this moral sense or "sentiment" if we are properly to praise or blame anyone for anything.[79]

Thus when Joseph Lathrop observed that "there is nothing more evident from reason, revelation and common experience, than the tendency of virtue to the happiness, and the tendency of vice to the misery of mankind, both in private and social life,"[80] he restated common American assumptions concerning the nature and relevance of natural law. Reason was one, but only one, tool in the constant attempt to divine the will of the creator. Also important in this task were "revelation"—a nonrational faith in the Word of God—and "common experience"—a prudent reading of the character of human experience. Both these latter faculties, faith and prudence, bespeak an instinctive recognition of the nature of things (as willed by "nature's God"). Both indicate that man's instinctive sense of what is moral will guide him to proper conduct.

This is not a treatise on natural law. But it should be clear that these men were not calling on us to follow merely some voice inside of us, secure in the knowledge that whatever we will will be right. Instead they called on us to truly listen to our inner instincts and to work, through faith, science, and prudence, to learn what we should do.

When communitarians call on us to fulfill ourselves they unwittingly invite us to lose ourselves to the passions and appetites that too often rule even the most rationally minded. Pride is the particular vice of intellectuals, and it is one that is particularly damaging to the traditions that hold communities together. Those who would ignore our natural limits, and in particular our need for the guidance of faith and custom, undermine the mutual accommodation and acceptance on which mutual affection relies. They sap the sources of the communal feelings they crave.

Wills's great rhetorical leader cannot replace God. He cannot provide enduring standards of conduct because he is only too human—fallible and likely to change his opinions over time. He cannot lead a free people.[81] In the end he must either bow to their opinions or force them to bow to his. And the more he seeks to reshape them in his own image, to reengineer them into good communitarians, the more socially adrift and vice-ridden they will become.

Communities exist because they have a purpose. If government takes over their function, communities will expire. If government takes over the role of charity—if we come to think with Cuomo that we "as a *government*" must be our brother's keeper—then the Golden Rule, the admonition to love one's neighbor as oneself, easily can be reduced to the paying of taxes. "I pay half my salary to the government," it might be (and often is) said, "so why should I deny myself leisure and luxuries to take care of others, such as the homeless? That's the government's job."

The family itself exists because it has a purpose: to conceive and form the characters of children so that they will become good and virtuous adults. Seen in this light, the government funding on which Cuomo says families depend actually may harm them because it ensures that family members no longer need one another. Of course even good families may need a helping hand at times. But when the government replaces, as it in large part has, the personal charity of church, extended family, and neighborhood, our natural sense of responsibility and obligation is dulled. Financial support becomes a "right" instead of a debt to be repaid with efforts toward personal and financial responsibility.

Many of us no longer feel that we need our families because we now look to the state for support. We even consider religious charity demeaning because it entails moral obligations of gratitude and efforts to be worthy of a voluntary gift. Small wonder we come to fear our neighbors as we lose our attachment to our families and even our churches. Mutual need and the corresponding recognition of mutual obligation among our fellows disappears as we come to see the state as the source of all that is good and necessary. After all, can the state not take care of us and teach us and our children all we really need to know—about money, about sex, and between these two about all that is important in life?

By fostering this kind of reasoning, bureaucratic charity kills virtue and kills the communities in which good lives are led. It reduces mutual obligation and affection to a contest of political power between interests, perhaps even between champions of rich and poor. It turns neighborhoods into ghettos beset by selfishness, greed, and violence.

We learn to treat our neighbors well by interacting with them. The personal attachments from which thinking acts of virtue grow, from which we learn habits of mutual dependence, accommodation, and affection, are not political. They are, in fact, "selfish" if one deems the work of mankind to be the "perfection" of God's creation through political means.

Politics may need to take on many of the aspects of family and religious life, but it is not the ultimate source of goodness, let alone religious principle. Perhaps the greatest blessing of liberty is that it leaves room for the private and social institutions that shape our character and our life together. As Tocqueville noted 150 years ago, liberty in America has been a great benefit to spiritual life and to the formation of virtue:

> The free institutions of the United States and the political rights
> enjoyed there provide a thousand continual reminders to every
> citizen that he lives in society. At every moment they bring his
> mind back to this idea, that it is the duty as well as the interest of
> men to be useful to their fellows. . . . At first it is of necessity
> that men attend to the public interest, afterward by choice. By

dint of working for the good of his fellow citizens, he in the end acquires a habit and taste for serving them.[82]

Free to form their own attachments without state interference, Americans in earlier times sought to serve those they knew and loved, to do unto others as they would have done unto them. In part the motivation for such virtue was practical—it is unwise to cheat one's neighbor. But this fact of practical life always has been recognized as a blessing because it helps us recognize our duty, leads us to act rightly, and allows us to learn through experience that it is both pleasant and good to do so. In this way we learn the habits of virtue. In this way we form communities.

Before he can have freedom man must have order. He must have a place in his family, in his community, and in the universe. Freedom itself is empty. It means merely a lack of constraints. But well-ordered liberty constitutes a way of life; one deeply embedded in our culture; one to which our community habitually was attached.

We cannot construct or reconstruct communities in the space of a few years or even generations. The tragedy of our current social breakdown is that what took only a few years to destroy will takes centuries to rebuild. And the advent of mass culture, which denigrates and even attacks the local attachments necessary for the formation of good character, may make recovery all but impossible.

Communities in the end are, as Aristotle said, based on friendship. We need not love everyone with whom we come in contact even on a daily basis. But there must be that mutual trust that comes only from shared expectations of one another. And these expectations do not come from the pen of the intellectual. They come from the traditions of the people; they grow over time in the course of human interaction in our families, churches, and local associations.

Standards do not, however, come about "dialogically." There are standards by which we all must abide, and the list includes more than Etzioni's rule of nondiscrimination. Cultures share in common a demand that we love our own and show, where possible, kindness and magnanimity to strangers. Cultures also share the demand that we join in worshipping the divine presence that orders the universe and gives meaning to our lives.

Only when we share the same general moral vision can we maintain our trust for one another and thereby our community. To argue, then, that we may "outgrow" the centuries-old civilization that gave birth to our nation and its culture is to dabble in intellectual delusions. Better, then, to look to our own past to recapture our lost sense of community and the lost sense of the holy that once supported it.

America always has made room for those who want to join in a life of well-ordered liberty. Indeed the country's strictly *political* creed—the list of political propositions one must accept in order to be a "true" American—is too thin and shallow to maintain any cohesive community. Tolerance and civility form the heart of this creed. But they are possible only as habituated expressions of mutual respect among full and active religious and ethnic communities. There is room for great diversity among America's towns and neighborhoods, but our social fabric will tear if bereft of local and religious ties.

America has tolerated great differences in cultural background and made room for many different forms of life. The nation even allows certain peoples, like the Old Order Amish, to opt out of much of public life. But there are limits to this tolerance. Few Americans, for example, are willing to tolerate polygamy on a large scale. The Supreme Court rejected the practice a hundred years ago as a violation of our most basic religious and cultural beliefs. Some of those beliefs have changed, but today as we fight to keep our families alive, few Americans argue that we must stretch the definition of "family" to include polygamy.

Words do not have the power communitarians ascribe to them. We are as much creatures of habit and passion as of intellect. Even if the intellectual classes change a word's definition or attempt to kill it altogether, the concept will remain—if only the practice remains. Virtue never died, despite the disuse of the word, because it never died as a practice—it merely was transformed into "decency," "civility," and other terms for still existing conduct in accord with the Golden Rule.

However, beliefs have great power. If we come to believe that polygamy is good, we will begin practicing it and our civilization will change. Likewise, if we come to believe we can mold our own characters, shape our own destinies, and even change reality through the clever use of language, we will become enamored of our own skills and lose respect for God, parental authority, and tradition. These latter three forces largely shape our character. But if we believe only in the power of ourselves and our language we will come to ignore them. Then the institutions through which God, parental authority, and tradition shape our character—church, family, and local association—will fall into disorder. The result: our society and our very souls also will become disordered, all because we came to believe that we needed no authority outside our own wills to guide us.

Pride always has been man's greatest sin, and it always has brought disaster. To accept our limits, then, is not to pursue despair. It is rather to value the goods we may enjoy over those that, however perfect in theory, lie outside our reach. It is the beginning of maturity and the basis for the hope that by seeing the fragility of virtue, society, and even our neighbor, we may learn to be kinder to all three.

Notes

Introduction

1. Remarks delivered November 13, 1993, by President Clinton at Masonic Temple, Memphis, Tennessee.

2. Liz Carpenter Lectureship series, April 6, 1993, University of Texas, Austin, Texas.

3. William J. Bennett, *The Index of Leading Cultural Indicators: Facts and Figures on the State of American Society* (New York: Simon and Schuster, 1994).

4. The figures are from the Department of Health and Human Services and Lynne A. Wardle, "No-Fault Divorce and the Divorce Conundrum," *Brigham Young Law Review* 79 (1991): 139–42, 97, 107. On the causal link between liberalized divorce law and increasing rates of divorce see, for example, Thomas B. Marvell, "Divorce Rates and the Fault Requirement," *Law and Society Review* 23 (1989): 543, 546. For a more complete discussion of the relationship between liberalized expectations, liberal legislation, and family breakdown see Bruce Frohnen, "The End of the Family?" in Peter Augustine Lawler and Robert Martin Schaefer, eds., *The American Experiment: Essays on the Theory and Practice of Liberty* (Savage, MD: Rowman and Littlefield, 1994), 401–15.

5. Lenore Weitzman, *The Divorce Revolution* (New York: Free Press, 1985), 337–39.

6. Barbara Dafoe Whitehead, "Dan Quayle Way Right," *Atlantic Monthly* (April 1993): 47–84.

7. This is the title of the Introduction in Amitai Etzioni, *The Spirit of Community: Rights, Responsibilities, and the Communitarian Agenda* (New York: Crown, 1993).

8. The decision to exclude MacIntyre and Nisbet from this discussion goes against the weight of the literature on communitarianism. See, for example, Daniel Bell, *Communitarianism and Its Critics* (Oxford: Oxford University Press, 1994),

237

and Derek Phillips, *Looking Backward: A Critical Appraisal of Communitarian Thought* (Princeton: Princeton University Press, 1993).

Most critics focus on the communitarian critique of liberal individualism. They emphasize recent communitarian opposition to self-absorbed materialism and the economic and political structures that encourage it. But conservative "communitarian" criticism of the atomizing influences of individualism dates back many decades (Nisbet traces it at least as far back as the French conservative reaction to the French Revolution). And conservative criticism of individualism rests on reverence for tradition and for a variety of local communities and associations, most of which do not live up to "new" communitarian demands concerning commitment to democracy and individual rights.

It is futile to attempt to "save" the term communitarian for thinkers like Nisbet and MacIntyre. These men should in any event be comfortable enough with labels like conservative and traditionalist. Instead we must attempt to understand just what the term communitarian has come to mean in the hands of its new masters.

9. This and all other references to the communitarian platform can be found in the Appendix in Etzioni, *The Spirit of Community.*

10. Ibid., 109: "Nobody considers it moral to abuse children, rape, steal (not to mention commit murder), be disrespectful of others, discriminate, and so on and on." Note also that these duties are phrased in the negative—we have duties *not* to abuse children.

11. John Adams, "Letter to the Officers of the Guilford Regiment of Militia," in Adams, *Works* (Boston: Little, Brown, 1854), 9:229.

Chapter One. A Liberal Community?

1. Karl Marx, *Theses on Feuerbach,* in *The Marx-Engels Reader,* ed. Robert C. Tucker (New York: Norton, 1978), 145; emphasis in original.

2. All references to Robert Shapiro are taken from "The End of Entitlement," *New Democrat* 4 (July 1992): 19.

3. John Stuart Mill, *On Liberty* (Indianapolis: Hackett, 1978), 103–6. Mill also recommends government-sponsored achievement tests for various fields and purposes. He sees these tests as a substitute for direct state control of education, apparently feeling such control to be unnecessary and perhaps counterproductive, without seeing any possibility that private licensing agencies might carry on the task of designing examinations to test individuals' command of various fields of knowledge in a "morally neutral" fashion.

4. John Stuart Mill, "Chapters on Socialism," in *On Liberty and Other Writings,* ed. Stefan Collini (Cambridge: Cambridge University Press, 1989); see especially p. 273. Note also the following quotation from Mill's *Principles of Political*

Economy: "Mankind are capable of a far greater amount of public spirit than the present age is accustomed to suppose possible. History bears witness to the success with which large bodies of human beings may be trained to feel the public interest their own. And no soil could be more favourable to the growth of such a feeling, than a Communist association, since all the ambition, and the bodily and mental activity, which are now exerted in the pursuit of separate and self-regarding interests, would require another sphere of employment, and would naturally find it in the pursuit of the general benefit of the community" (quoted in David Levy, "Libertarian-Communists, Malthusians, and J. S. Mill—Who Is Both," *Independent Journal of Philosophy* 4 [1983]). Mill's only warnings against government control of the economy stem from his fear that *total* control might lead to abuse of power and stifling of individual initiative. See, for example, *On Liberty*, p. 109.

5. See especially Milton Friedman, *Capitalism and Freedom* (Chicago: University of Chicago Press, 1962), chap. 1.

6. Charles Taylor, "Cross-Purposes: The Liberal-Communitarian Debate," in Nancy L. Rosenblum, ed., *Liberalism and the Moral Life* (Cambridge: Harvard University Press, 1989), 160, footnote omitted.

7. William A. Galston, *Liberal Purposes: Goods, Virtues, and Diversity in the Liberal State* (Cambridge: Cambridge University Press, 1991), 221.

8. Taylor, "Cross Purposes," 165, 171–74.

9. John Stuart Mill, *Three Essays* (Oxford: Oxford University Press, 1975), 83.

10. John Stuart Mill, *On Liberty*, in *On Liberty and Other Writings*, 13–14.

11. J. G. A. Pocock, "Virtue and Commerce in the Eighteenth Century," *Journal of Interdisciplinary History* 3 (1972): 119–34; Gordon Wood, *Creation of the American Republic, 1776–1787* (Chapel Hill: University of North Carolina Press, 1969).

12. Quoted in Derek L. Phillips, *Looking Backward: A Critical Appraisal of Communitarian Thought* (Princeton: Princeton University Press, 1993), 25.

13. George W. Carey, *The Federalist: Design for a Constitutional Republic* (Champaign: University of Illinois Press, 1989), 159–60.

14. John Locke, *Second Treatise of Government* (London: Dent, 1924; Arlington Heights, IL: Harlan Davidson, 1982), 4.

15. Ibid., 45.

16. Theodore J. Lowi, *The End of Liberalism: The Second Republic of the United States*, 2d ed. (New York: Norton, 1979), xvi.

17. Ibid., xi.

18. Theodore J. Lowi, "Liberal and Conservative Theories of Regulation," in Gary C. Bryner and Dennis L. Thompson, eds., *The Constitution and the Regulation of Society* (Albany: State University of New York Press for Brigham Young University, 1988), 16–17.

19. See especially Galston, *Liberal Purposes*, 283.

20. Ibid., 6.

21. References to the communitarian platform can be found in the appendix of Amitai Etzioni, *The Spirit of Community: Rights, Responsibilities, and the Communitarian Agenda* (New York: Crown, 1993).

22. William A. Galston, "Family Matters," *New Democrat* 4 (July 1992): 19.

23. Russell Kirk, *The Politics of Prudence* (Bryn Mawr, PA: Intercollegiate Studies Institute, 1993).

24. Robert A. Nisbet, *The Quest for Community: A Study in the Ethics of Order and Freedom* (New York: Oxford University Press, 1953), 53.

25. Galston, *Liberal Purposes*, 222.

26. Ibid.

27. Ibid., 284. Note also p. 285, where Galston differentiates child-rearing from adult cohabitation in arguing that government should support only heterosexual unions. "Lifestyle choices" are good, according to Galston, but where they will have social effects, such as on the formation of citizen character, society must decide what it shall support. And empirical evidence shows that heterosexual couples provide the best chance for the formation of healthy liberal character. Amitai Etzioni, in *The Spirit of Community*, also defends the two-parent family but is careful to label "sexist" any notion of male and female sex-roles: see especially p. 61. Daniel Bell, in *Communitarianism and Its Critics* (Oxford: Oxford University Press, 1994), argues at length that homosexual unions should be sanctioned, on the grounds that they constitute communities in which the members develop and fulfill their identities.

28. Galston, *Liberal Purposes*, 286–87.

29. Ibid., 301.

30. Ibid., 9.

31. Charles Taylor, *The Ethics of Authenticity* (Cambridge: Harvard University Press, 1991), 15, 26.

32. Ibid., 3. Note also Taylor's discussion of the relationship between the "aesthetically realized life" and standards of morality in *Sources of the Self: The Making of the Modern Identity* (Cambridge: Harvard University Press, 1989), 499, 510. Here he states that no one after Schopenhauer can fail to raise the question of whether "artistic epiphany draws us to the same things that morality demands." But this does not mean, for Taylor, that we should abandon objective rules altogether. "It is just that [the effort to surmount subjectivism] remains a continuing task, which cannot be put behind us once and for all, as with the public order of former times." We must construct standards, knowing that we will have to reconstruct them time and again.

33. Galston, *Liberal Purposes*, 280.

34. Ibid., 254.

35. Ibid., 255.

36. Ibid.
37. Charles Taylor, "Cross-Purposes: The Liberal-Communitarian Debate," in Nancy L. Rosenblum, ed., *Liberalism and the Moral Life* (Cambridge: Harvard University Press, 1989), 163.
38. Ibid., 82.
39. Ibid., 51–53.
40. Ibid.
41. Taylor, "Cross-Purposes," 182. See also Taylor's *Multiculturalism* (Princeton: Princeton University Press, 1994) 59.
42. Taylor, *Multiculturalism,* 62, 64–67.
43. Taylor, *Ethics,* 105.
44. Ibid., 106–7.
45. Ibid., 5.
46. Material in this paragraph and the next two is from ibid., 46–48.
47. Taylor, "Cross Purposes," 117, 113.
48. Ibid., 174–75.
49. Etzioni, *Spirit of Community,* appendix.
50. Taylor, *Ethics,* 119.
51. Etzioni, *Spirit of Community,* appendix.
52. Galston, *Liberal Purposes,* 229–30.
53. Ibid., 243–44.
54. Ibid., 265; emphasis in original.
55. Ibid., 267. Galston also identifies American mores with the "culture" of white Anglo-Saxon males but does not develop the point.
56. Ibid., 279.

Chapter Two. From Social Cohesion to Radical Reform

1. Niccolò Machiavelli, *Discourses on the First Ten Books of Titus Livius* (New York: Modern Library, 1950), bk. 2, 5.
2. Ibid., bk. 2, 15.
3. Strauss makes his opinion on this matter most clear in "On a Forgotten Kind of Writing," in Leo Strauss, *What Is Political Philosophy?* (Chicago: University of Chicago Press, 1959), 221.
4. Philosophers are intellectuals in the sense in which I am using the term here. To the extent that they abandon the pursuit of knowledge for its own sake in order to reconstruct our political life, philosophers abandon their special status and become technicians of ideas and institutions.
5. Robert N. Bellah, Richard Madsen, William M. Sullivan, Ann Swidler and Steven M. Tipton, *Habits of the Heart: Individualism and Commitment in American Life* (Berkeley: University of California Press, 1985), 335.

6. Ibid., viii.

7. Ibid., 217–18.

8. Robert N. Bellah, *The Broken Covenant: American Civil Religion in Time of Trial* (New York: Seabury Press, 1975), 135–36.

9. Ibid., 123.

10. Robert N. Bellah, Richard Madsen, William M. Sullivan, Ann Swidler, and Steven M. Tipton, *The Good Society* (New York: Knopf, 1991), 209, 183.

11. Bellah et al., *Habits of the Heart*, 239–41.

12. Ibid., 242.

13. Robert N. Bellah, *Beyond Belief: Essays on Religion in a Post-Traditional World* (New York: Harper and Row, 1970), 253.

14. Bellah, *Broken Covenant*, 159–60.

15. Bellah, *Beyond Belief*, 202.

16. Taylor has said that a renewed "Judaeo-Christian theism" would provide "a divine affirmation of the human, more total than humans can ever attain unaided." But religious belief remains for him only one possible "thing that matters." Taylor, by far the most openly religious of the communitarians, sees the possibility that worship of the divine and life plans influenced by religious mores may point to a better, more fulfilling life than can other things that matter. But by his moral reasoning he seeks mainly to promote not religion and religiously based morality but commitment; we must find our own thing that matters and follow it (*Sources of the Self: The Making of the Modern Identity* [Cambridge: Harvard University Press, 1989], 507, 521).

17. Bellah et al., *The Good Society*, 209.

18. Charles Taylor, "Religion in a Free Society," in James Davison Hunter and Os Guiness, eds., *Articles of Faith, Articles of Peace: The Religious Liberty Clauses and the American Public Philosophy* (Washington, DC: Brookings Institution, 1990), 97.

19. Robert N. Bellah, "The Revolution and the Civil Religion," in Jerald C. Brauer, ed., *Religion and the American Revolution* (Philadelphia: Fortress Press, 1976), 57.

20. Bellah, *Beyond Belief*, 168.

21. Bellah, *Broken Covenant*, ix–x.

22. Bellah, *Beyond Belief*, 175–76.

23. Catherine L. Albanese, *Sons of the Fathers: The Civil Religion of the American Revolution* (Philadelphia: Temple University Press, 1976), 4.

24. Ibid., 8.

25. Ibid., 19.

26. Ibid., 7.

27. Bellah, *Beyond Belief*, 180–81.

28. Ibid., 175, 179.

29. Bellah, "The Revolution and the Civil Religion," in Brauer, *Religion and the American Revolution*, 62.

30. Ibid., 60.

31. Ibid., 62.

32. Ibid., 65–66.

33. Ibid., 68–69.

34. Bellah, *Beyond Belief*, 172.

35. Ibid., 181.

36. Bellah, *Broken Covenant*, ix.

37. Bellah, *Beyond Belief*, 186, 182.

38. Ibid., 182.

39. Bellah, *Broken Covenant*, 62.

40. Ibid., 54–55.

41. See Raoul Berger, *Government by Judiciary: The Transformation of the Fourteenth Amendment* (Cambridge: Harvard University Press, 1977), for a devastating critique of the claim that the Fourteenth Amendment was intended to desegregate American schools, let alone promote far-reaching egalitarian programs such as those Bellah ascribes to the amendments.

42. Bellah, *Broken Covenant*, 54–55.

43. Bellah et al., *Habits of the Heart*, 212–13.

Chapter Three. Rhetorical Foundings and the Great Leader

1. See especially Robert N. Bellah, "The Revolution and the Civil Religion," in Jerald C. Brauer, ed., *Religion and the American Revolution* (Philadelphia: Fortress Press, 1976).

2. See Patrick Allitt, *Catholic Intellectuals and Conservative Politics in America, 1950–1985* (Ithaca: Cornell University Press, 1993), 248.

3. Garry Wills, *Certain Trumpets: The Call of Leaders* (New York: Simon and Schuster, 1994), 14; emphasis in original.

4. Ibid., 15; emphasis in original.

5. Allitt, *Catholic Intellectuals*, 284–85.

6. Wills, *Certain Trumpets*, 121.

7. Ibid., 15.

8. Garry Wills, *Under God: Religion and American Politics* (New York: Simon and Schuster, 1990), 116–17.

9. Ibid., 382–83.

10. Ibid., 56, 60.

11. Ibid., 379–80.

12. Ibid., 275–78.

13. Ibid., 302; emphasis in original.

14. Ibid., 337.

15. Wills, *Certain Trumpets*, 182.

16. Wills, *Under God*, 358.

17. Gary Wills, *Explaining America: The Federalist* (Garden City, NY: Doubleday, 1981), 268–69.

18. Derek L. Phillips, *Looking Backward: A Critical Appraisal of Communitarian Thought* (Princeton: Princeton University Press, 1993).

19. Garry Wills, *Inventing America: Jefferson's Declaration of Independence* (Garden City, NY: Doubleday, 1978), xxiv.

20. Ibid., xiv.

21. Ibid., xiii.

22. Ibid.; see especially p. 334.

23. Ibid., 333.

24. Ibid., 342, 339.

25. Ibid., 346–48.

26. Ibid., 357.

27. Ibid., xiv.

28. Ibid., xix.

29. Ibid., xxii, xxiv.

30. Ibid., xix.

31. Ibid.; see especially part 1, chap. 3 (188–93), and p. 265.

32. Ibid., 265; emphasis in original.

33. Ibid., 267. Wills planned to write a volume examining the constitutional ratifying conventions. It has yet to appear.

34. See Jefferson's letter to his nephew, November 30, 1790. Jefferson opposed the practical *Federalist* to Locke's more theoretical *Second Treatise*.

35. Wills, *Explaining America*, 268.

36. The quotations in this paragraph and the extract in the next are from ibid., 54; emphasis in original.

37. *Annals of Congress*, 4th Cong., April 6, 1796, 776.

38. Wills, *Explaining America*, 31–33.

39. Ibid., 265.

40. Ibid., 270.

41. Garry Wills, *Lincoln at Gettysburg: The Words That Remade America* (New York: Simon and Schuster, 1992), 174–75; emphasis in original.

42. Ibid., especially pp. 145 and 172.

43. Ibid., 38, 40.

44. Ibid., 39.

45. Ibid., 146–47.

46. Ibid., 101.

47. References in Lincoln's work to Americans' legal obligations, and to the moral obligation of upholding the Constitution, are legion. On the specific issues

of the fugitive slave laws, the principle of federal noninterference with state slave practices, and the constitutionally dictated federal role in regulating slavery in the territories, see especially *The Collected Works of Abraham Lincoln*, ed. Roy P. Basler (New Brunswick, NJ: Rutgers University Press, 1953), 1:348; 2:255–56, 270, 272, 471, 492–93; 3:87, 131–32, 222; 4:168–69.

48. Wills, *Lincoln at Gettysburg*, 102; emphasis in original.

49. Ibid., 81–2, 80.

50. Wills, *Inventing*, 188; emphasis in original. Again, the point is not the accuracy of Wills's interpretation but its role in his thought and in his political program.

51. Ibid., 194–96.

52. Material in this paragraph to the end of this section is from Wills, *Certain Trumpets*, 218–19; emphasis in original.

53. Quotations in this paragraph and the next are from Mario Cuomo, *More Than Words* (New York: St. Martin's Press, 1993), 86, 178.

54. Ibid., 7.

55. Mario M. Cuomo and Harold Holzer, eds., *Lincoln on Democracy* (New York: HarperCollins, 1990), xxiv.

56. Don E. Fehrenbacher, ed., *Lincoln: Speeches and Writings, 1832–1858* (New York: Library of America, 1989), 302.

57. Cuomo, *More Than Words*, 98.

58. Anyone believing this is a misprint and that Cuomo actually said "equality *of* opportunity" may wish to look at ibid., 97, where he also refers to "equality *and* opportunity."

59. Ibid., 96.

60. Ibid., 88.

61. Ibid., 208.

62. Ibid., 23, 207–10.

63. Ibid., 18.

64. Ibid., 29.

65. Ibid., 70–71.

66. Ibid., 69–70.

67. Ibid., 24; emphasis in original.

68. Ibid., 67.

69. Ibid., 226–27; emphasis in original.

70. Ibid., 23.

71. Ibid., 25.

72. Ibid., 249.

73. Alexis de Tocqueville, *Democracy in America*, ed. J. P. Mayer, trans. George Lawrence (Garden City, NY: Doubleday, 1969), 511.

74. Ibid.

75. Cuomo, *More Than Words*; see especially pp. 39–40 and 60.

76. The quotations in this paragraph and the next are from ibid., 46, 40; emphasis in original.

77. Ibid., 274–75, 278.

78. Ibid., 38–39.

79. Tocqueville, *Democracy*, 450.

80. John Courtney Murray, *We Hold These Truths: Catholic Reflections on the American Proposition* (Kansas City, MO: Sheed and Ward, 1960).

81. Cuomo, *More Than Words*, 45.

82. Ibid., 224.

83. See especially ibid., xiv.

Chapter Four. The Politics of Community Life

1. Robert N. Bellah, Richard Madsen, William M. Sullivan, Ann Swidler, and Steven M. Tipton, *The Good Society* (New York: Knopf, 1991), 10.

2. Robert N. Bellah, Richard Madsen, William M. Sullivan, Ann Swidler, and Steven M. Tipton, *Habits of the Heart: Individualism and Commitment in American Life* (Berkeley: University of California Press, 1985), 39.

3. See especially Bruce Frohnen, "Robert Bellah and the Politics of 'Civil' Religion," *Political Science Reviewer* 21 (Fall 1992): 148–218.

4. For a full explication of this reading of Tocqueville see Bruce Frohnen, *Virtue and the Promise of Conservatism: The Legacy of Burke and Tocqueville* (Lawrence: University Press of Kansas, 1993), chaps. 4 and 5.

5. Bellah et al., *The Good Society*, 7.

6. Ibid., 20–22.

7. Ibid., 32.

8. Bellah et al., *Habits of the Heart*, 13.

9. Mario Cuomo, *More Than Words* (New York: St. Martin's Press, 1993), 29; emphasis in original.

10. Bellah et al., *The Good Society*, viii.

11. Bellah et al., *Habits of the Heart*, 177, 170–75.

12. Ibid., 43.

13. Ibid., 233–34. Bellah's textual interest in Tocqueville appears limited almost exclusively to the French philosopher's analysis of individualism. *Individualism and Commitment in American Life: Readings on the Themes of Habits of the Heart* (New York: Harper and Row, 1987) by Bellah and co-authors Richard Madsen, William M. Sullivan, Ann Swidler, and Steven M. Tipton contains only one selection from Tocqueville's voluminous writings—three pages on individualism.

14. Bellah et al., *Habits of the Heart*, 218.

15. Bellah et al., *Individualism and Commitment in American Life*, 6, and *Habits of the Heart*, viii.

16. Bellah et al., *Habits of the Heart*, 285–87.

17. See especially Alexis de Tocqueville, *Democracy in America*, ed. J. P. Mayer, trans. George Lawrence (Garden City, NY: Doubleday, 1969), 189.

18. Bellah et al., *Habits of the Heart*, 217–18.

19. Ibid., 214.

20. Ibid., 216.

21. Charles Taylor, "The Dangers of Soft Despotism," *Responsive Community* (Fall 1993): 30.

22. Bellah et al., *Habits of the Heart*, 38.

23. Bellah et al., *The Good Society*, 81.

24. Bellah et al., *Habits of the Heart*, 6.

25. Ibid., 214.

26. Bellah et al., *The Good Society*, 275.

27. Bellah et al., *Habits of the Heart*, 15.

28. Allan Bloom, *The Closing of the American Mind: How Higher Education Has Failed Democracy and Impoverished the Souls of Today's Students* (New York: Simon and Schuster, 1987), 144.

29. Bellah et al., *The Good Society*, 168.

30. Ibid., 126.

31. Ibid., 50.

32. Robert N. Bellah, *The Broken Covenant: American Civil Religion in Time of Trial* (New York: Seabury Press, 1975), 159.

33. Bellah et al., *Habits of the Heart*, 110–11.

34. This quotation and those following are from Bellah et al., *The Good Society*, 47–49.

35. Bloom, *Closing of the American Mind*, 142.

36. See Jean Jacques Rousseau, "The Social Contract," in *The Social Contract and Discourses*, trans. G. D. H. Cole (London: Dent, 1973), 184–85.

37. Bellah et al., *The Good Society*, 184.

38. Rousseau, *Social Contract*, 273, 272.

39. Bellah et al., *The Good Society*, 9.

40. Bellah et al., *Habits of the Heart*, 153.

41. Ibid., 306.

42. Ibid., 140–41.

43. Bellah, *Broken Covenant*, 104.

44. Amitai Etzioni, *The Spirit of Community: Rights, Responsibilities, and the Communitarian Agenda* (New York: Crown, 1993), especially 230–31.

45. Bellah et al., *Habits of the Heart*, 212–13.

46. See Etzioni, *The Spirit of Community*, 204–6.

47. Charles Taylor, *The Ethics of Authenticity* (Cambridge: Harvard University Press, 1991), 2.

48. Taylor, "Dangers of Soft Despotism."

49. Taylor, *Ethics of Authenticity,* 4.
50. Bellah et al., *Habits of the Heart,* 231.
51. Ibid., 235.
52. Ibid.
53. Ibid., 233–34.
54. Bellah et al., *The Good Society,* 14.
55. Tocqueville, *Democracy in America,* 451–52.
56. Ibid., 453.
57. Bellah et al., *Habits of the Heart,* 221.
58. Ibid., 153.
59. Bellah et al., *The Good Society,* 208.
60. Bellah et al., *Habits of the Heart,* 237.

Chapter Five. Liberalism as Social Movement

1. Quotations are from Amitai Etzioni, *The Spirit of Community: Rights, Responsibilities, and the Communitarian Agenda* (New York: Crown, 1993), 18–20; emphasis in original.
2. Ibid., 230.
3. Charles Taylor, "The Dangers of Soft Despotism," *Responsive Community* (Fall 1993): 24.
4. Etzioni, *Spirit of Community,* 232.
5. David Osborne and Ted Gaebler, *Reinventing Government: How the Entrepreneurial Spirit Is Transforming the Public Sector* (New York: Plume, 1993), xviii–xix.
6. See especially Charles Murray, *Losing Ground: American Social Policy 1950–1980* (New York: Basic Books, 1984), part 3.
7. As Bellah argued, for communitarians, we must dwell on the *injustices* of the past to form a kind of negative consensus, one that opposes tradition and prods us to pursue social justice. See the discussion in Chapter 2.
8. Speech delivered at the University of Chicago, November 13, 1991.
9. Etzioni, *Spirit of Community,* 99–100.
10. Ibid., 204–6.
11. Leon Wieseltier, "Total Quality Meaning," *New Republic* (1993): 16, 20.
12. Taylor, "Dangers of Soft Despotism," 24–25, 30.
13. Clarke E. Cochran, "The Thin Theory of Community: The Communitarians and their Critics," *Political Studies,* 32 (1989): 422–35; examples are my own.
14. Charles Taylor, *Sources of the Self: The Making of the Modern Identity* (Cambridge: Harvard University Press, 1989), 507; footnotes omitted. Taylor relies heavily on Bellah in making this point.

15. "Hey I'm Terrific," *Newsweek*, February 17, 1992, 46–51. One more general discussion of the nature and problem of the self-esteem mania is provided in Charles Murray, *In Pursuit of Happiness and Good Government* (New York: Simon and Schuster, 1988); see especially pp. 112–31 and notes therein. I should note that Michael Walzer, a leading communitarian philosopher, has criticized self-esteem for being too subjective (*Spheres of Justice: A Defense of Pluralism and Equality* [New York: Basic Books, 1983], 278–79). But Walzer's goal and program make clear that he is not, in fact, rejecting the communitarian notion of self-esteem. He objects to much of the current emphasis on self-esteem because he believes it lacks objective standards. But Walzer's alternative conception—democratic self-respect—provides only communitarian values as standards. Self-esteem is too relativistic, for Walzer, because it is based on inequality. We love ourselves on account of our status—because we are nobles rather than peasants, and so on. Democracy makes such self-esteem highly unstable because status is so fleeting and malleable. What we need, then, are democratic standards that individuals can meet and thereby gain respect. Such standards are provided, in Walzer's view, by the pursuit of social justice (the democratic common good) and the standards erected by the various groups to which we happen to belong at a given time. Of course these groups, for Walzer as for other communitarians, cannot be allowed to violate the democratic values of equality, tolerance, and inclusiveness (pp. 272–77). Note especially Walzer's statement (p. 272) that preventive detention is unjust precisely because we have defined it so; that the community creates its own "objective" standards and can change them.

15. William Kilpatrick, *Why Johnny Can't Tell Right from Wrong* (New York: Simon and Schuster, 1992), 48.

16. Ibid., 41.

17. Ibid., 45.

18. Quoted in ibid., 42.

19. "Hey I'm Terrific," *Newsweek*, February 17, 1992, 49.

20. Ibid.

21. John Dewey and James H. Tufts, *Ethics* (1908), quoted in Robert B. Westbrook, *John Dewey and American Democracy* (Ithaca: Cornell University Press, 1992), 157. Westbrook explains (p. 152) that Dewey wrote the key sections of this text, leaving Tufts to write the historical introduction and a section on economic and family life foreshadowed by chapters Dewey himself wrote. I heavily rely on Westbrook's analysis here because it is complete, well constructed, and friendly toward Dewey.

22. Dewey and Tufts, *Ethics*, 272, 357; quoted in Westbrook, *John Dewey*, 158–59.

24. Dewey even constructs a list of liberal democratic virtues emphasizing self-control in the interests of the common good, courage, fairness, impartiality,

and honesty, along with reasoned judgment (*Ethics*, 363–79; quoted in Westbrook, *John Dewey,* 161).

25. Dewey, *Ethics,* 392; quoted in Westbrook, *John Dewey,* 165.

26. Dewey, "Teaching That Does Not Educate" (1909), and "Education, Direct and Indirect" (1904); quoted in Westbrook, *John Dewey,* 169.

27. Dewey, *How We Think* (1910); quoted in Westbrook, *John Dewey,* 169.

28. Dewey, "The Moral Significance of the Common School Studies," 208, and "History for the Educator" (1909); quoted in Westbrook, *John Dewey,* 171.

29. Westbrook, *John Dewey,* 98–101.

30. Dewey, "Progressive Education and the Science of Education" (1928); quoted in Westbrook, *John Dewey,* 502.

31. See Westbrook, *John Dewey,* 505.

32. Katherine Mayhew and Anna Edward, *The Dewey School* (1936); quoted in Westbrook, *John Dewey,* 106.

33. Westbrook, *John Dewey,* 111–13.

34. *Newsweek,* February 22, 1993, 44.

Chapter Six. Covenant, Contract, and the Power of Interpreters

1. In this, as in much else, communitarianism bears a striking resemblance to the Social Gospel movement of the late nineteenth and early twentieth centuries. This connection is made clear in David B. Danbom, *"The World of Hope": Progressives and the Struggle for an Ethical Public Life* (Philadelphia: Temple University Press, 1987). Danbom's hagiography of the Social Gospelers and their influence on Progressivism rests on communitarian assumptions concerning the weakness of individualism, the evils of capitalism, and our civil religious duty to strive after a perfectly moral and just society in this world; see especially chap. 2.

2. Plato, *The Republic,* trans. G. M. A. Grube (Indianapolis: Hackett, 1974), 83, 415a–d.

3. William Kilpatrick, *Why Johnny Can't Tell Right from Wrong* (New York: Simon and Schuster, 1992). See especially pp. 22–23, where Kilpatrick notes that administrators and social scientists often tell teachers to rename their self-esteem programs so that parents will not know that they still are being used.

4. William A. Galston, *Liberal Purposes: Goods, Virtues, and Diversity in the Liberal State* (Cambridge: Cambridge University Press, 1991), 52.

5. Amitai Etzioni, *The Spirit of Community: Rights, Responsibilities, and the Communitarian Agenda* (New York: Crown, 1993), 166–67.

6. Alexander Hamilton, James Madison, and John Jay, *The Federalist Papers,* ed. Clinton Rossiter (New York: Mentor, 1961), 278.

7. John Locke, *Second Treatise of Government* (Arlington Heights, IL: Harlan Davidson, 1982), 83–84.

8. See, for example, Washington's farewell address: "If in the opinion of the People, the distribution or modification of the Constitutional powers be in any particular wrong, let it be corrected by an amendment in the way in which the Constitution designates. But let there be no change by usurpation; for though this, in one instance, may be the instrument of good, it is the customary weapon by which free governments are destroyed. The precedent must always greatly overbalance in permanent evil any partial or transient benefit which the use can at any time yield"; quoted in Raoul Berger, *Government by Judiciary: The Transformation of the Fourteenth Amendment* (Cambridge: Harvard University Press, 1977), 299.

9. Mary Ann Glendon, *Rights Talk: The Impoverishment of Political Discourse* (New York: Free Press, 1991), 45.

10. For this and other suggestions for reform, see ibid., chap. 4.

11. Ibid., 45.

12. Ibid., 100–101.

13. Ibid., 165.

14. Ibid., 153–54.

15. Quoted in Berger, *Government by Judiciary*, 288.

16. *Federalist* 78, 467: "There is no position which depends on clearer principles than that every act of a delegated authority, contrary to the tenor of the commission under which it is exercised, is void. No legislative act, therefore, contrary to the Constitution, can be valid."

17. Quoted in Berger, *Government by Judiciary*, 287. The other states with constitutional provisions paralleling this from Massachusetts were New Hampshire, North Carolina, Pennsylvania, and Vermont.

18. Ibid., 289.

19. *Federalist* 25, quoted in Berger, *Government by Judiciary*, 299.

20. Quoted in Berger, *Government by Judiciary*, 364. In the passage from which this quotation is taken Story notes "that the government of the United States is one of limited and enumerated powers; and . . . a departure from the true import and sense of its powers is pro tanto, the establishment of a new Constitution. It is doing for the people, what they have not chosen to do for themselves. It is usurping the functions of a legislator."

21. Quoted in ibid., 291. The Massachusetts House insisted that their constitution was "fixed" in 1768, while they still were ruled by a supposedly omnipotent Parliament and Crown. They demanded that legislative acts not overreach the authority given to the legislature by higher law documents in the British tradition. Ibid.

22. Quoted in ibid., 367.

23. Quoted in ibid., 367.

24. Quoted in ibid., 370.

25. Quoted in ibid., 296.

26. Quoted in ibid., 288, n. 22.

27. *Griswold v. Connecticut*, 381 U.S. 479, 484 (1965). See also Judge Hand's discussion of Justice Black's misreading of the intent of the Fourteenth Amendment—a misreading based on faulty attempts to glean the framers' own intentions—in *Jaffree v. Board of School Commissioners of Mobile County*, 554 F.Supp. 1104, 1109 n. 26 (1983).

28. This is not to say that I, personally, believe that states should prevent individuals or couples from obtaining contraceptive devices. My opinion on that matter is irrelevant here. But the discussion thus far should make clear my view that local communities must make such fundamental moral decisions for themselves, rather than bowing to an unelected federal body, if they are to retain their independence and moral cohesion.

29. This argument is stated most forthrightly in William J. Brennan, Jr., "The Constitution of the United States: Contemporary Ratification," in Jack N. Rakove, ed., *Interpreting the Constitution: The Debate over Original Intent* (Boston: Northeastern University Press, 1990), 25.

30. H. Jefferson Powell, "The Original Understanding of Original Intent," *Harvard Law Review* 98 (1985): 885, 888.

31. Ibid., 901.

32. For example, *res ipsa loquitur*—"the thing speaks for itself"—actually is not a bit of legal arcanum. This legal doctrine is rather simple and necessary for fair and coherent decision-making. It states merely that some events clearly provide answers to certain legally important questions. If someone walking by a warehouse window has a barrel of flour dropped on him it is safe to assume that it came from the warehouse rather than the heavens, and that a barrel of flour would not fly out of a window unless it were thrown, dropped or placed in an inappropriate, unsafe place or fashion. Thus a common understanding—that barrels of flour do not fall of their own accord from the skies—is summed up in a rule of law.

33. Powell, "The Original Understanding," 904.

34. Brennan, "The Constitution of the United States," in Rakove, *Interpreting the Constitution*, 25, 23.

35. Louis Dupré, "The Modern Idea of Culture: Its Opposition to Its Classical and Christian Roots," in Ralph McInerny, ed., *Modernity and Religion* (Notre Dame: Notre Dame University Press, 1994), 2.

36. This is the theme of Bruce Frohnen, *Virtue and the Promise of Conservatism: The Legacy of Burke and Tocqueville* (Lawrence: University Press of Kansas, 1993). In the interest of space I refer the reader to that work for more complete explications of several points I make here.

37. Dupré, "The Modern Idea of Culture," in McInerny, *Modernity and Religion*, 7–8.

38. Ibid., 4.

39. Ibid., 9.
40. Ibid., 8; emphasis in original.
41. Ibid., 8–9; emphasis in original.
42. Ibid., 7–8; emphasis in original.

Chapter Seven. Religion and the Ends of Communal Life

1. See Ellis Sandoz, *A Government of Laws: Political Theory, Religion, and the American Founding* (Baton Rouge: Louisiana State University Press, 1990), 227.

2. Patrick Henry, "Speech Before the Virginia Ratifying Convention," June 5, 1788, in Ralph Ketcham, ed., *The Antifederalist Papers and the Constitutional Convention Debates* (New York: New American Library, 1986), 208.

3. In *The Myth of American Individualism: The Protestant Origins of American Political Thought* (Princeton: Princeton University Press, 1994), Barry Alan Shain argues that the social and political structure of early America can best be summed up as local, Protestant communalism. A variety of self-regulating associations were joined together to form the local community. In this context individuals were seen as parts of numerous groups, seeking to lead godly lives in common with their fellows. One led a good life by fulfilling one's various stations in life. "Individual autonomy, as it is understood today, would have been viewed as inconsistent with human flourishing—in fact, it would have been seen as a form of sinful degeneration"; see especially pp. xvi, 21, 50.

4. See Shain, *The Myth of American Individualism*, especially p. 66, where he argues that all local communities in America sought religious and moral homogeneity. The right to dissent was recognized principally as the right to leave one community for another (or to found a new community) that would regulate life in a manner more in keeping with one's own convictions. See also ibid., 30.

5. Donald S. Lutz, "Religious Dimensions in the Development of American Constitutionalism," *Emory Law Journal* 39 (1990): 22.

6. Perry Miller, *The Puritans* (New York: Harper and Row, 1963), 199–200. See also Anson P. Stokes, *Church and State in the United States* (New York: Harper and Row, 1950), 121. Stokes cites Roger Williams's description of the church as a kind of corporation.

7. Samuel West in Charles S. Hyneman and Donald S. Lutz, eds., *American Political Writing During the Founding Era*, 2 vols. (Indianapolis: Liberty Press, 1983), 1:419.

8. Lutz, "Religious Dimensions," 25.

9. Ibid.

10. See especially the discussion of early political and religious arrangements in *Jaffree v. Board of School Commissioners of Mobile County*, 554 F.Supp. 1104, 1114–15 (1983) and the sources cited therein.

11. See especially Michael McConnell, "Accommodation of Religion," *Supreme Court Review* 1985: 1, 23. The five states with religious test oaths at the turn of the century were North Carolina, South Carolina, Texas, Arkansas, and Mississippi.

12. Harold J. Berman, "Religious Freedom and the Challenge of the Modern State," *Emory Law Journal* 39 (1990): 149, 151–55, 157.

13. Ibid., 149–50. Noonan is quoted in ibid., 150.

14. John Locke, *Second Treatise of Government* (Arlington Heights, IL: Harlan Davidson, 1982), 4–5, 17–18.

15. See Chapter 3, especially around note 21.

16. For an introduction to the mythical voice in life and literature see, for example, Russell Kirk, "The Salutary Myth of the Otherworld Journey," *The World and I*, 10 (October 1994): 424.

17. Perhaps the best set of arguments for the notion that we can live together in peace only after accepting the truth of religion is presented in C. S. Lewis, *The Abolition of Man* (New York: Macmillan, 1947). Civilization and reason itself, for Lewis, assume the existence of a transcendent natural law. We all put forward arguments based on our vision of what is good and true. Even those who argue that all structures are merely collections of power go on to argue for particular reforms. Even those who deny the meaning of any social structure or set of social structures praise the courage and creativity of the exceptional individual who lives with this knowledge. Civilized life, however, requires certain beliefs, primarily that we must practice benevolence to strangers but especially to those we know and love, and that barring special circumstances we should deal honestly and openly with our fellows. All men recognize these natural laws and know they should follow them. Conflict arises over whether there exist special circumstances allowing for harsh, partial treatment (e.g., one should not be benevolent toward a murderer because this is unjust and endangers one's innocent fellows). To argue that the fact that natural laws should be applied differently in different circumstances and may be objects of disagreement proves that they do not exist is to deny the importance of prudence, the faculty of fitting rules to circumstances, and free will. It is to demand a perfection that does not exist in this world.

18. John Locke, *A Letter Concerning Toleration* (Indianapolis: Hackett, 1983), 51. Locke also refused toleration for Catholics on the grounds that they owed their allegiance to a "foreign prince"—the pope. References among the founding generation concerning the necessity of religion for virtue and of virtue for liberty are so numerous they should not require citation. Unfortunately, only recently have the political sermons in which the argument is most common been made easily accessible. See especially Ellis Sandoz, ed., *Political Sermons of the American Founding Era* (Indianapolis: Liberty Press, 1991), and Hyneman and Lutz, *American Political Writing*. A. James Reichley notes that "at the time of the revolution,

at least 75 percent of American citizens had grown up in families espousing some form of Puritanism" (*Religion in American Public Life* [Washington, DC: Brookings Institution, 1985], 53). This may explain the scant notice given such proponents of extreme religious liberty, including toleration of atheists, as William Penn and Roger Williams. See John Witte, Jr., "The Integration of Religious Liberty," *Michigan Law Review* 90 (1992): 1377, n. 53.

19. Jacob Rush, "The Nature and Importance of an Oath—The Charge to a Jury," in Hyneman and Lutz, *American Political Writing*, 1018.

20. On Gad Hitchcock see ibid., 282, 285. For references to atheists see, for example, ibid., 1005, where Peres Fobes asserts that the atheistic argument that religion is merely a tool to awe men into obedience to government is proof of religion's social utility, and ibid., 1204, where John Leland praises the federal ban on religious tests for allowing pagans, Turks, Jews, Christians, and Deists all to serve and mentions atheists not at all.

21. Ibid., 122; emphasis in original.

22. Ibid., 285.

23. Samuel West, "On the Right to Rebel Against Governors," in ibid., 434.

24. Ibid., 114.

25. Ibid., 119.

26. Abraham Williams in ibid., 8–9.

27. Samuel West in ibid., 424.

28. Abraham Williams in ibid., 15.

29. Zabdiel Adams in ibid., 555. See also Anonymous in ibid., 39–40, who argues that the teaching of virtue "chiefly depends upon the *good government and instruction of families* . . . if every family was duly instructed and governed; if the youth were restrained by those who have the care of them at *home*, from acting in public, contrary to the declared mind of the public, there would be less occasion to put the laws in severe execution: but when the laws of God and man are openly violated, and those who are entrusted with the execution of them, are abused and insulted, it is high time for all orderly citizens to unite in a proper defence of them." Also see pp. 581–82, where Anonymous argues that man's duty toward God ought to be taught in parish and "petty district" schools and particularly in the college that South Carolina should establish as soon as financially possible. Note also Benjamin Rush, "A Plan for the Establishment of Public Schools and the Diffusion of Knowledge in Pennsylvania; to Which Are Added, Thoughts upon the Mode of Education, Proper in a Republic (Philadelphia, 1786)" in ibid., 675–92, arguing that education promotes religion by combating superstition and promotes liberty by spreading learning.

30. See Ketcham's introduction to *The Antifederalist Papers*, 47.

31. Peres Fobes in Hyneman and Lutz, *American Political Writing*, 994.

32. Simeon Howard in ibid., 202–3.

33. Ibid., 665.

34. Ibid.

35. Letter from John Adams to Abigail Adams (October 29, 1775), quoted in John R. Howe, Jr., *The Changing Political Thought of John Adams* (1966), 156–57; also in Witte, "The Integration of Religious Liberty," 1382.

36. "The Preceptor" in Hyneman and Lutz, *American Political Writing*, 175.

37. Ibid., 128.

38. Ibid., 915. Theophilus Parsons argues that these often disparate rights could best be protected by requiring that measures concerning both individuals and property receive support from a majority representing both propertied and individual interests; ibid., 493.

39. Ibid., 961.

40. Ibid., 10. See also "U," pp. 33–36, arguing that the privileges accorded to men of station in civil life teach us the manners that separate us from the animals. Also note Shute's references to the classic notion of a great chain of being, according duties to each of us according to our station in life—a station itself dictated by nature; ibid., 110. The early Americans, whatever their stance in relation to the Constitution, were not at all averse to utilizing the language of class. See, for example, "The Federal Farmer," in Ketcham, *The Antifederalist Papers*, 260–61, who argues that aristocratic elements were using the current unrest in order to secure more than their proper due from the "democratic part of the community."

41. Hyneman and Lutz, *American Political Writing*, 278.

42. See, for example, Demophilus in ibid., 340; Braxton, ibid., 330–31; and Anonymous, ibid., 381.

43. Note also the discussion of Garry Wills in Chapter 3. Wills, of course, argues that the Declaration of Independence asserts only the equality of Americans *as a people* on a par with the English and other peoples.

44. William Whiting addressed the "people" of Berkshire County and argued for preservation of Massachusetts Bay's "political society" (Hyneman and Lutz, *American Political Writing*, 461–62. The Declaration of Independence might have annihilated the Massachusetts Constitution, Whiting argued, but it had not destroyed the "compact among the people" (pp. 467, 472). To say that destruction of a constitution destroys the political community is wrong, according to Whiting, because constitutions have only limited effects and purposes; the destruction of a constitution will not change the character of such underlying, fundamental institutions as the system of law (p. 474). The people of Berkshire County unquestionably belonged to the natural, local society of their county. Their attachment to the state of Massachusetts was less natural and more a matter of political convenience. The Berkshiremen *could* legitimately secede from the political society of Massachusetts, but they must do so explicitly and through appropriate means—they must receive Congress's permission.

45. Samuel West in ibid., 436, 442. Social attachments were more intimate at the locality and more distant and interest-based as the institutions involved

became more distant. But man was called to participate in all of these associations. In his lectures on the nature and purpose of law, James Wilson presented
man as an individual whose natural social affection made him become a member
of a particular society, confederation, and also "the great commonwealth of nations." Men owed allegiance to a variety of authorities, each within its appropriate jurisdiction. Thus Wilson discusses forms of law—of nature, of nations, and
of the municipality as well as the common law—corresponding to the variety of
associations in which men naturally participate (*Works*, ed. Robert Greene Mc-
Closkey, 2 vols. [Cambridge: Harvard University Press, 1967], 2:195, 230–31.

46. "The Impartial Examiner" vol. 1, pt. 2, in Bernard Bailyn, ed., *The Debate over the Constitution*, 2 vols. (New York: Library of America, 1993): 2:251–55.

47. Lutz, "Religious Dimensions," 23–24; citations omitted.

48. Ibid., 21, 22; emphasis in original.

49. Wilson, *Works*, 1:149. Jefferson is quoted in Herbert W. Schneider, *A
History of American Philosophy* (New York: Columbia University Press, 1946), 95.
Adams's argument can be found in Hyneman and Lutz, *American Political Writ-
ing*, 402.

50. Herbert J. Storing, *What the Antifederalists Were For*, vol. 1 of *The Complete
Antifederalist* (Chicago: University of Chicago Press, 1981), 10.

51. Ibid., 9.

52. See Brutus, Essay I, where Brutus argues that "although the government reported by the [Constitutional] convention does not go to a perfect and
entire consolidation, yet it approaches so near to it, that it must, if executed, certainly and infallibly terminate it" (Ketcham, *The Antifederalist Papers*, 271). The
new central government's absolute authority in the realm of treaty-making,
maintenance of armed forces, taxing, regulating trade, and instituting courts,
combined with its right to do all that is necessary and proper to fulfill these functions, will lead it to usurp all state power. "It is a truth confirmed by the unerring
experience of ages, that every man, and every body of men, invested with power,
are ever disposed to increase it, and to acquire a superiority over every thing that
stands in their way" (p. 275). Indeed, Brutus's subsequent arguments concerning the corrupting influences of the constitutional structure rest on his assumption that it will usurp state power and authority. See especially p. 279: "In a republic of such vast extent as the United States, the legislature cannot attend to
the various concerns and wants of its different parts." See also "The Federal
Farmer," in ibid., 263–64, where a prominent Antifederalist argues that the new
system constitutes a consolidation of government, and that "one government
and general legislation alone, never can extend equal benefits to all parts of the
United States: Different laws, customs, and opinions exist in the different states,
which by a uniform system of laws would be unreasonably invaded." See also
Patrick Henry, in ibid., 199, where he rejects any government that is not a compact between states as inherently consolidationist.

53. "The colonists indeed on account of local circumstances, have been in-dulged to form into little distinct states under the same head, and to make laws and execute them, restricted at the same time by the laws and dependent upon the supreme power of the nation as far as it is consistent with the essential rights of *British* subjects and necessary to the well-being of the whole" (in Hyneman and Lutz, *American Political Writing*, 129; emphasis in original). See also ibid., where Shute argues that the colonies are children of Great Britain—they came from the motherland but are not integral, subservient parts thereof. Demophilus (ibid., 345–50), provides an instructive early American theory of federalism based on an interpretation of Saxon social and political organization. According to Demophilus, the Saxons were organized into tribes, allied with one another through mutual defense agreements. The Saxons occasionally formed larger units whose size and character depended upon the reasons for their formation. If the interest involved was that of the "people at large," all of the tribes would join in serving it. The primary interest of the people at large being defense, mutual defense in effect became the basis of the Saxon kingdom. This left much room for local autonomy. Yet each tribe, despite being a "distinct people," had the same basic form of government. Largely self-contained, these tribes maintained their own parliaments, magistrates, and generous electoral laws. In this way the variety of local organizations were alike in their protection of citizens' natural rights. The townships in which tribal life was formed and carried on served as the essence of society and the proper basis of wider associations. Demophilus in fact used his history of the Saxons to argue that their form of organization—building from the locality upward—remained natural and showed that the town-ship was-the natural basis for the Pennsylvania Constitution then at issue. See also Shain, *Myth of American Individualism*, chap. 3, for a discussion of the gener-ally dichotomous relationship between localism and individualism.

54. Publius, in *Federalist* 51, argues that the people must be the primary con-trol of any government, but that auxiliary precautions also will be needed. With the constitutional system of separated powers, he argues, "the private interest of every individual may be a sentinel over the public rights" (Alexander Hamilton, James Madison, and John Jay, *The Federalist Papers*, ed. Clinton Rossiter [New York: Mentor, 1961], 320). See also George W. Carey, *The Federalist: Design for a Constitutional Republic* (Champaign: University of Illinois Press, 1991), 159–60.

55. *The Federalist Papers*, 127, 126.

56. Ibid., 321.

57. Ibid., 322. Note also the Antifederalist argument made by Brutus: "The great art . . . in forming a good constitution, appears to be this, so to frame it, as that those to whom the power is committed shall be subject to the same feelings, and aim at the same objects as the people do, who transfer to them their author-ity" (in Ketcham, *Antifederalist Papers*, 325). All legislatures, argues Brutus, will contain members who will seek their own rather than the public interest. The

task of constitution makers, then, was to prevent such self-interested governors from forming dangerous combinations. Brutus's criticism of the Constitution on this point was that its legislature would be too small to prevent such combinations. Indeed, any truly national legislature in America would be too distant from the people and too limited in its representation to fulfill its function of preventing the formation of oppressive factions (ibid., 326–29).

58. *Federalist*, 10, 66–67.

59. Charles Murray, preface to Marvin Olasky, *The Tragedy of American Compassion* (Washington, DC: Regnery Gateway, 1992), xi.

60. In *A Shopkeeper's Millennium: Society and Revivals in Rochester, New York, 1815–1837* (New York: Hill and Wang, 1978), at 49–50, Paul E. Johnson points out the increasing economic segregation of Rochester neighborhoods during the 1820s and 1830s caused by increased trade and industrialization. As mass production came into vogue, the old pattern of young apprentices living with their masters gave way to separate living quarters and lifestyles, resulting in anxiety for all concerned. But the resulting segregation was minimal by contemporary standards. More catastrophic was the effect of federal urban renewal programs, particularly in the South where white leaders often used them as an excuse to destroy poor blacks' housing (up until then interspersed with more well-to-do whites' housing) and move blacks to concentrated, segregated parts of town. See Theodore J. Lowi, *The End of Liberalism: The Second Republic of the United States*, 2d ed. (New York: Norton, 1979), especially 238–46.

61. Hyneman and Lutz, *American Political Writing*, 20, 36.

62. Quoted in ibid., 60.

63. Ibid., 153, 102.

64. Ibid., 103.

65. See especially ibid., 6–7.

66. Ibid., 40.

67. Quoted in ibid., 43, 61.

68. Ibid., 30, 34.

69. Ibid., 31.

70. Ibid., 72, 71.

71. The best treatment of social Darwinism in America remains Robert C. Bannister, *Social Darwinism: Science and Myth in Anglo-American Social Thought* (Philadelphia: Temple University Press, 1979).

72. Olasky, *The Tragedy of American Compassion*, 121, 120.

73. Social Gospel leader Walter Rauschenbush put it succinctly: "God is against capitalism"; quoted in ibid., 138.

74. Ibid., 121–22, 127–29.

75. Ibid., 137–38.

76. Ibid., 144–45.

77. Ibid., 101–13.

78. See especially Morton G. White, *The Philosophy of the American Revolution* (New York: Oxford University Press, 1978), 106, 108, 111, 114; Garry Wills, *Inventing America: Jefferson's Declaration of Independence* (Garden City, NY: Doubleday, 1978); and Wilson, *Works*, 1:143, 148. That Scottish enlightenment thinking is in keeping with supposedly "instrumentalist" Lockean principles is pointed out in Thomas L. Pangle, *The Spirit of Modern Republicanism: The Moral Vision of the American Founders and the Philosophy of Locke* (Chicago: University of Chicago Press, 1988), 37–38. I leave aside for current purposes my qualms concerning the transformation of conscience into a "moral sense." As I note above, Taylor points to this transformation as the basis of the culture of authenticity. But the founding generation for the most part seems to have used "conscience" and "moral sense" more or less interchangeably and clearly looked to external standards of right and wrong.

79. Wilson, *Works*, 1:141.

80. Hyneman and Lutz, *American Political Writing*, 665.

81. See Chapter 3, above.

82. Alexis de Tocqueville, *Democracy in America*, ed. J. P. Mayer, trans. George Lawrence (Garden City, NY: Doubleday, 1969), 512–13.

Selected Bibliography

Adams, John. *Works.* 10 vols. Boston: Little, Brown, 1854.

Albanese, Catherine L. *Sons of the Fathers: The Civil Religion of the American Revolution.* Philadelphia: Temple University Press, 1976.

Allitt, Patrick. *Catholic Intellectuals and Conservative Politics in America, 1950–1985.* Ithaca: Cornell University Press, 1993.

Bailyn, Bernard, ed. *The Debate over the Constitution.* 2 vols. New York: Library of America, 1993.

Bannister, Robert C. *Social Darwinism: Science and Myth in Anglo-American Social Thought.* Philadelphia: Temple University Press, 1979.

Bell, Daniel. *Communitarianism and Its Critics.* Oxford: Oxford University Press, 1994.

Bellah, Robert N. *Beyond Belief: Essays on Religion in a Post-Traditional World.* New York: Harper and Row, 1970.

————. *The Broken Covenant: American Civil Religion in Time of Trial.* New York: Seabury Press, 1975.

Bellah, Robert N., Richard Madsen, William M. Sullivan, Ann Swidler, and Steven M. Tipton. *The Good Society.* New York: Knopf, 1991.

————. *Habits of the Heart: Individualism and Commitment in American Life.* Berkeley: University of California Press, 1985.

————. *Individualism and Commitment in American Life: Readings on the Themes of* Habits of the Heart. New York: Harper and Row, 1987.

Bennett, William J. *The Index of Leading Cultural Indicators: Facts and Figures on the State of American Society.* New York: Simon and Schuster, 1994.

Berger, Raoul. *Government by Judiciary: The Transformation of the Fourteenth Amendment.* Cambridge: Harvard University Press, 1977.

Berman, Harold J. "Religious Freedom and the Challenge of the Modern State." *Emory Law Journal* 39 (1990): 149–64.

Bloom, Allan. *The Closing of the American Mind: How Higher Education Has Failed*

Democracy and Impoverished the Souls of Today's Students. New York: Simon and Schuster, 1987.

Brauer, Jerald C., ed. *Religion and the American Revolution*. Philadelphia: Fortress Press, 1976.

Carey, George W. *The Federalist: Design for a Constitutional Republic*. Champaign: University of Illinois Press, 1989.

Cochran, Clarke E. "The Thin Theory of Community: The Communitarians and Their Critics." *Political Studies* 32 (1989): 422–35.

Cuomo, Mario. *More Than Words*. New York: St. Martin's Press, 1993.

Cuomo, Mario M., and Harold Holzer, eds. *Lincoln on Democracy*. New York: Harper Collins, 1990.

Danbom, David B. *"The World of Hope": Progressives and the Struggle for an Ethical Public Life*. Philadelphia: Temple University Press, 1987.

Etzioni, Amitai. *The Spirit of Community: Rights, Responsibilities, and the Communitarian Agenda*. New York: Crown, 1993.

Friedman, Milton. *Capitalism and Freedom*. Chicago: University of Chicago Press, 1962.

Frohnen, Bruce. "Robert Bellah and the Politics of 'Civil' Religion." *Political Science Reviewer* 21 (Fall 1992): 148–218.

———. *Virtue and the Promise of Conservatism: The Legacy of Burke and Tocqueville*. Lawrence: University Press of Kansas, 1993.

Galston, William A. "Family Matters." *New Democrat* 4 (July 1992): 19–22.

———. *Liberal Purposes: Goods, Virtues, and Diversity in the Liberal State*. Cambridge: Cambridge University Press, 1991.

Glendon, Mary Ann. *Rights Talk: The Impoverishment of Political Discourse*. New York: Free Press, 1991.

Griswold v. Connecticut. 381 U.S. 479 (1965).

Hamilton, Alexander, James Madison, and John Jay. *The Federalist Papers*. Ed. Clinton Rossiter. New York: Mentor, 1961.

Hunter, James Davison, and Os Guiness, eds. *Articles of Faith, Articles of Peace: The Religious Liberty Clauses and the American Public Philosophy*. Washington, DC: Brookings Institution, 1990.

Hyneman, Charles S., and Donald S. Lutz, eds. *American Political Writing During the Founding Era*. 2 vols. Indianapolis: Liberty Press, 1983.

Jaffree v. Board of School Commissioners of Mobile County. 554 F.Supp. 1104 (1983).

Johnson, Paul E. *A Shopkeeper's Millennium: Society and Revivals in Rochester, New York, 1815–1837*. New York: Hill and Wang, 1978.

Ketcham, Ralph, ed. *The Antifederalist Papers and the Constitutional Convention Debates*. New York: New American Library, 1986.

Kilpatrick, William. *Why Johnny Can't Tell Right from Wrong*. New York: Simon and Schuster, 1992.

Kirk, Russell. *The Politics of Prudence.* Bryn Mawr, PA: Intercollegiate Studies Institute, 1993.

————. "The Salutary Myth of the Otherworld Journey." *The World and I* 10 (October 1994): 424–37.

Lawler, Peter Augustine, and Robert Martin Schaefer, eds. *The American Experiment: Essays on the Theory and Practice of Liberty.* Savage, MD: Rowman and Littlefield, 1994.

Levy, David. "Libertarian-Communists, Malthusians, and J. S. Mill—Who Is Both." *Independent Journal of Philosophy* 4 (1983).

Lewis, C. S. *The Abolition of Man.* New York: Macmillan, 1947.

Lincoln, Abraham. *The Collected Works of Abraham Lincoln.* Ed. Roy P. Basler. 9 vols. New Brunswick, NJ: Rutgers University Press, 1953.

————. *Speeches and Writings, 1832–1858.* Ed. Don E. Fehrenbacher. New York: Library of America, 1989.

Locke, John. *A Letter Concerning Toleration.* Indianapolis: Hackett, 1983.

————. *Second Treatise of Government.* London: Dent, 1924; Arlington Heights, IL: Harlan Davidson, 1982.

Lowi, Theodore J. *The End of Liberalism: The Second Republic of the United States.* 2d ed. New York: Norton, 1979.

————. "Liberal and Conservative Theories of Regulation." In Gary C. Bryner and Dennis L. Thompson, eds., *The Constitution and the Regulation of Society.* Albany: State University of New York Press for Brigham Young University, 1988.

Lutz, Donald S. "Religious Dimensions in the Development of American Constitutionalism." *Emory Law Journal* 39 (1990): 21–40.

McClellan, Edward B. *Schools and the Shaping of Character: Moral Education in America 1607–Present.* Indianapolis: ERIC Clearinghouse, 1992

McConnell, Michael. "Accommodation of Religion." *Supreme Court Review* (1985): 1–60.

Machiavelli, Niccolò. *Discourses on the First Ten Books of Titus Livius.* New York: Modern Library, 1950.

McInerny, Ralph, ed. *Modernity and Religion.* Notre Dame: Notre Dame University Press, 1994.

Marvell, Thomas B. "Divorce Rates and the Fault Requirement." *Law and Society Review* 23 (1989): 543–68.

Marx, Karl. *The Marx-Engels Reader.* Ed. Robert C. Tucker. New York: Norton, 1978.

Mill, John Stuart. *On Liberty.* Indianapolis: Hackett, 1978.

————. *On Liberty and Other Writings.* Ed. Stefan Collini. Cambridge: Cambridge University Press, 1989.

————. *Three Essays.* Oxford: Oxford University Press, 1975.

Miller, Perry. *The Puritans.* New York: Harper and Row, 1963.

Murray, Charles. *In Pursuit of Happiness and Good Government.* New York: Simon and Schuster, 1988.

―――. *Losing Ground: American Social Policy 1950–1980.* New York: Basic Books, 1984.

Murray, John Courtney. *We Hold These Truths: Catholic Reflections on the American Proposition.* Kansas City, MO: Sheed and Ward, 1960.

Nisbet, Robert A. *The Quest for Community: A Study in the Ethics of Order and Freedom.* New York: Oxford University Press, 1953.

Olasky, Marvin. *The Tragedy of American Compassion.* Washington, DC: Regnery Gateway, 1992.

Osborne, David, and Ted Gaebler. *Reinventing Government: How the Entrepreneurial Spirit Is Transforming the Public Sector.* New York: Plume, 1993.

Pangle, Thomas L. *The Spirit of Modern Republicanism: The Moral Vision of the American Founders and the Philosophy of Locke.* Chicago: University of Chicago Press, 1988.

Phillips, Derek L. *Looking Backward: A Critical Appraisal of Communitarian Thought.* Princeton: Princeton University Press, 1993.

Plato. *The Republic.* Trans. G. M. A. Grube. Indianapolis: Hackett, 1974.

Pocock, J. G. A. "Virtue and Commerce in the Eighteenth Century." *Journal of Interdisciplinary History* 3 (1972): 119–34.

Powell, H. Jefferson. "The Original Understanding of Original Intent." *Harvard Law Review* 98 (1985): 885–948.

Rakove, Jack N., ed. *Interpreting the Constitution: The Debate over Original Intent.* Boston: Northeastern University Press, 1990.

Reichley, A. James. *Religion in American Public Life.* Washington, DC: Brookings Institution, 1985.

Rosenblum, Nancy L., ed. *Liberalism and the Moral Life.* Cambridge: Harvard University Press, 1989.

Rousseau, Jean Jacques. *The Social Contract and Discourses.* Trans. G. D. H. Cole. London: Dent, 1973.

Sandoz, Ellis. *A Government of Laws: Political Theory, Religion, and the American Founding.* Baton Rouge: Louisiana State University Press, 1990.

Sandoz, Ellis, ed. *Political Sermons of the American Founding Era.* Indianapolis: Liberty Press, 1991.

Schneider, Herbert W. *A History of American Philosophy.* New York: Columbia University Press, 1946.

Shain, Barry Alan. *The Myth of American Individualism: The Protestant Origins of American Political Thought.* Princeton: Princeton University Press, 1994.

Shapiro, Robert. "The End of Entitlement." *New Democrat* 4 (July 1992): 16–19.

Stokes, Anson P. *Church and State in the United States.* New York: Harper and Row, 1950.

Storing, Herbert J. *What the Antifederalists Were For.* Vol. 1 of *The Complete Antifederalist.* Chicago: University of Chicago Press, 1981.

Strauss, Leo. *What Is Political Philosophy?* Chicago: University of Chicago Press, 1959.

Taylor, Charles. "The Dangers of Soft Despotism." *Responsive Community* (Fall 1993).

_____. *The Ethics of Authenticity.* Cambridge: Harvard University Press, 1991.

_____. *Multiculturalism.* Princeton: Princeton University Press, 1994.

_____. *Sources of the Self: The Making of the Modern Identity.* Cambridge: Harvard University Press, 1989.

Tocqueville, Alexis de. *Democracy in America.* Ed. J. P. Mayer, trans. George Lawrence. Garden City, NY: Doubleday, 1969.

Walzer, Michael. *Spheres of Justice: A Defense of Pluralism and Equality.* New York: Basic Books, 1983.

Wardle, Lynne A. "No-Fault Divorce and the Divorce Conundrum." *Brigham Young Law Review* (1991): 79–142.

Weitzman, Lenore. *The Divorce Revolution.* New York: Free Press, 1985.

Westbrook, Robert B. *John Dewey and American Democracy.* Ithaca: Cornell University Press, 1992.

White, Morton G. *The Philosophy of the American Revolution.* New York: Oxford University Press, 1978.

Wills, Garry. *Certain Trumpets: The Call of Leaders.* New York: Simon and Schuster, 1994.

_____. *Explaining America: The Federalist.* Garden City, NY: Doubleday, 1981.

_____. *Inventing America: Jefferson's Declaration of Independence.* Garden City, NY: Doubleday, 1978.

_____. *Lincoln at Gettysburg: The Words That Remade America.* New York: Simon and Schuster, 1992.

_____. *Under God: Religion and American Politics.* New York: Simon and Schuster, 1990.

Wilson, James. *Works.* Ed. Robert Greene McCloskey. 2 vols. Cambridge: Harvard University Press, 1967.

Witte, John, Jr. "The Integration of Religious Liberty." *Michigan Law Review* 90 (1992): 1363–83.

Wood, Gordon. *Creation of the American Republic, 1776–1787.* Chapel Hill: University of North Carolina Press, 1969.

Index

267

—